Civil Disob

Key Concepts Series

Barbara Adam, *Time*
Alan Aldridge, *Consumption*
Alan Aldridge, *The Market*
Jakob Arnoldi, *Risk*
Will Atkinson, *Class*
Colin Barnes and Geof Mercer, *Disability*
Darin Barney, *The Network Society*
Mildred Blaxter, *Health 2nd edition*
Harriet Bradley, *Gender 2nd edition*
Harry Brighouse, *Justice*
Mónica Brito Vieira and David Runciman, *Representation*
Steve Bruce, *Fundamentalism 2nd edition*
Joan Busfield, *Mental Illness*
Damien Cahill and Martijn Konings, *Neoliberalism*
Margaret Canovan, *The People*
Andrew Jason Cohen, *Toleration*
Alejandro Colás, *Empire*
Patricia Hill Collins and Sirma Bilge, *Intersectionality*
Mary Daly, *Welfare*
Anthony Elliott, *Concepts of the Self 3rd edition*
Steve Fenton, *Ethnicity 2nd edition*
Katrin Flikschuh, *Freedom*
Michael Freeman, *Human Rights 2nd edition*
Russell Hardin, *Trust*
Geoffrey Ingham, *Capitalism*
Fred Inglis, *Culture*
Robert H. Jackson, *Sovereignty*
Jennifer Jackson Preece, *Minority Rights*
Gill Jones, *Youth*
Paul Kelly, *Liberalism*
Anne Mette Kjær, *Governance*
Ruth Lister, *Poverty*
Jon Mandle, *Global Justice*
Cillian McBride, *Recognition*
Anthony Payne and Nicola Phillips, *Development*
Judith Phillips, *Care*
Chris Phillipson, *Ageing*
Robert Reiner, *Crime*
Michael Saward, *Democracy*
John Scott, *Power*
Timothy J. Sinclair, *Global Governance*
Anthony D. Smith, *Nationalism 2nd edition*
Deborah Stevenson, *The City*
Leslie Paul Thiele, *Sustainability 2nd edition*
Steven Peter Vallas, *Work*
Stuart White, *Equality*
Michael Wyness, *Childhood*

Civil Disobedience

William E. Scheuerman

polity

Copyright © William E. Scheuerman 2018

The right of William E. Scheuerman to be identified as Author of this Work has been asserted in accordance with the UK Copyright, Designs and Patents Act 1988.

First published in 2018 by Polity Press

Polity Press
65 Bridge Street
Cambridge CB2 1UR, UK

Polity Press
101 Station Landing
Suite 300,
Medford, MA 02155, USA

ISBN-13: 978-1-5095-1862-3
ISBN-13: 978-1-5095-1863-0(pb)

A catalogue record for this book is available from the British Library.

Library of Congress Cataloging-in-Publication Data

Names: Scheuerman, William E., 1965- author.
Title: Civil disobedience / William E. Scheuerman.
Description: Malden, MA : Polity Press, 2018. | Includes bibliographical references and index.
Identifiers: LCCN 2017021115 (print) | LCCN 2017023718 (ebook) |
    ISBN 9781509518654 (Mobi) | ISBN 9781509518661 (Epub) |
    ISBN 9781509518623 (hardback) | ISBN 9781509518630 (pbk.)
Subjects: LCSH: Civil disobedience–Juvenile literature.
Classification: LCC JC328.3 (ebook) | LCC JC328.3 .S254 2018 (print) |
    DDC 303.6/1–dc23
LC record available at https://lccn.loc.gov/2017021115

Typeset in 10.5 on 12 pt Sabon by Toppan Best-set Premedia Limited
Printed and bound in the UK by CPI Group (UK) Ltd, Croydon

For further information on Polity, visit our website: politybooks.com

For my parents

Contents

Acknowledgments

The initial inspiration for writing this volume came from Edward Snowden, whose 2013 whistleblowing jolted me out of my scholastic slumbers and forced me to think hard about politically motivated lawbreaking and how to make sense of it. Donald Trump's ascendancy later provided a frightening reminder of why it remains vital that we understand civil disobedience.

Robin Celikates and Maeve Cooke accompanied the journey, generously supporting my efforts and commenting on components of the manuscript, as have two colleagues, Russell Hanson and Jeffrey Isaac. I have learned a great deal from all of them.

I presented earlier versions of the ideas developed here at my home institution, Indiana University, and Amsterdam University, Copenhagen Business School, *Forschungskolleg Humanwissenschaften* (Bad Homburg), Goethe University (Frankfurt), Hamburg University, Humboldt University (Berlin), Notre Dame University (Indiana), Seoul National University, University College Dublin, University of Memphis, University of Pennsylvania, University of Toronto, and the University of York (UK). As always, the annual Prague critical theory conference on philosophy and social sciences, for which I have been fortunate to serve as co-director, provided ample opportunities to garner critical feedback. Lively audiences there and elsewhere forced me to think more clearly about what I was trying to say. Special thanks to Kimberley Brownlee, Simone Chambers, Gabriella Coleman, Aurelian Craiutu, Verena Erlenbusch, Alessandro Ferrara, Rainer Forst, Jeffrey Green, Joohyung Kim, Poul Kjaer, Mihaela Mihai, Brian Milstein, Darrel Moellendorf, Peter Niesen, Niklas Olsen, Danielle Petherbridge, Maria Pia Lara, Martin Sauter, Sandra Shapshay, Jon Simons, Jiewuh Song, Ernesto Verdeja, Susan Williams, and Theresa Züger.

During the summer and fall of 2016, the idyllic *Forschungskolleg Humanwissenschaften* in Bad Homburg, Germany, hosted my family. I thank Rainer Forst for making the visit possible, and Beate Sutterlüty, Iris Koban, and Andreas Reichhardt for their patience and support. Without their efforts, I would never have completed the volume. The Humboldt Stiftung, the German-American Fulbright Commission, and Indiana University helped finance the research stay. Seyla Benhabib and Nancy Fraser generously endorsed my fellowship applications.

Some sections of articles from *Journal of International Political Theory*, *Journal of Political Philosophy*, *New Political Science*, and *Philosophy and Social Criticism* have been reworked into this text. Thanks to a host of anonymous reviewers, and Jocelyn Borycka, Bob Goodin, Patrick Hayden, and David Rasmussen, for providing sound editorial advice at earlier stages. At Polity, Louise Knight and Nekane Tanaka Galdos were a pleasure to work with.

My debts to Julia, Zoe, and Lily transcend my limited literary and stylistic talents.

Finally, I dedicate this book to my parents, Bill and Louise, with the hope that we will enjoy another great half century together. Thank you.

Introduction

Why civil disobedience?

A loose collection of activists targeting police racism and brutality, Black Lives Matter (BLM) got its name from Alicia Garza, who first used the term in a July 2013 Facebook post criticizing the acquittal of George Zimmerman, who had shot and killed Trayvon Martin, a black teen. The 2014 police killings of Michael Brown and Eric Garner, followed by other widely publicized incidents of police violence, rapidly ignited protests organized by younger black activists. Beyond the usual mix of demonstrations, marches, and vigils, BLM soon embraced more controversial tactics, including some deemed illegal by public authorities and, not surprisingly, culminating in arrests. Protestors occupied police stations and police union offices, blockaded major highways and mass transit systems, interrupted political speakers (including Hillary Clinton and Bernie Sanders), and disrupted shoppers in large malls and downtown shopping districts. Though its activities have generally been nonviolent, some have resulted in the destruction of property and scuffles with police (Lowery 2016).

BLM has generated sympathy among political progressives, some of whom view it as a rightful heir to the 1960s US civil rights movements and Martin Luther King's vision of nonviolent civil disobedience. On the political right, in sharp contrast, prominent figures – including President Donald Trump – accuse the group of instigating violence against police officers, describing its actions as reckless and incongruent with the "rule of law," an idea conservatives tend to conflate with "law and order."[1] Right-wing pundits often draw clear lines between a saintly King and what they deplore as BLM's propensity for violence and white-bashing.

A third – and more sophisticated – response comes from an older generation of African-American activists, some of whom marched with King yet worry the movement has abandoned his ideas. They accuse its proponents of lacking the requisite spiritual orientation and failing to appreciate why conscientious lawbreaking demands public displays of dignity, decorum, and self-discipline. BLM, on their view, has not done enough to delineate its actions from those of street thugs and looters. It needs to think harder about how to mobilize majority support for its grievances. Recent activists have given lucid expression to legitimate black frustration, but not enough thought as to how best to funnel it in morally sound and politically productive ways (Kennedy 2015; Reynolds 2015).

While also claiming inspiration from King, BLM has responded by distancing itself from his patriarchal and occasionally conservative religious views. The group rejects the "respectability politics ethos" of older civil rights activism, touting its own preference for less hierarchical, centralized organizational forms. In contrast to the electoral reformism of the present-day black political elite (and its close ties to the Democratic Party), the activists doubt that "the American system is salvageable, because it is so deeply rooted in ideas of racial caste."[2] Accordingly, the movement has spurned efforts by elected leaders and other political figures to embrace its cause, seeing in them a real danger of cooptation. Its defenders have also pushed back against sanitized readings of King's tactics, pointing out that he and his followers were also frequently accused of fomenting unrest and violence (Sebastian 2015).

What should we make of these competing interpretations? BLM has in fact broken the law and engaged in behavior that has sometimes rattled even sympathizers. Should we highlight the movement's apparent disdain for legality? Does it make sense to view its endeavors as essentially lawless and criminal? Though the movement's participants have by no means always categorized their activities as civil disobedience, the term appears frequently in discussions of them. One reason is that the concept "civil disobedience" possesses a moral and political cachet that alternatives – most obviously, "crime" or "illegality" – lack. With this moral and political capital also come some modest legal gains: when politically motivated lawbreakers convince a judge or jury that their actions constitute civil disobedience, in some jurisdictions they can count on less severe treatment than those who fail to do so.[3] Protestors may get off with a reduced sentence, or some realistic expectation of clemency in the not-too-distant future. They can also successfully claim the mantle of iconic practitioners of civil disobedience such as King and Mahatma Gandhi, in the process garnering a valuable measure of public recognition for their actions.

Our answers to these questions, in short, are politically consequential, and the stakes for real-life activists high. BLM's case, to be sure, is of special interest to US citizens (and, of course, people everywhere repulsed by racism).[4] Yet parallel questions emerge in many other contexts. We are witnessing a proliferation of politically motivated illegalities, some familiar and some less so, with activists, their supporters, and critics regularly debating whether the illegalities in question deserve to be described as *civil disobedience*.

A similar controversy, for example, has broken out about whether mass migrations of peoples across state borders, like those that have recently brought millions to Germany, Greece, Turkey, and smaller countries such as Austria and Sweden, might be sensibly characterized as civil disobedience. Those illegally crossing borders in search of a decent job, for example, apparently view legal entry requirements as unjust, and when violating laws prohibiting their free movement do so nonviolently. Even when crossing borders covertly, they may subsequently take on occupations making them visible to a broader public. Their actions also generate public debate about immigration and refugee policies, spurring calls for legal changes. On one interpretation, illegal migrants are implicitly appealing to some nascent idea of global or cosmopolitan justice that favors human rights over national prerogatives (Cabrera 2010: 131–53). Since their acts seem to meet some of the usual tests of legitimate civil disobedience, why not describe them as such?

This and related queries seem increasingly inescapable. Given substantial popular dissatisfaction with the normal workings even of longstanding liberal democracies, large numbers of people are now willing to pursue unconventional and legally suspect protest. In well-functioning liberal democracies, political decisions should be made via normal lawmaking channels; those seeking legal and policy changes should not be driven to break the law in personally risky ways. Unfortunately, it is no longer clear that many liberal democracies are in fact sufficiently well-functioning. The present crisis of democracy, as manifest in burgeoning mass apathy, populist rage against political elites, and the decline of mainstream political parties, likely portends a growing prominence for politically motivated lawbreaking. Alarming authoritarian trends also probably mean that incidents of grassroots or oppositional lawbreaking will increase, as citizens push back against top-down attacks on civil liberties and democracy.

We need to understand civil disobedience, its key components, what they entail, and how and why it involves a special type of lawbreaking, one that in principle may be deserving of our respect even when we find the political cause or activists behind it disagreeable. Why does it matter? Since Gandhi and King, the concept of civil disobedience has appealed especially to those hoping to bring about positive social change. Responsible political action today – as in the past – presupposes conceptual and terminological clarity. We want a notion of civil disobedience that potentially allows us to situate it coherently within a broader field of related political terms, even if messy social realities unavoidably get in the way of airtight conceptual distinctions. For both political and theoretical reasons, to be examined below, one tendency in recent years has been a certain blurring of the lines between notions of civil disobedience, on the one hand, and other politically motivated illegalities, on the other. Both normative and empirical literatures now speak broadly of *political resistance*, nonviolent or otherwise.[5] In contemporary political discourse as well, *resistance* functions as a diffuse catch-all concept, masking a diversity of competing political tactics and ideological perspectives. Unfortunately, this trend sometimes comes with a hidden price tag: we risk losing a sufficiently precise understanding of civil disobedience and its distinctive traits.[6]

Unlike those that jettison the term "civil disobedience" for generic and potentially less precise conceptual alternatives, this book tries to hold on to it. To do so successfully, we need to explore the concept's nuances as well as possible ambiguities and frailties.

Which civil disobedience?

One way to proceed would be offer another full-fledged political philosophy of civil disobedience. To their credit, some contemporary authors are pursuing this approach. One of their project's more striking oversights, however, suggests the virtues of a more modest starting point.

Civil disobedience has long been the subject of wide-ranging controversy. Philosophically inclined writers are again revisiting the topic; later we take a careful look at their efforts (chapter 7). Though multifaceted, the ongoing exchange seems motivated to a great degree by a skeptical reading of the allegedly hegemonic liberal model of civil disobedience, and especially the influential account provided by the philosopher John Rawls in his classic *A Theory of Justice* (1971). The ongoing debate's premise is that only by transcending the orthodox liberal model of civil disobedience can we accommodate contemporary political realities and realize a sufficiently supple conceptual alternative. Preoccupied with knocking Rawls off his pedestal, critics tend to revert to cramped interpretations of a rich body of prior political and theoretical reflections. They simplify key ideas about civil disobedience, liberal or otherwise. They make things too easy for themselves by obscuring the concept's complex history.

There is no *single* classical or orthodox idea of civil disobedience: rival political traditions have formulated overlapping yet basically different models of civil disobedience. Consequently, this volume examines four separate accounts of civil disobedience – namely, competing religious-spiritual, liberal, democratic, and anarchist concepts.[7] Ideas about civil disobedience have been articulated in diverging and indeed conflicting ways. Civil disobedience's presuppositions, normative justifications, and political aspirations can only be properly grasped when situated in the context of four rival traditions, each of which has made some notable contributions. My exposition is both analytic and roughly chronological: we can view the longstanding debate about civil disobedience as a learning process of sorts, with succeeding generations of activists and thinkers trying to correct the real (or at least perceived) mistakes of their predecessors, and then improving on them. By proceeding in this fashion, we can gain a better sense of how more recent notions of civil disobedience – in particular its impressive *democratic* variant – represent real conceptual and political progress. We should also eventually be able to see where contemporary philosophical analysis goes astray.

For religious believers Gandhi and King, civil disobedience was principally a device to counter evil, a form of divine witness requiring of practitioners a suitably demanding spiritual comportment. Every element of this original model, accordingly, possessed a directly *religious-spiritual* significance (chapter 1).[8] In contrast, the *liberal* model of civil disobedience, as fashioned by Rawls and other liberals in the 1960s and early 1970s, struggled to free civil disobedience from its initial religious bearings, recognizing that it could only remain politically relevant when reconfigured in accordance with modern pluralism. In the process, liberals came to interpret civil disobedience primarily as a useful corrective to overbearing political majorities that periodically threaten minority rights (chapter 2). The *democratic* model of civil disobedience, whose most significant defenders have included Hannah Arendt and Jürgen Habermas, challenged liberalism's narrow understanding of democracy and its insufficiently critical diagnosis of the liberal political status quo. Civil disobedience, on their wide-ranging and sometimes politically radical account, could help overcome far-reaching democratic deficits and open the door to extensive political and social reform (chapter 3). Finally, the *anarchist* model, as practiced by generations of political militants, and recently reformulated by self-described philosophical anarchists, defied core presuppositions about the state and law on which previous approaches rested. Posing a profound challenge to all prior accounts, contemporary anarchism remains deeply conflicted about civil disobedience as conventionally understood (chapter 4).

This typology hardly denies the existence of vital alternative ideas about civil disobedience. The women's movement, for example, has made significant practical and intellectual contributions (Perry 2013: 126–56). Nonetheless, the four frameworks discussed here (religious, liberal, democratic, anarchist) remain hugely influential and theoretically most decisive. Feminists who write fruitfully about civil disobedience, in fact, often rely on them.[9]

Notwithstanding differences between and among rival models, we can identify crucial commonalities, especially among its religious, liberal, and democratic renditions. Despite its plural conceptual formations, civil disobedience rests on some shared components and aspirations.

Most importantly, religious, liberal, and democratic accounts all view civil disobedience as a distinctive mode of lawbreaking predicated, however paradoxically, on a deeper respect for law or legality. As King eloquently commented in "Letter from Birmingham City Jail"

> I submit that an individual who breaks a law that conscience tells him is unjust, and willingly accepts the penalty by staying in jail to arouse the conscience of the community over its injustice, is in reality expressing the very highest respect for the law. (King 1991 [1963]: 74)

With the notable exception of most anarchists, activists and intellectuals from Gandhi to Habermas have typically offered some rendition of the idea that civil disobedience means not only morally or politically motivated lawbreaking, but also lawbreaking demonstrating fidelity to – or respect for – law. Absent some version of this notion of lawbreaking for the sake of law, or illegality in the name of legality, King and many others suggested, it would prove difficult to counter the commonplace criticism, recently rehashed by Trump and others hostile to BLM, that civil disobedience represents deplorable lawlessness or shameful criminality. As I intend to document, this simple but powerful intuition has been formulated in a diversity of more-or-less plausible ways. It remains, in fact, hard to imagine a sound concept of civil disobedience without it, despite creative efforts by recent writers to do just that.

Competing models of civil disobedience, despite their sizable disagreements, also make use of a joint conceptual language, even as they employ that language for different purposes. Even some anarchists, when push comes to shove, implicitly suggest that lawbreaking's legitimacy depends on *civility, conscientiousness, nonviolence,* and *publicity,* though they interpret such preconditions in ways dissimilar from those in competing religious, liberal, and democratic approaches. One of the more surprising features of the story I retell below is how many elements of Gandhi's original model of civil disobedience tend to resurface, in novel and sometimes barely recognizable forms, in subsequent accounts. Civil disobedience is not, at any rate, an empty pot into which rival political and theoretical traditions simply pour their own potions. Its exponents depend on a common analytic language. Even when speaking that language in ways that are so heavily accented by their own political and philosophical views that others may find them hard to comprehend, theirs remains a common tongue. As such, it provides some minimal yet meaningful constraints on what can or cannot be meaningfully expressed by it.

Just as an ordinary English speaker hoping to communicate successfully would not arbitrarily reclassify the word "dog" to mean "cat," so too would those interpreting "civility" to cover verbal or physical harassment, or "nonviolence" to enable corporal abuse, seem confused and perhaps incomprehensible to standard users of civil disobedience's conceptual language.[10] Civility, conscientiousness, nonviolence, and publicity, within civil disobedience's pluralistic conceptual discourse, take on different and sometimes antagonistic connotations. Yet they remain shared ideational mainstays.

Whither civil disobedience?

Lest readers have already become vexed that I intend to provide a Panglossian story about civil disobedience, let me put your worries – or rather *lack of* worries – to rest. In fact, standard (religious, liberal, and democratic) versions are under strain today; there are many grounds for anxiety about their prospects. Some strains result from a now widespread anti-statism and anti-legalism, a trend motored by a resurgence of anarchist (and libertarian) currents. For those who view state and law as congenitally illegitimate, King's view of civil disobedience as intrinsically linked to the "very highest respect for law" must seem hopelessly naïve. Other strains derive from the ongoing *postnationalization* and *privatization* of public authority, fundamental shifts in state/society relations that work to undermine the nation-state-centered or Westphalian presuppositions of mainstream thinking about civil disobedience (chapter 5). One reason why many illegal protests today no longer mesh neatly with conventional ideas of civil disobedience is that their implicit social and institutional presuppositions are dissipating. Present-day activists face the unattractive task of applying "old-fashioned" notions of civil disobedience to a "newfangled" political and social context by no means conducive to their efforts, and the results can prove messy.

Parallel quagmires tend to plague digital disobedience, or politically motivated digital or online lawbreaking. Prominent digital lawbreakers such as Edward Snowden have occasionally categorized their acts under the rubric of civil disobedience. In some scenarios, there may be sound reasons for endorsing this claim. Nonetheless, it remains unclear whether concepts designed with physical or "on-the-street" lawbreaking in mind can or should be seamlessly applied to digital lawbreaking. There are real perils in stretching the concept of civil disobedience to capture phenomena probably better analyzed by alternative means. By overextending it, we rob the concept of the requisite analytic and normative contours, denying ourselves tools we need to respond to political challenges in a responsible, well-informed manner. Civil disobedience is an essential piece of the puzzle of contemporary politics. Yet that puzzle contains many other pieces as well.

What then about BLM, global migrants, or countless other contemporary examples that potentially come to mind? Does it make sense to employ the term civil disobedience when analyzing them? What do we gain – and potentially lose – by doing so? Answering these questions requires a lengthy detour. That detour begins with the religious-spiritual model of civil disobedience sketched so vividly by Gandhi and King.

1

Divine Witness

Civil disobedience was probably invented by religious believers who envisaged it as a sacred duty forced upon them by their God. Principled lawbreaking in the face of immoral laws represented not just a moral right but a divine obligation, ignored only at a terrible spiritual cost. Although this model of civil disobedience can trace some roots to the distant past, it was the great twentieth-century political figures Mohandas K. Gandhi and Martin Luther King, Jr. who vividly outlined, via their actions and closely related writings, what rapidly became the canonical exemplar of religious civil disobedience.[1] In more recent decades, their ideas have inspired a diverse range of activists who openly violate laws allegedly inconsonant with God's will.

Properly conducted lawbreaking, operating as a corrective to a social world plagued by sin and evil, is conceived as tapping directly into divine forces. Outlining a series of demanding conditions for legitimate civil disobedience, Gandhi, King, and their disciples view each component in decidedly spiritual terms. Civil disobedience represents a religious quest requiring of practitioners a proper moral bearing. During the famous "salt *satyagraha*" (1930–1), Gandhi slept in the open with only the barest material necessities, traveling from town to town where he and his disciples repeatedly violated a salt tax they viewed as embodying British colonial exploitation. Gandhi saw this as a sacred pilgrimage in which discipline and purity were essential. Indeed, a religious aura surrounded the whole enterprise. He and his followers kept quoting the Gospels, presumably drawing comparisons between Gandhi and Christ deliberately setting his face towards Jerusalem and confrontation with the authorities; the sale of Bibles among Ahmedabad Hindus shot up. The government noted that Gandhi's position in the public mind was completely different from that of any ordinary political leader. (Brown 1989: 237)

US civil rights activists who broke segregation statutes in the late 1950s and early 1960s were recruited heavily from African-American churches and sang spirituals when carted off to jail. King, no less than Gandhi, viewed his movement as religiously inspired. In this respect, as in so many others, he creatively adapted Gandhi's ideas to US conditions.

We start by analyzing this religious conception of civil disobedience because of its massive historical and intellectual impact. Subsequent, more secular, liberal, democratic, and anarchist accounts of civil disobedience all implicitly start with Gandhi's and King's ideas, trying to preserve their skeletal features while fitting them with a new philosophical and political body. They take up many pieces of the puzzle Gandhi and King constructed, but then remake it. Given the spiritual contours of the original, their more secular orientation sometimes means they have had a hard time doing so.

Special attention is paid to the fertile idea that civil disobedience represents neither ordinary lawbreaking nor mere criminality, but instead, as King put it in "Letter from Birmingham City Jail," action exemplifying "the very highest respect for law" (1991 [1963]: 74). The notion of civil disobedience as premised on respect for law vividly emerged in Gandhi's thinking, as did the soon commonplace intuition that civil disobedience demands "a willingness to be identified and to accept punishment" (Perry 2013: 15). To understand the lasting appeal of these ideas we need to examine their original religious rendition.

Many virtues notwithstanding, religiously based civil disobedience suffers from serious flaws. Its spiritual underpinnings raise difficult questions for modern pluralism. They also risk inviting troublesome – and no longer identifiably *civil* – lawbreaking.

Civil disobedience and *satyagraha*

Though Gandhi was perhaps never fully satisfied with the term "civil disobedience," he used it to describe politically motivated contraventions of the law, like many others wrongly attributing its invention to the nineteenth-century American dissident Henry Thoreau.[2] Alongside boycotts, noncooperation, pickets, strikes, and walkouts, civil disobedience represented one particularly effective type of *satyagraha*, or political action motivated by "love" or "truth-force," whose divine strictures gave moral meaning to the universe. In its most literal sense, satyagraha entailed "insistence on truth, and the force derivable from such insistence" (Gandhi 2008 [1919]: 324). "The universe would disappear without the existence of that force," Gandhi claimed (1986a [1909]: 244). Gandhi accordingly described his own life-long spiritual quest and activities as "experiments with truth" (1993 [1957]).

How best to practice and thereby advance divine truthfulness? Our inner voice, or moral conscience, provided access to divinity and thus was by nature indubitable. God is ready to speak to each of us personally and directly (Sorabji 2014: 200). Yet one could only properly recognize that voice by means of the "strictest discipline. Irresponsible youngsters therefore ... have no conscience, nor therefore have all grown-up people" (Gandhi 1986b [1924]: 125). Those who engaged in rigorous processes of self-purification, where both mind and body were subjected to mental and physical discipline (a strict diet and sexual abstinence, or *brachmacharya*), would alone prove receptive to godly conscience.

By necessity, civil disobedience was always *conscientious* lawbreaking: Gandhi never delineated civil disobedience from what liberals and others later called *conscientious objection*. Rightful lawbreaking had to rest directly on "the voice of God, of Conscience, of Truth, or the Inner Voice" (1986b [1933]: 131). It had to be *civil*, not because it entailed common or civic obligations to a community of political equals, but because its practitioners should abide rigorous norms of proper moral behavior and decorum. Why? Because God demanded nothing less.

In Gandhi's reworked version of Hinduism, "God is Truth," and genuine religious faith entailed an unceasing quest for absolute truth, and by necessity principled indifference to anything (for example, material well-being or sexual pleasure) getting in the way of that quest. The search for absolute truth should not, however, engender disdain for others. Because no mortal could ever legitimately assert that he or she had fully approximated divine truth, or that conscience spoke decisively to him or her alone, a basic respect for others – Gandhi, following Leo Tolstoy (1967), in this context generally refers to *love* – was required of anyone hoping to avoid sinful hubris. "[C]onduct based on truth is impossible without love. Truth-force then is love-force" since *no* human being was qualified or competent to harm or punish, by destructive or violent means, others similarly situated (2008 [1919]: 324; also, Bondurant 1958). Truth, love, and nonviolence (*ahimsa*) were intimately intermingled because the quest for absolute truth presupposed an acknowledgment of human cognitive and moral limitations. Human fallibility required nonviolence, since only the hubristic mistakenly believed that they were entitled to do violence to others. Those rightly attuned to the human capacity for error instead refused to force on their peers their own potentially mistaken "experiments with truth."

Civil disobedience represented spiritual truth-seeking in action, a sacred duty in the face of morally corrupt laws. When the law humiliates or discriminates, makes arbitrary or unfair distinctions, or rests on mere brute force, it clashes with divine Truth or Soul-Force. If secular powers successfully resist attempts to change or abrogate such laws when pursued by alternative channels (for example, economic boycotts or negotiations with power holders), then it becomes obligatory on divine truth-seekers to repair a damaged moral order. "That we should obey laws whether good or bad is a new-fangled notion" (1986a [1909]: 246). Even laws made by powerful political majorities can be unjust since democracy and majority rule provide no guarantee of moral rectitude (1986a [1909]: 247). When and how it was best to engage in lawbreaking, Gandhi conceded, raised difficult political questions. Yet it remained a moral – and ultimately divine – obligation to do so.[3]

In part because of its risks, and in part its spiritual preconditions, Gandhi tended to suggest conscientious lawbreaking should only occur after ordinary political and legal channels had been properly exhausted. Lawbreaking was a serious matter, and when recklessly committed could easily generate violence or chaos. At crucial junctures – for example, when opposing colonial anti-sedition statutes passed during 1919 – Gandhi abruptly broke off his endeavors precisely because of such fears. "Every possible provision should be made against an outbreak of violence or general lawlessness" (1987 [1922]: 99). Gandhi doubted the likelihood of advantageous political outcomes when lawbreakers lacked the requisite religious and spiritual discipline. Since "he alone can offer satyagraha who has true faith in religion," any idea of civil disobedience as a morally neutral technique deployable by any activist, spiritually inclined or otherwise, was anathema to him (2008 [1909]: 329).

Highlighting his strategic acumen, recent commentators have pushed back against the stereotypical view of Gandhi as an idealistic moral crusader (Mantena 2012). Such interpretations build on prior attempts to uproot Gandhi's political methods and techniques from their spiritual soil, an approach surely in part responsible for his ideas' successful global dispersion (Sharp 1973; Shridharani 1972 [1939]). Gandhi, in fact, frequently relied on military and strategic metaphors; he possessed a keen eye for the mechanisms of power. Principally committed to nonviolence, he still conceded that in a spiritually imperfect world, *some* violence remained unavoidable. Nonviolence not just vis-à-vis other human beings but also in relation to animals – the source of Gandhi's vegetarianism – was a counsel of perfection that we should heed but could not always completely achieve, even if morally obliged to try to do so (Sorabji 2014: 198).

Construing Gandhi as a closeted political realist, however, obfuscates the fact that *every* feature of his account of civil disobedience was spiritually constructed. His nonviolence, for example, rested on much more than strategic or political considerations. Nor is there any sense in Gandhi's thinking of politics as *autonomous* or relatively distinct from morality. "Politics cannot be divorced from religion. Politics divorced from religion becomes debasing" (1986a [1915]: 374). His spiritual commitments probably encouraged him to expect that if civil disobedients were "right with God," political benefits would tend to follow. Divine truth was destined to win out over injustice and evil: those called to act on God's behalf, and who then did so properly, would likely *convert* – a religious term Gandhi favored over conventional political ones – opponents. Gandhi also saw no distinction between "public" and "private," or state and society, since on his account every arena of human social activity was legitimately subjected to the quest for divine truth.[4]

Civil disobedience should be *open* or *public*, not primarily because disobedients had to convince or persuade opponents, but because divine "truth hates secrecy" (1986b [1931]: 191). Fraud, lying, and deceit were inconsonant with religious faith. Consequently, Gandhi sometimes favored providing advance notice of lawbreaking to political authorities. Even when opponents deemed protests confrontational or disruptive, their main purpose remained moral instruction. As a consequence, disobedience had to be *civil*, meaning "gentle, truthful, humble, knowing, willful yet loving, never criminal and hateful," since only then could it advance God's work (2008 [1922]: 360). Nor could it be permitted to become rancorous, rude, or rowdy. Sabotage and the destruction of property were to be avoided. Participants should "observe perfect chastity, adopt poverty, follow truth, and cultivate fearlessness" (2008 [1909]: 322, 329). Spiritual activists should harbor no anger against their opponents or those who imprisoned them. Rather, they were expected willingly and even joyfully to *accept whatever punishment* or abuse they faced, "even unto death" (2008 [1930]: 332). A sacred duty, civil disobedience might demand martyrdom.

Love and truth-force demanded *strict nonviolence*, a principled and not merely pragmatic feature of civil disobedience. Nonviolence morally cleansed those practicing it while preserving political opponents' moral and spiritual integrity (Brown 1989: 84). Demanding both mental and physical prowess, and respect for the basic integrity of all of God's creations, nonviolence was never for the weak-willed or spiritually irresolute, but instead solely for disciplined souls animated by the quest for divine truth. *Willingness to sacrifice and suffer*, even in the face of injustice, demonstrated one's moral sincerity and jolted those complicit in evil into reconsidering their positions; its strategic advantages could sometimes prove decisive. Its core justification remained spiritual: a divinely based law of nonviolence undergirded our moral universe just "as the earth is held in her position by gravitation," and we are obliged to follow it just as we follow the laws of gravity (1986b [1939]: 425). Like a modern-day moral Newton, Gandhi thought it his responsibility to fill his contemporaries in on the existence of that law.

Civil disobedience funneled latent and potentially destructive political energies: "Civil disobedience will be but a purifying process and may bring to the surface what is burrowing under and into the whole body" (1987 [1930]: 107). Responsible lawbreaking could help reduce the prospect of political violence by disciplining and redirecting the uncorked emotions that often motivated it. When properly conducted, it could engender far-reaching change and eventually a total overhaul of society. Gandhi sought not just an independent India but one that someday would be an exemplar of practical nonviolence, with a spiritually reborn India a moral beacon to the whole world. Simultaneously, he insisted: "I want no revolution. I want ordered progress ... I want no chaos. I want real order to be evolved out this chaos which is misrepresented to me as order" (2008 [1920]: 354). Circumventing the ills of violent revolution, civil disobedience potentially permitted radical and indeed massive change not just to the state but also to family and the economy. When, instead, poorly conducted, it constituted a "denial of our oath and sin against God," an irreligious act likely to have counterproductive consequences (2008 [1922]: 364).

Principled lawbreaking

Given Gandhi's disdain for colonialism and preference for a radical overhaul of modern society, why his worries about lawlessness and disorder? Why his insistence on the need to distinguish civil disobedience sharply from other forms of lawbreaking? And why the seemingly "legalistic" preoccupation with demonstrating his and his followers' respect for law?

Gandhi's views on state and law are complex and controversial; the scholarly literature is too massive to summarize here.[5] In his reflections, however, we can disclose a subtle version of the idea that morally principled lawbreaking necessarily rests on some deeper respect for law. It strengthens rather than weakens our underlying commitments to the fundamental ideal of a law-based order, which for Gandhi always represented a valuable social good.[6]

One reason Gandhi thought civil disobedience should often focus on specific laws or government measures was that lawlessness and violence too often went hand in hand. Committed to nonviolence, and concerned that any more general disdain for law opened the door to its opposite, he defended a "tender willing obedience to laws which might even be considered irksome but not immoral" (1986b [1927]: 189). Even when immoral laws had to be challenged, "[s]ubmission to the state law is the price a citizen pays for his personal liberty" (1987 [1921]: 96). To a young lawyer residing in South Africa, still hopeful that British constitutional ideals could be mobilized against colonial injustice, fidelity to the law meant diligently obeying *most* but not *all* laws, even when morally and politically irksome to do so (Brown 1989: 63–5). Later, having returned to India and decidedly more radical, Gandhi defended a frontal assault on the status quo: submission "to a state wholly or largely unjust" constituted "an immoral barrier for liberty" (1987 [1921]: 96).

What, then, distinguished this quest for a total societal reconstruction from more conventional revolutionary strategies? Part of the answer concerns Gandhi's ideas about law.

Conscientious nonviolent lawbreakers *anticipated* the creation of a future legal order where voluntary consent, love, and nonviolence would more fully permeate social and political affairs. Civil disobedience meant "obedience of the higher law of our being – the voice of conscience" (1987 [1917]: 91).[7] Under contemporary political conditions, laws were obeyed mechanically and out of fear of potentially violent sanctions. In a prospective and more fully divine legal order, state coercion's role could be sizably reduced. Law then would garner an appropriate spiritual and more clearly consensual basis. A very different type of police force and mode of enforcement, subservient to the populace and perhaps "with some kind of arms," might remain necessary, Gandhi admitted, yet force then would "be rarely used, if at all" (1986b [1940]: 436). A basically nonviolent order would require legality and – for the foreseeable future – some devices for enforcement.[8] The divinely structured universe, after all, rested on law: "God is not a person. He is the Law and also the Law-Giver" (1986a [1945]: 589). Not surprisingly, a more fully divine political order would need law as well.

Conscientious lawbreakers who followed Gandhi's prescriptions contributed directly to the creation of this superior legal and political alternative. To succeed they *already* had to embody the ethos of the new legal order they hoped to create:

> The right to civil disobedience accrues only to those who know and practise the duty of voluntary obedience to laws whether made by them or others. Obedience should not come from fear of the consequences of the breach but because it is the duty to obey with all our heart and not merely mechanically. Without the fulfilment of this preliminary condition, civil disobedience is civil only in name. (1986b [1938]: 419)

Those properly schooled in civil disobedience prefigured the ideals of voluntary (vs. mechanical or fearful) consent and nonviolence on which Gandhi's desired future order would directly build. In possession of the proper spiritual comportment, their lawbreaking pointed the way to that new order:

> A Satyagrahi obeys the laws of society intelligently and of his own free will, because he considers it to be his sacred duty to do so. It is only when a person has thus obeyed the laws of society scrupulously that he is in a position to judge as to which particular rules are good and just and which unjust and iniquitous. Only then does the right accrue to him of the civil disobedience of certain laws in well-defined circumstances. (1993 [1957]: 470)

How best to demonstrate that lawbreakers had chosen wisely in abrogating the law, and that their acts rested on respect for legality? The answer, Gandhi posited, was for disobedients not only to accept legal penalties but to do so with the right spiritual and corresponding civil bearing. Gandhian lawbreakers were expected to be model prisoners, respectful of their jailers and diligently doing whatever tasks were required, expecting no special favors or dispensations: "Our triumph consists in thousands being led to the prisons like lambs to the slaughter-house" (1987 [1921]: 94). Ordinary criminals, in contrast, evaded punishment and often sought special treatment. Proper civil disobedients hated injustice but not the officials sanctioning them. If their actions followed a suitably spiritual blueprint, they might bring officials over to their cause, in the process effectively disarming the colonial state's violent apparatus. State officials would find it difficult to justify harsh treatment of lawbreakers who had the right moral comportment.[9]

Gandhi goes to America

Gandhi's ideas were imported by radical US labor, peace, and anti-racist activists, before eventually finding a secure home in the civil rights movement and then, during the successful 1956 boycott of segregated buses in Montgomery (Alabama), their most impressive public advocate in Reverend Dr. Martin Luther King.[10] As he commented in *Stride Toward Freedom*, where King introduced his ideas to a broader public, "Christ furnished the spirit and motivation, while Gandhi furnished the method" (1986a [1958]: 85). Our brief discussion in this chapter emphasizes how King repositioned Gandhi's framework within prophetic Christianity, which he viewed as consistent with – and probably indispensable to – core US political and constitutional ideals. The resulting political mix produced a potent though sometimes messy brew.

King, like Gandhi, viewed nonviolent civil disobedience as one among many militant types of direct political action, including peaceful demonstrations, picketing, and economic boycotts. Lawbreaking – illegal sit-ins at segregated lunch counters, for example – should only typically occur after lawful protests, efforts to negotiate with opponents, and regular political channels had stalled. Even then, prospective disobedients had to meet a demanding set of moral tests taken from Gandhi. They should "collect the facts" as a way of identifying suitable targets, while "self-purification" required practical workshops where protestors faced hard questions: "Are you able to accept blows without retaliating? Are you able to endure the ordeal of jail?" (1991 [1963]: 70). Non-violent lawbreaking demanded in reality more discipline and self-control than violent political action, with both King and Gandhi regularly suggesting that it was not passive but instead "active" – and for them correspondingly "manly."[11]

King also spoke of converting rather than defeating his foes, and for him as well willingness to suffer was a crucial means of demonstrating respect and even love for opponents. Civil disobedience brought potentially destructive latent social tensions to the surface, constructively funneling them. It was in fact those who preached blind obedience to "law and order," not nonviolent lawbreakers, who invited disorder: it was only a matter of time before an oppressive social order violently exploded. Following Gandhi, King insisted that "[o]ne who breaks a law must do it openly, lovingly (not hatefully as the white mothers did in New Orleans when they were seen on television screaming 'nigger, nigger, nigger'), and with a willingness to accept the penalty" (1991 [1963]: 74). Conscientious lawbreaking demanded *civility*. By publicly and "lovingly" violating the law, disobedients provided proof of their good Christian will, offering a sharp public contrast between their actions and those of sinful segregationists who shamefully committed violent acts under the cover of darkness (1991 [1963]: 74). Lawbreakers evinced respect for the law by conducting themselves in an orderly, public, and respectful manner, before willingly suffering whatever penalties officials imposed (1991 [1963]: 74). While their actions disrupted an unjust social order's everyday operations, they simultaneously prefigured a superior future order based directly on *agape*, or

> disinterested love … *Agape* does not begin by discriminating between worthy and unworthy people, or any qualities people

possess. It begins by loving others *for their sakes*. It ... dis-
covers the neighbor in every man it meets. Therefore, *agape*
makes no distinction between friend and enemy; it is directed
toward both. (King 1986a [1958]: 104–5)

King, again like Gandhi, took a backseat to none when
defending civil disobedience's radical possibilities. "The
thing to do is to get rid of the system and thereby create
a moral balance within society" (1986b [1961]: 47). "The
system" included not just racial segregation but militarism
and a capitalist economy that eventually had to be replaced
by democratic socialism (Dyson 2000; Jackson 2007; King
2016).[12] Providing an answer to the "long debated question of gradualism versus immediacy," civil disobedience
helped transcend the conventional binary divide between
narrow or limited reformism and maximalist revolutionary politics (1986a [1958]: 221). An instrument of radical
or transformational reformism, it offered substantial possibilities for social change seemingly more radical (violent
or conventionally revolutionary) approaches could not in
fact match.[13]

King's account has become so familiar that it is easy to
underplay spiritual traits overlapping but also differing from
Gandhi's original.[14] Christians owed ultimate allegiance not
to secular authorities but to God, and laws conflicting with
"His will" had to be challenged (King 1986a [1958]: 117).
Opposing unjust law, in sum, constituted a spiritual obligation. *Agape*, the energy or life-force giving moral meaning
to an otherwise sinful world, represented "the love of God
operating in the human heart," with King relying heavily
on Christian scripture to explain its meaning (1986a [1958]:
104). Fittingly, King and his disciples typically made sure to
wear their Sunday finest when protesting and facing arrest.
Activists who suffered at the hands of unjust state officials and cheerfully accepted legal penalties followed Jesus'
example of unearned but redemptive suffering. By filling
the jails and potentially overwhelming the state's coercive
apparatus, they bore Christian moral witness and taught
"a callous public of the inhumanities its complacency con-
doned" (Farmer 1965: ix; also, Pineda 2015). Civil disobedience, King told hostile skeptics, was exemplified by "early

Christians who were willing to face hungry lions and the excruciating pain of chopping blocks, before submitting to certain unjust laws of the Roman empire" (1991 [1963]: 74–5).

Nonviolence was "Christianity in action," "witness to the truth," and it was Christ's divine presence, King claimed in describing his own activities in Montgomery, "as I had never experienced Him before," that inspired him to act (1986a [1958]: 89, 134, 216). Less restrictive than Gandhi's original, his Christian rendition of nonviolence no longer dictated celibacy, strict dieting, or vegetarianism. King also occasionally implied stricter prohibitions on violence against persons than on property:

> I am aware that there are many who wince at a distinction between property and persons – who hold both sacrosanct. My views are not so rigid. A life is sacred. Property is intended to serve life, and no matter how much we surround it with rights and respect, it has no personal being. It is part of the earth man walks on; it is not man. (King 2016 [1968]: 148)

He and his closest advisers also periodically calculated how to get maximum political mileage from violent white backlashes, and they occasionally exploited white fear of black violence to gain concessions, facts that have encouraged some recent commentators to view his nonviolent commitments with some skepticism (Ginsberg 2013; Nimtz 2016).

Responding to contemporaries who already anticipated one version of this skeptical take, he countered:

> Isn't this like condemning the robbed man because his possession of money precipitated the evil act of robbery? ... Isn't this like condemning Jesus because His unique God-Consciousness and never-ceasing devotion to His will precipitated the evil act of crucifixion? ... Society must protect the robbed and punish the robber. (1991 [1963]: 76)

Good Christians who conscientiously broke evil laws could not be held responsible for sinners who responded by resorting to violence to uphold an unjust system. Inasmuch as lawbreakers maintained strict discipline when faced with police brutality or mob violence, they continued to occupy the moral high ground. Their actions, in short, remained both identifiably nonviolent and divinely inspired.

Even as he Christianized Gandhi, King's intonation frequently underwent a decisive shift. He spoke of the need to *persuade* fellow citizens and appeal not just to the nation's moral conscience but also to *national opinion* (1991 [1963]: 76). King participated in a shared community of believers and as a prospective equal citizen in a political order that was failing to live up to its own ideals. Civil disobedience entailed spiritual civility as well as shared civic duties as an equal citizen. King, in sum, fused prophetic Christianity with liberal and democratic – and some distinctly US – political and legal ideas.

When delineating just from unjust laws, he appealed to Christian ideas of natural law: "[a]ny law that uplifts human personality is just. Any law that degrades human personality is unjust" (1991 [1963]: 74).[15] Student activists who broke unjust laws were "obstetricians at the birth of a new order," since their conduct anticipated a future order where Christian love and the sacredness of each human being were taken seriously (1986b [1961]: 118, 165). Yet, King also regularly zeroed in on US democracy's specifically political and legal failings:

> An unjust law is a code inflicted upon a minority which that majority has no part in enacting or creating because they did not have the unhampered right to vote. Who can say that the legislature of Alabama which set up segregation laws was democratically elected? (1991 [1963]: 74)

Civil disobedience was legitimate not only as divine witness but when countering the existing order's failure to live up to its own democratic ideals. Defending his view of conscientious lawbreaking as based on respect for law, King referred to "the magnificent words" of the *Declaration of Independence* and the US Constitution, describing them as "a promissory note to which every American was to fall heir. This note was the promise that all men, yes, black men as well as white men, would be guaranteed the unalienable rights of life, liberty, and the pursuit of happiness" (1986b [1963]: 217).

Civil disobedients were belatedly cashing in on that note. Theirs was an effective political technique for reigniting the incomplete enforcement of standing US constitutional law, for example, the landmark *Brown v. Board of Education* (1954) case mandating school desegregation, but belligerently obstructed by southern segregationists and acquiescent government officials (1986b [1961]: 43–53). Lawbreakers could successfully rivet public attention on an unsettling scenario in which rulings by the nation's highest judicial body were being de facto invalidated by hostile officials and their racist political allies. By scuttling the Supreme Court's forward-looking and racially progressive decisions, King pointed out, it was rabid segregationists who were getting away with egregious violations of the law. When nonviolent lawbreakers abrogated local segregation statutes and other racist legal pillars, they were doing so only to counter fundamental violations of constitutional law.

The federal government, of course, had to do better at enforcing constitutional law in the face of local intransigence. Against those who tended to discount law, King emphasized its necessary role: "It may be true that morals cannot be regulated, but behavior can be regulated. The law may not change the heart, but it can restrain the heartless ... The habits, if not the hearts, of people have been, and are being, altered every day by federal action" (1986b [1962]: 100–1). Nonetheless, he conceded, "the law needs help." Fortunately,

> [n]onviolence can touch men where the law cannot reach them ... The courts can order desegregation of the public schools. But what can be done to mitigate the fears, to disperse the hatred, violence, and irrationality gathered around school integration, to take the initiative out of the hands of racial demagogues, to release respect for the law? In the end, for laws to be obeyed, men must believe they are right. (1986a [1958]: 215–16)

Civil disobedience helped counter a long tradition of racial mistrust and violence by morally disarming its antagonists. Looking to the future, King prophesied that desegregation would eventually "break down the barriers, and bring men together physically. But something must happen so to touch the hearts and souls of men" (1986a [1958]: 219–20). Non-violent lawbreaking transformed "hearts and souls," bringing about racial reconciliation and the creation of a "beloved community" built on *agape* and mutual respect. Only in such a prospective community could Americans realistically hope for universal respect for the law since only then would the law *deserve* to be respected by everyone.

Civil disobedience anticipated a pacific and socially just order where law could rest on firmer foundations. Without it, politically and socially divided communities could never expect the downtrodden and oppressed to embrace the law as their own.

For King, the requirement that lawbreakers must express respect for law was more than a strategic device for swaying skeptical, law-obeying whites. Based on a forward-looking and potentially radical political dynamic, it contributed to the creation of a more just legal order deserving of universal respect. Weaving together religious and more secular political ideas, King hoped that civil disobedience could directly advance core legal and constitutional ideals, ideals which he hoped a superior political order would better instantiate than the terribly flawed status quo.[16] Law remained for him, as for Gandhi, a valuable social good worth fighting to perfect.

This hardly meant accepting "the legitimacy of the [existing] judicial order" or the legal status quo (Milligan 2013: 99). On the contrary, for King principled lawbreaking catalyzed political change, appealing to both public opinion and the nation's moral conscience against reactionary politicians blocking reform. By zooming in on grave injustices, lawbreakers could help America finally live up to the "idea of the dignity and worth of human personality ... expressed eloquently and unequivocably" in its founding documents, which King, following the nineteenth-century abolitionist Frederick Douglas, interpreted as starting points for potentially radical change (1986b [1956]: 135–44; [1962]: 119).

Latent tensions between Christian and potentially non-religious political elements in King's thinking probably never irritated him for the simple reason that he believed, like many of his mid-century contemporaries, that the liberal and democratic ideals he endorsed cohered with – and perhaps rested on – Christianity. Writing about the *Declaration of Independence*, for example, he wrote: "[n]ever has a sociopolitical document proclaimed more profoundly and eloquently the sacredness of human personality" (1986b [1962]: 119). Though an internationalist who despised smug exceptionalist views of his country, King himself occasionally endorsed the misleading idea of the US as fundamentally Christian.[17]

Not surprisingly perhaps, even today commentators remain divided over King's legacy, with some emphasizing his religiosity and others his more secular political commitments (Dyer and Stuart 2013; Richards 2004). In a sense, both sides in the debate are probably right, but only because King himself was contradictory.

Getting right with God – or your fellow citizens?

Gandhi and King soon became global icons, with their religiously based model of civil disobedience motivating activists fighting unjust laws in an astonishing variety of settings. Proffering a sturdily built launching pad for morally principled lawbreaking, both figures transcended their provincial roots.[18] Because of their heroic efforts and huge impact, the world is surely a better place. Their ideas have also served as a basis for more recent accounts of civil disobedience. In chapters to follow, we analyze subsequent (liberal, democratic, and anarchist) revisions. Yet before doing so, we need to grasp why and how their model, despite its strengths and vast appeal, suffers from some real limitations.

Its most obvious problem is that it remains unclear how the model can ever speak persuasively to those uncomfortable with its spiritual foundations. In fairness, Gandhi and King both regularly countered the accusation of narrow sectarianism. King appealed, as noted, directly to liberal and democratic political ideals, while Gandhi asserted that "I hold my conduct to be in utter agreement with universal religion" (1986a [1930]: 511). King, whose followers included many secular activists, revealingly commented that

> even these persons [i.e., non-believers within the ranks of the civil rights movement] believe in the existence of some creative force that works for universal wholeness. Whether we call it an unconscious process, an impersonal Brahmin, or a Personal Being of matchless power and infinite love, there is a creative force in this universe that works to bring the disconnected aspects of reality into a harmonious whole. (1986a [1958]: 107)

Neither thinker ultimately offers a satisfactory retort to sympathetic critics vexed by their dependence on controversial religious ideas, or the fact that their movements – by no means coincidentally – effectively took the form of spiritual revivals, with both men revered by co-religionists as saint-like charismatic figures possessing quasi-divine authority.[19] Such features understandably frustrated secular allies; they also generated divisive internal political conflicts. Gandhi had a notoriously difficult time attracting Muslim support, while King was satirically labeled "The Lawd" [sic] by young radicals unhappy with what they viewed as his authoritarian and patriarchal leadership style.

More significantly, it hardly exemplifies love or mutual respect to deny, as Gandhi and King sometimes did, that morally principled lawbreaking could be legitimately committed by those without faith in the existence of some divine or "creative force." This position belittles the idea of equal moral personhood to which both figures otherwise subscribed, reducing those who allegedly lack the requisite spiritual comportment to second-class status.

In a global context where religion continues to flourish, this model will continue to have a wide appeal. Yet ours also remains a universe with sharply competing religious and non-religious moral communities; some real problems result for this view.

Social movements scholars can help us identify them. Looking at 1980s anti-nuclear protestors, the sociologist Barbara Epstein identified a tension between spiritual and more strategic approaches to political action, with religious activists inspired by Gandhi and King privileging the former over the latter (Epstein 1991: 222–6).[20] Their disdain for matters of political strategy and disinterest in the messy give-and-take of democratic politics sometimes got in the way of their own efforts. Civil disobedience as moral witness and self-sacrifice did not seamlessly overlap with the need for compromise and negotiation between and among individuals and groups with sharply contrasting viewpoints. Spiritual activists sometimes exhibited "moral elitism" incongruent with democratic politics. Within anti-nuclear movements

> radical Christians believe in leadership by example; but for the Christians example is tinged with a heroism that is often incompatible with collective action. In believing that faith and willingness to take special risks give them a special claim to morality, the radical Christians implicitly set up moral hierarchies that are antithetical to the spirit of grass roots democracy and that coexist uneasily with the consensus process. Debates in jail about whether or not to accept relatively lengthy sentences often turn into debates about moral superiority and inferiority. (1991: 225)

The remarkable successes of movements such as Gandhi's and King's probably helped obscure latent tensions between absolutist appeals of (godly) moral conscience, on the one hand, and messy, situational questions of political judgment, strategy, and the weighing of consequences, on the other. An underlying conflict between what the German social thinker Max Weber dubbed the "ethics of conviction," defined as an absolute commitment to moral ideals, regardless of consequences, versus the "ethics of responsibility," where political actors try primarily to "answer for the (foreseeable) consequences" of their actions, tends to get submerged within the religious model of civil disobedience (2004 [1919]: 83). Implicit in it was always the hopeful yet perhaps naïve belief, famously stated by King, "that the universe is on the side of justice," and that conscientious lawbreakers could count on heaven as an ally (1986a [1958]: 106).[21] For King, as for Gandhi before him, sacred lawbreaking was destined, if perhaps only in the final instance, to produce desirable political consequences: good moral judgment and successful politics tended to coalesce because human affairs could track divine law. For those who do not share this expectation, however, things are unavoidably more complicated.

The religious model's moral elitism was also partly hidden by Gandhi's and King's remarkable talents at mobilizing mass movements. But what happens when divinely inspired law-breakers' efforts fail to gain the hoped-for mass support? What path are those who believe themselves to be divinely appointed then likely to follow when popular opposition to their cause hardens? Then the model's built-in preference for the moral conversion of those in need of spiritual tutelage over the persuasion of political and moral equals becomes manifest, with potentially unsettling results.

Take, for example, the case of militant anti-abortion activists, many initially inspired by Gandhi and King and who early on modeled their efforts accordingly.[22] The story is a complicated one, yet some evidence points to a growing moral stridency, along with a concomitant tendency to sacrifice conscientious lawbreaking's familiar civil traits, when activists failed to shatter a rough consensus favoring the legalization of abortion. By the late 1980s in the US and elsewhere, militant anti-abortion activists harassed and physically threatened abortion providers, damaged (and sometimes even bombed) health clinics, and failed to treat women seeking terminations in a "loving" or respectful fashion. They justified their activities with literalist readings of scripture, claiming divine sanction for "rescuing" unborn babies from a morally horrific and murderous "holocaust" (Maxwell 2002; Risen and Thomas 1998). Randall Terry, onetime leader of the militant Operation Rescue, believed that God directly commanded him to lead a religious army against abortion. "You are dealing with sacred history!" Randall thundered, before egging his disciples on to vandalize clinics and harass their opponents (quoted in Risen and Thomas 1998: 220).

As even commentators opposed to legalized abortion soon pointedly noted, however, such lawbreaking could not be plausibly viewed as justified by Gandhi's or King's ideas. Activists in "Operation Rescue have given no sign to the public of the humility of which Gandhi so eloquently wrote" (DiSalvo 1991: 224). Nor did such militants show appreciation for the crucial intuition that civil disobedients should be expected to demonstrate respect for law. Instead, they crudely prioritized a sectarian interpretation of divine law, relying on tendentious readings of sacred texts, ignoring spiritual reasons, so vital to Gandhi and King, for a qualified obedience to problematic types of human law.[23] They engaged in violent acts that both Gandhi and King would have categorically condemned.

It would be unfair to draw a straight line from Gandhi and King to religiously motivated lawbreakers who scream hateful epithets at their opponents and commit physical violence. Nonetheless, degraded renditions of spiritually based civil disobedience can help identify some of the original model's weaknesses. Gandhi and King always believed that conscientious lawbreakers were obliged to make the case that their actions potentially strengthened law; lawbreakers were expected to accept legal penalties. Yet what if one sees divine law as systematically violated by the existing (secular and sinful) legal order, and therefore as unworthy of even token recognition? Not surprisingly perhaps, more radical religious lawbreakers have sometimes undertaken militant actions under the cover of darkness or gone into hiding to circumvent legal penalties.[24] Like one of the church leaders interviewed by Epstein, they seem to think that "You don't vote on morality," because "[m]orality will lose every time" (quoted in Epstein 1991: 226). Religiously based notions of civil disobedience tend to presuppose at best a qualified but by no means categorical defense of democratic politics and law. When push comes to shove, God – or at least: what one's subjective and always fallible "inner voice" tells any given individual about God – trumps competing political and legal claims, potentially including the fundamental ideal of equal moral and political personhood on which democracy builds.

We will need to see if civil disobedience can be successfully placed on less sectarian and more secure foundations. To do so, we turn to liberal ideas about civil disobedience, as they emerged in the shadows of the US civil rights movement and the political upheavals of the 1960s and early 1970s.

2
Liberalism and its Limits

During the 1960s and early 1970s, mostly US-based Anglophone intellectuals set about ambitiously recasting religious notions of civil disobedience as a novel liberal model better suited to what John Rawls, its most prominent philosophical architect, famously diagnosed as the fact of pluralism (1971). Because liberals typically began by trying to make sense of religiously motivated lawbreaking, outward appearances initially seemed unaltered. The liberal model's stipulations for justifiable civil disobedience were for the most part directly cribbed from its spiritual predecessor. Nonetheless, their connotations underwent major changes (Haksar 1986; 2003; MacCallum 1970). Civil disobedience came to signify something very different for liberals than it had for earlier religious practitioners.

Stimulated by Gandhi, King, and their growing band of anti-war, civil rights, and pacifist disciples, the liberal debate was no mere academic exercise. By the early 1960s, the UK-based Campaign for Nuclear Disarmament (CND) was organizing well-publicized mass civil disobedience at air force bases deploying nuclear weapons, as well as at the offices of the Ministry of Defence and prominent public sites such as London's Trafalgar Square. Across the Atlantic, activists inspired by Gandhi tried to board nuclear submarines docked at Groton, Connecticut and staged illegal sit-ins at atomic bases in Omaha, Nebraska. Most importantly, at least for

US intellectuals, King's Gandhian-inflected version of civil disobedience briefly succeeded in gaining the sympathy of moderate whites, eventually preparing the way for major reforms such as the 1965 Voting Rights Act. Later in the decade, civil disobedience was widely employed by opponents of the Vietnam War. Young activists burned draft cards in opposition to military conscription, while their middle-aged sympathizers violated repressive laws barring them from encouraging young men from doing so.[1]

Our discussion of the liberal model poses some challenges. First, "liberalism" is a term notoriously difficult to define, with substantial libraries filled with tomes defending alternative characterizations. For our limited aims, Duncan Bell's handy contextualist rendition seems apt: in the most general terms, liberalism represents "the sum of the arguments that have been classified as liberal, and recognized as such by other self-proclaimed liberals, across time and space" (Bell 2014: 689–90). The thinkers discussed in this chapter generally described themselves and their opinions as "liberal." More specifically, they theorized in the shadows of the mid-twentieth-century reconfiguration of liberalism as the ideological "other" of totalitarianism, a reconfiguration in which liberalism was envisioned as a "politico-intellectual tradition centered on individual freedom in the context of constitutional government" (2014: 699). Despite some major theoretical and political disagreements, the liberals analyzed below situated their views of civil disobedience in a setting where maintaining individual freedom, constitutional government and the rule of law, and representative (or liberal) democracy constituted indispensable starting points. They also presupposed the existence of a plurality of competing moral, ethical, and religious ideas and conceptions of the good life. As the liberal political theorist Judith Shklar observed, pluralism should be "treated as a social actuality" and simultaneously "as something that any liberal should rejoice in and seek to promote, because it is in diversity alone that freedom can be realized" (1986 [1964]: 5).

Second, the wide-ranging character of the liberal debate, in which myriad philosophical viewpoints were advanced by an impressive array of rival voices,[2] means that any attempt to distill the model's key elements risks obscuring nuances and perspectives. Against a tendency in the recent literature to downplay the liberal model's many nuances, I place it in the best possible light.[3] Though I concede that my account probably downplays discordant ideas and voices, it not only proffers an accurate portrayal of liberalism's main features but one that captures its underlying intuitions. The liberal model remains a necessary starting point for any fruitful analysis of civil disobedience. It is important that we do justice to it.

Liberalism's most basic achievement has already been mentioned: it acknowledges, amid a political universe with extensive moral and religious pluralism, the necessary limitations of religious justifications. As noted by the political theorist Carl Cohen, a key figure in the 1960s philosophical exchange, Gandhi and others mistakenly relied on spiritual

> knowledge claims that are practically impossible to defend. They pretend to know what the higher law demands of all men [sic], but their argument, such as it is, is convincing only to those who already share their [religious] views. Many men – perhaps most men – do not share their views and cannot be given satisfactory rational grounds for acknowledging the authority of their alleged supernatural commands or criteria. (1971: 115–16)

Sectarian views of civil disobedience suffer from epistemological barriers surmountable only by an alternative route based not on religious inspiration but on general rational principles, potentially subject to falsification, freely debatable, and capable of being endorsed by anyone, believer or otherwise. Resting on non-sectarian principles, the liberal model also strives to circumvent the prior religious account's occasional non-democratic connotations. As Rawls pointed out, when instead appropriately envisioned as a form of political participation between free and equal persons, civil disobedience makes no sense to believers in a divine order. There

> the sovereign is held to govern by divine right as God's chosen lieutenant, [since] then his subjects have only the right of suppliants. They can plead their cause but they cannot disobey should their appeal be denied. To do this would be to rebel

against the final legitimate moral (and not simply legal) authority. (1971: 383)

When society is properly conceived as a system of coopera-tion among equals, "those injured by serious injustice need not [simply] submit" to authorities claiming divine sanction. In a liberal and democratic polity, civil disobedience but-tresses efforts by free and equal citizens to counter unfair laws "within the limits of fidelity to law" (1971: 383). Illegal but normatively legitimate action "at the outer edge" of law, it potentially helps ward off unfair attacks on basic liberties (Rawls 1971: 366).

This influential liberal model, as we shall see, includes sizable political and conceptual strengths. By separating civil disobedience from its original sectarian frame, it gives both believers and the secular-minded reasons for embracing it. Recasting civil disobedience within the contours of modern pluralism, liberalism highlights its core persuasive and com-municative functions. It also thoughtfully restates the intu-ition that some types of political illegality, when properly conducted, can successfully express an underlying attachment to law.

Yet the liberal approach still suffers from flaws. Although in decisive ways less restrictive than its religious predecessor, liberals tend to tether civil disobedience to a circumscribed and overly complacent brand of political reformism. Before we consider such weaknesses, however, we need to lay out liberalism's advances vis-à-vis its religious precursor.

Civil disobedience vs. conscientious objection

Because the liberal model forsakes religious foundations, some critical commentators see in it a drive to secularize civil disobedience (Milligan 2013: 14). Indeed, vast distances sepa-rate liberals from Gandhi and King. If secularization means expunging *all* spiritual traits from civil disobedience, however, the criticism is misplaced. The liberal model aspires to take moral and religious pluralism seriously, not coercively legis-late an intolerant one-size-fits-all secularism (or "secular humanism"). In seeking to do justice to modern pluralism, the liberal approach takes two main moves. First, it distinguishes civil disobedience from conscientious objection. Second, it insists that religious and spiritual justifications should play a secondary and largely subordinate role within civil disobedience.

Liberalism rejects the idea, defended by Gandhi and King, that civil disobedience is always at its core conscientious lawbreaking, a spiritual obligation based on moral conscience (that is, as the voice of God). For the liberal, the religious model confusedly conflates civil disobedience and conscientious objection, two related yet different variants of normatively justifiable lawbreaking. Gandhi and others misleadingly confused sacred disobedience to evil law with disobedience as a voluntary civil or political act between and among equals.[4] That confusion, the liberal believes, needs to be cleaned up.

Civil disobedience is no longer an "experiment with (divine) truth" aiming at the spiritual conversion of those complicit in moral evil. It now refers specifically to political lawbreaking, where activists try to persuade their legal and political equals (on the basis, for example, of some shared conception of justice) to bring about changes to law and policy. In conscientious objection, participants seek noncompliance with laws they deem immoral, without necessarily aiming to motivate others to follow their example or alter policy (Brownlee 2012b; Rawls 1971: 368–71; Raz 2009 [1979]: 262–92; Russell 1961). Because civil disobedience is a political act it is also necessarily public, whereas conscientious objection can in principle remain private or secret. The former is civil because focused on common or political affairs, and typically with the protection of basic rights. Conscientious objection similarly enjoins respect for our political peers and their rights. However, it does not necessarily entail civility in the sense of invoking shared civic or political commitments. In civil disobedience, controversial moral or religious views do not suffice as a justification. They are adequate, however, for conscientious objection:

> The primary purpose of conscientious objection is not public education but private exemption, not political change but

(to put it bluntly) personal hand-washing. When the conscientious objector violates the law, he or she does so primarily in order to avoid conduct condemned by personal conscience even though required by public law. (Bedau 1991: 7)

Liberalism's delineation of civil from conscientious disobedience built directly on the longstanding practice of providing some legal protections to those – paradigmatically, pacifists refusing military service – who hoped to circumvent legal injunctions on religious grounds. Yet liberalism did not simply offer a philosophical codification of existing practices. Some liberals inferred that only extreme or manifestly intolerant moral and spiritual practices (i.e., those blatantly harmful to others) should be viewed as inconsonant with an appropriately expansive view of conscientious objection. Though circumscribed, conscientious objection's limits were set by broad political principles that furnished grounds for tolerating many controversial moral and religious views (Rawls 1971: 370).

Conscientious objection, on this approach, offered a potentially extensive arena in which those committed to unpopular moral and religious ideals could disobey law. Like those exempted from military duties but still expected to perform substitute services, conscientious objectors could not expect to get off scot-free even when they had successfully made their case. Nonetheless, for those whose moral or religiously tinged "experiments with truth" might prove deeply unpopular, and where "no basis for mutual understanding" with political peers could be found, conscientious objection provided a way to keep one's hands morally clean (Rawls 1971: 369; also, Cohen 1971: 41–2).

In effect, liberalism funneled religiously motivated law-breaking into what it viewed as the more suitable channel of conscientious objection. For the liberal, civil disobedience proper is political: individuals or groups counter egregious injustices by addressing existing political majorities and eventually those officials responsible for implementing policy. They appeal to public and not private authorities because the former decisively "affect permanently men's [sic] prospects in life" (Rawls 1971: 222). The state alone possesses a "comprehensive scope" and "substantial regulative powers with respect to other institutions" (Rawls 1971: 236). Political battles are waged in the final instance on the terrain of state institutions because they are vital to the realization of a common understanding of justice.

In Rawls' influential formulation, as a "conscientious yet political act" directed at swaying majorities, civil disobedience is "guided and justified by political principles, that is, by the principles of justice" regulating the broad contours of political and social life (1971: 364–5). Those pursuing civil disobedience can reasonably expect that broad agreement with their political peers, present disagreements notwithstanding, is achievable. Their lawbreaking potentially takes any of a broad array of either direct or indirect forms. In the former, an unjust law is itself violated (for example, segregation laws violated by civil rights activists). In the latter, ancillary laws, albeit ones ideally related to a contested injustice, are broken (for example, trespassing laws at a military base as part of protests against defense policies). Disobedients may refuse to pay taxes, ignore military conscription rules, violate traffic laws, or disturb the peace: what remains pivotal is that they do so with the aim of convincing an existing political majority that existing laws are unjust and urgently need to be altered.[5]

As the overlapping definitional language suggests, civil disobedience still deploys *conscience*. Even if civil disobedience no longer necessarily rests on religious convictions, nothing precludes appeals based in part on moral and spiritual grounds (Rawls 1971: 385). The liberal model's aim is not, as noted, to advance a one-size-fits-all secularism but instead to take moral and religious differences seriously. Appeals derived from one's idea of divinity or private morality necessarily play a reduced role in civil disobedience, since they cannot – and indeed should not – be expected to persuade those who do not share them. In deeply pluralistic societies where the voice of conscience speaks unavoidably in different and oftentimes inconsonant tongues, civil disobedience cannot rest exclusively or even primarily on sectarian appeals. Misguided attempts to make it do so, the liberal claims, potentially deny political peers a chance to provide their own independent answers to fundamental moral and religious questions, opening the door to moral elitism and political paternalism. Politically motivated lawbreaking can only contribute in most instances to changes in attitudes (and, ultimately, policy) by demonstrating its congruence with the community's general or overriding normative and political commitments. Controversial religious and moral ideas, in contrast, only go so far in a pluralistic polity.

Not surprisingly perhaps, most participants in the liberal debate tended to prefer King over Gandhi, reinterpreting the former's approach as exemplifying their own more secular ideas. Rawls, for example, conceded that "[r]eligious doctrines clearly underlie King's views and are important in his appeals." Nonetheless, he continued, King's religious views were "expressed in general terms: and they fully support constitutional values and accord with public reason" (1993: 250). For Rawls and other liberals, King's exemplary status derived from his ability to address not just fellow Christians but the overall political community and its constitutional underpinnings (Richards 2004). Religiously motivated or otherwise, disobedients should be expected to follow King's example and make their appeals on general political principles, though individual moral convictions might cohere with and help buttress them (Rawls 1971: 365).

Among the liberal model's proponents, internal differences quickly emerged concerning the pivotal question of how best to interpret the shared political principles disobedients were expected to invoke. Where could citizens locate them, and how might they be satisfactorily grounded? How could the principles best guide politically oriented lawbreakers? To what extent were they already implicit in – or instead perhaps transcended – existing law?

One answer, already intimated by King and eagerly appropriated by liberals struggling to place his ideas on sturdier non-religious foundations, was to associate them with what Marshall Cohen described as "the constitutions of modern states," and especially "the constitution as interpreted by the courts" (Cohen 1972: 298–9; also, Kateb 1983: 104). Civil disobedience meant violating the law while doing so in sync with fundamental principles already instantiated in existing constitutional jurisprudence. Because civil disobedience presupposed an underlying commitment to a constitutional order implicitly endorsed by one's fellow citizens, direct appeals to it, unlike sectarian moral or religious appeals, possessed a real chance of garnering majority support. Law-breakers merely recalled shared constitutional standards that had been misconstrued by existing legislative majorities or other powerful political forces.

Dissonant voices soon identified some worrisome implications. If civil disobedients simply appeal to existing legal or constitutional frameworks, were they not simply testing or trying out alternative interpretations of the law? Why then even describe their actions as illegal, when in fact they were merely proposing alternative views of existing law?

These and related questions generated a massive debate (Dworkin 1977: 202–22; Fortas 1968; also, Allen 1967; Cohen 1971: 94–105; Freeman 1966). Many liberals ultimately came around to some version of the view that it sufficed for definitional purposes if state authorities directly involved in the protest interpreted the acts at hand as illegal, regardless of subsequent determinations by the courts or their relationship to "higher" or more fundamental constitutional norms or principles (Zashin 1972: 112). An ex post facto vindication of a protest's legality did not a priori preclude its exclusion from the category of civil disobedience (Rawls 1971: 365).

Nonetheless, even a left-liberal like Rawls still inferred that politically motivated lawbreakers should appeal to an already existing common or shared sense of justice, as though civil disobedience merely aimed at correcting a majority's misunderstandings about preexisting ideals of justice. But how could this position vindicate the more radical political aspirations of Gandhi, King, and many others? Why envision civil disobedience as little more than a dramatic "post-it" note to a forgetful political majority? What about its possible role, for example, in igniting major challenges to influential views of justice or other political and constitutional ideals?

The liberal approach gained a rigorous philosophical bite missing from its religious predecessor. To its credit, it also freed the idea of civil disobedience from narrow spiritual bearings. Yet it occasionally did so at the price of a narrowing of political horizons.

Pace Gandhi and King, civil disobedience is depicted as most suitable to what Rawls and others envisaged as a basically sound liberal and democratic political order, where sizable injustices and rights violations remained, yet for the most part a palatable common vision of political justice had been realized.[6] It helps stabilize and preserve such systems and thereby ward off "uncivil" lawbreaking (Rawls 1971: 384).[7] For this reason as well, civil disobedience remains exceptional: in liberal societies political minorities should generally be able to identify meaningful opportunities for pursuing reform via ordinary channels. Activists should first typically exhaust those channels, and only when confronted with egregious injustices, and normal political devices fail to provide recourse, consider civil disobedience. Even then it might prove politically counterproductive (Rawls: 1971: 351, 363).

For Rawls, civil disobedience concerns injustices relating to basic civil and political liberties but not matters of social and economic policy; the latter are "best left to the [ordinary] political process" (1971: 373).[8] In the face of relatively minor injustices or rights violations, or complicated questions of social and economic policy, civil disobedience is inapt:

> civility imposes a due acceptance of the defects of institutions and a certain restraint in taking advantage of them. Without some recognition of this duty mutual trust and confidence are liable to break down. Thus in a state of near justice at least, there is normally a duty ... to comply with unjust laws provided that they do not exceed certain bounds of injustice. (1971: 355)

Social and political institutions, in short, are imperfect. The existence of a basically just order cannot guarantee that laws and policies will always be sound or fair. If we ignore this fact of political life and exploit institutional frailties by breaking laws whenever we deem them unsatisfactory, the mutual trust and confidence on which our common institutions depend will likely dissipate.

Gandhi and King also interpreted civil disobedience as a political last resort, but not because they viewed existing institutions as fundamentally sound. Civil disobedience for them was a radical reformist technique capable of generating nonviolent yet wide-ranging political and social change. In principle, it could be successfully employed in both liberal and authoritarian contexts (Haksar 1986).[9] Nor did they exclude from its purview social and economic matters: King devoted his final years to figuring out how mass civil disobedience could empower poor and working-class people as part of a multiracial movement (Jackson 2007: 329–58).

To be sure, dissenting voices within the 1960s and 1970s liberal debate occasionally echoed this politically more radical position. Michael Walzer, for example, claimed that private corporations operate as quasi-governmental institutions vis-à-vis those subject to their decisions: "corporations collect taxes on behalf of the state, maintain standards required by the state, spend state money, and above all enforce a great variety of rules and regulations with the silent acquiescence" of the state (1970 [1969]: 26). Those ruled over by corporate authority, however, typically possess limited possibilities to alter its policies or replace its officers: corporate officials "preside over what are essentially authoritarian regimes" (1970 [1969]: 26; also, McWilliams 1969). Why then deny those with principled concerns about undemocratic corporate power a right to undertake militant types of politically motivated lawbreaking, beyond those narrowly prescribed by liberalism? Within the contours of the liberal state, citizens usually have some – perhaps insufficient – channels for political change. But workers subject to corporate autocracy lack even those.

By day's end, however, liberalism tended to push such dissenting voices aside and draw a strict border between reform and revolution, with civil disobedience interpreted as consonant with the former but not the latter (C. Cohen 1971: 42–8; M. Cohen 1969: 211–12; 1972; Rawls 1971: 366–8; Raz 2009 [1979]: 265–65). Its relatively limited reformist aims suited supposedly advanced liberal societies that needed to do little more than ward off occasional rights violations by powerful political groups. Outside the boundaries of basically just liberal polities, to be sure, more militant – and possibly violent – resistance or revolution might make sense. However, in a more-or-less well-functioning liberal democracy with basically decent institutions, civil disobedience and its cousin, conscientious objection, remained normatively privileged modes of lawbreaking.

Recasting the die

To better grasp the ramifications of the liberal model's super-session of its religious forerunner, we can usefully zero in on Hugo Adam Bedau's cogent summary of its elements. Writing in 1970 after nearly a decade of intense debate, Bedau reca-pitulated what by then had become the conventional liberal wisdom:

> civil disobedience I take to be acts which are illegal (or pre-sumed to be so by those committing them, or by those coping with them, at the time), committed openly (not evasively or covertly), nonviolently (not intentionally or negligently destructive of property or harmful of persons), and consci-entiously (not impulsively, unwillingly, thoughtlessly, etc.) within the framework of the rule of law (and thus with a willingness on the part of the disobedient to accept the legal consequences of his act...) and with the intention of frus-trating or protesting some law, policy, or decision (or the absence thereof) of the government (or of some of its officers). (1991 [1970]: 51)

At first glance, Gandhi or King might easily have endorsed this definition. Its components (civility, openness or publicity, nonviolence, conscientiousness, respect for the law, accep-tance of legal penalties) overlap directly with their account. So wherein precisely lie the differences?

Our discussion has already partly answered this question. By delineating conscientious objection from civil disobedi-ence, while also rethinking conscience's role within the latter, the liberal model systematically overhauls the conscientious-ness requirement. As Bedau's definition illuminates, the liberal approach invites civil disobedients to demonstrate conscien-tiousness in a variety of ways. It now potentially suffices if their actions exhibit a modicum of considerate or thought-ful (moral) reflection, or what Mulford Sibley analogously characterized as a minimal "sense of responsibility" (1972 [1965]: 30). In the context of far-reaching moral pluralism, no more detailed – and thereby limiting and perhaps intoler-ant – standard for conscientiousness should be postulated. On this issue, as on a number of others we now consider, the liberal model proves to be significantly *less* restrictive than its religious predecessor.[10]

The civility standard similarly undergoes a dramatic facelift. Civility no longer refers to morally and religiously acceptable behavior, required of lawbreakers abiding their sacred duties and aspiring to serve as religious exemplars in a fallen world. Unlike King's disciples, one is required neither to be polite nor to wear one's "Sunday best." Instead, "civil" refers chiefly to the lawbreaker's political or civic orientation, her attempt to address matters of common concern, uphold basic rights, and maintain shared just institutions. It means that laws are broken not for narrow private gain but instead for the public good (Rawls 1969 [1966]: 246–7). People have come together to act in common to institute changes of public concern (Bay 1971 [1967]: 77). Correspondingly, liberalism no longer systematically privileges "proper" (that is, religiously acceptable) decorum among protestors. Lawbreaking can sometimes legitimately serve as a shock technique to unsettle a complacent political community (Sibley 1972 [1965]: 34; Cohen 1971: 17).

By the same token, activists should keep in mind that the whole point of civil disobedience is persuasion. They need to think hard about their action's likely intended as well as unintended consequences. Consequently, lawbreakers should avoid counterproductively alienating prospective allies, with their endeavors ideally exemplifying common political ideals (for example, some model of responsible, active citizenship). They ideally inspire onlookers and even adversaries (Bay 1971 [1967]: 77). Yet nothing in principle prohibits them from engaging in illegal actions likely to be viewed as unconventional. Nor does anything keep them from engaging in behavior some faith communities might consider unsuitable.

Liberalism's reconstruction of the civility requirement goes hand in hand with related revisions to the publicity and non-violence standards. Civil disobedients tackle common political concerns by addressing their political equals, with their actions structurally akin to public speech or communication. No longer a moral obligation, it is now closer in spirit to an exercise of a political right one can legitimately employ under certain conditions, albeit a right lacking standard legal and constitutional protections. If those making use of this right are to do so effectively, they need to be open or public, not because divine "truth hates secrecy," as Gandhi believed, but because the underlying rationale for civil disobedience is changing law or policy via open debate (1986b [1931]: 191). Ideally, "the forcefulness and drama of the act" itself should prove self-explanatory. Yet activists will usually need to provide some express public justification or statement explaining their endeavors (Cohen 1971: 17). In a community of political equals, publicity brings attention to injustices and is essential if others are to be convinced of the need for reform. In this vein, activists may decide to provide, as Gandhi and King sometimes recommended, advance notice to state authorities. In liberalism, however, they do so not to meet a religiously based moral obligation but to ignite public debate. If advance notice gives officials an unfair chance preemptively to block legitimate protest, keeping activists from making their case to the public, this stipulation can be sensibly overridden (Cohen 1971: 17).

What matters is not public attention focused on the person of the lawbreaker per se but instead the protest, its target, and the reasons behind it. Publicity directed at individual activists "is almost uniformly unfavorable and often quite damaging" (Cohen 1971: 16). Critics typically try to trivialize political disagreements by highlighting disobedients' personal foibles, real or otherwise. Protestors need to do whatever they can to make sure that public attention focuses on lawbreaking and its rationale. Part of the price they should be expected to pay if they hope to be taken seriously, public rather than secret action helps demonstrate their sincerity and conscientiousness (Rawls 1971: 367).

Gandhi and King, as we noted, sometimes struggled with the daunting task of sensibly interpreting and practicing nonviolence. On this hugely complicated matter the liberal approach similarly leaves some tough questions unanswered. Here I emphasize liberalism's break with prior religious ideas.[11]

Violence for the liberal model entails some tangible injury or harm, with the term often used interchangeably with others like "force."[12] Liberalism resists the claim that the term is too messy or ambiguous to serve useful purposes.

"The meaning of violence is itself unclear, but most plain men have a good idea of when it has and when it has not taken place. If I punch a policeman on the nose I am clearly violent" (Cohen 1971: 23). Civil disobedience should be minimally nonviolent in the sense of avoiding "directly and willfully injurious" harm to others, though it can still prove difficult sometimes to determine whether violence even in this narrow sense has occurred.[13] The existence of messy borderline cases need not distract us; some tension between conceptual constructs and real-life empirics is unavoidable. For some liberals, violence defined as relatively direct (and typically physical) harm or injury generally suffices (Cohen 1971: 23–4). Inflationary definitions of violence potentially limit nonviolence's scope, inadvertently deflating its legitimate sphere.

A related difficulty concerns the question of whether violence is best defined as concerning both persons and property. Bedau's statement suggests that nonviolence means avoiding harm to both, yet other liberals followed King in loosening the strict prohibition on harm to property: "the violence of symbolically important public property may be a dramatic, and not very dangerous, way, of lodging effective protests" (Cohen 1969: 217). When contributing to civil disobedience's persuasive functions, the destruction of property can in principle be tolerated. Implicit here is some idea of property as a means toward an end, justified primarily because it benefits persons. Destruction of property is worrisome when immediately linked to concrete harms accruing to persons (for example, when a private residence is torched and the owner left homeless). When it instead involves harm especially to public property, with no deleterious consequences for persons, in principle it differs. For example, when Vietnam-era activists damaged Reserve Officer Training Corps (ROTC) offices, or university-maintained draft records, no harm to persons resulted. Strictly prohibiting violence "especially against persons" makes sense (Rawls 1971: 366). Violence against property is a messier and more controversial affair about which reasonable persons might disagree.

For tactical and strategic reasons, however, many and probably most liberals ultimately suggested that violence against both persons and property should be avoided. Only then does an act's nonviolent character speak most clearly, since damage to property is too easily conflated with vandalism and criminality (Cohen 1971: 30). In the heat of political battle, conceptual subtleties tend to get lost. If disobedients are going to make a sufficiently clear case to their fellow citizens, it is probably best to avoid committing injury to either persons or property.

Significantly, liberalism stipulates nonviolence not on religious or spiritual grounds but instead chiefly because its core civil character demands it. Physical harm is prohibited not because of a general pacifist abhorrence of force but because it is incongruent with the respect we owe others as political and legal equals (Rawls 1971: 366; also, Zwiebach 1975). Nonviolence is essential since injury and harm to others clash with the objective of freely convincing them of the existence of injustices in need of correction. Coercion and force deny others their status as equals, undermining the possibility of common political agency on which democratic persuasion rests.[14] Nonviolence is a prerequisite of an "ideal political discourse" in which rational exchange, tolerance, and patience with one's political foes rightly should predominate (Bedau 1991: 8). Because violence especially against our peers endangers the foundations of our shared civil or public life, it should be kept at bay.

Even strictly nonviolent protests, to be sure, sometimes appear to precipitate violent responses. On one more recent philosophical view, nonviolence, in fact, is "rarely, if ever, conducted without elements of violence" (May 2015: 27). Liberalism tries to address this dilemma by demanding that prospective disobedients follow an ethic of responsibility: they need to think hard about the possible consequences of their actions, and do whatever can be reasonably expected of them to minimize unnecessary harm especially to innocent parties. At the same time, it would be unfair to deny activists, merely because their opponents prove reckless or violent, a fair chance to present their case to a broader public, particularly in the context of flagrant injustices. For this reason as well, the liberal tends to believe that nonviolence vis-à-vis both persons and property makes sense, since it generally proves most effective at minimizing even indirect culpability for ex post facto violence. If lawbreakers avoid *any* acts plausibly interpreted as violent, and make a due effort to avoid inciting violent responses, they cannot logically be accused of fomenting anarchy or violence (Cohen 1971: 33).

A final consequence is a certain skepticism about lawbreaking that blocks or paralyzes government offices, in the process crippling the state machinery and preventing the exercise of key functions. Gandhi and King, in some contrast, endorsed spiritually motivated yet potentially confrontational "noncooperation with evil" with precisely such disruptive goals in mind (Haksar 1986). "Our power is our ability to make things unworkable," US civil rights organizer – and sometimes mentor to King – Bayard Rustin once declared. "The only weapon we have is our bodies, and we need to tuck them in places, so wheels don't turn" (quoted in Engler and Engler 2016: 145).

Liberalism is decidedly more conflicted about militant, disruptive lawbreaking of this type. When protestors paralyze officials acting with the presumed support of a political majority, disabling and preventing them from carrying out their tasks, civil disobedience's core communicative and persuasive functions may take a backseat to coercion or force. Then political majorities are perhaps being sabotaged, not deliberatively addressed. Lawbreakers are no longer properly concerned with engaging peers in a free and open debate, but instead hindering them from acting. Such protests also typically ignite coercive responses – for example, calling in the police to drag away protestors – no one in fact, perhaps, desires. Because liberals, in short, emphasize civil disobedience's communicative role, they worry that disruptive lawbreaking can sometimes undermine its rationale (Cohen 1969: 215; Rawls 1971: 367–8).

How far can obstructive protests go before ceasing to represent acceptable civil disobedience? Liberalism suggests there is no easy answer (Cohen 1971: 67). Whether any given protest remains sufficiently communicative involves complex matters of political judgment. A general philosophical theory of civil disobedience can only take us so far in tackling difficult contextual questions of this type (Rawls 1971: 389).

Disobedience and the rule of law

For the liberals, as for Gandhi and King, politically motivated illegality needs to be sharply delineated from ordinary criminality. Only by demonstrating respect for law can disobedients expect to persuade peers of their civic-minded intentions. To its credit, liberalism places this familiar idea on sturdier non-spiritual foundations

As in its previous religious incarnation, the liberal model tends to weld legal fidelity to a "willingness to accept the legal consequences of one's conduct" (Rawls 1971: 366). Disobedients should typically expect to face legal repercussions and "pay a price" to highlight their deliberate and conscientious goals (Rawls 1971: 367). Lawbreaking means potentially facing legal penalties; no one can reasonably claim a prior exemption from possible sanctions (Woozley 1976: 329–31). Yet liberalism discards the religious intuition that they should expect to suffer or sacrifice to bear witness to divinity. Religiously inspired disobedients may opt, if they desire, to imitate Gandhi and King. Others may do so for tactical reasons. Yet liberalism insists that no one is obliged to do so.

More importantly, by accepting legal consequences disobedients show proper respect for the "legitimacy of the existing legal order as a whole" (Bay 1971 [1967]: 72). They seek to "vindicate the principle of law" (Sibley 1972 [1965]: 34). Accepting possible legal repercussions for their illegal acts, protestors confirm that they respect what liberals widely describe as the "rule of law" (Bedau 1991: 8)

Participants in the wide-ranging liberal debate offered competing accounts of precisely what such willingness properly entails. Some went so far as to assert that disobedients should count on being treated no differently from those violating laws for nonpolitical reasons, while others argued that civil disobedience's distinctive traits justified official leniency (Cohen 1971: 76–91; James 1973). Since liberal states should encourage citizens to cultivate independent judgments about complex issues, and because fidelity to the law cannot be equated with blind loyalty to a specific official's or institution's legal views, the state has a responsibility to soften the predicament of civil disobedients "whenever it can do so without great damage to other policies" (Dworkin 1977: 215). No government can realistically guarantee blanket immunity to lawbreakers. However, "when the practical reasons for prosecuting are relatively weak in a particular case, or can be met in other ways, the path of fairness lies in tolerance" (Dworkin 1977: 215–16).

Others argued that disobedients might simply deny legal wrongdoing altogether. Nonetheless, they should still be prepared to appear before authorities and "make a constitutional (or merely legal) defense" explaining their actions (Zashin 1972: 142). In extreme scenarios when there is "no right of public trial, and no possibility of using punishment for publicity purposes, or if punishments [are] made draconian in order to prevent dissenters from publicizing their views," the evasion of legal sanctions becomes justifiable (Singer 1973: 83–4). Willingness to appear before a tribunal only makes sense when independent of direct political pressures, and basic legal protections remain secure. Those who cooperate with kangaroo courts open themselves to becoming complicit in the prosecuting regime's own disdain for legality.

The debate's myriad complexities should not obscure the central point that liberalism views this matter differently from its religious precursors. Readiness to accept legal consequences no longer rests on an interpretation of civil disobedience as sacred witness, as potentially anticipating a novel order in which spiritual ideals are more completely instantiated. Liberalism endorses the more prosaic but also more plausible idea of a qualified duty or obligation to obey the law, grounded on the thesis that any normatively acceptable political order requires rule- or law-based government: "The life of every civilized community is governed by rules," or the rule of law (Cohen 1971: 2). Law-based government represents a valuable social good: if we sacrifice too many of its elements, egregious injustices are likely to occur (Fuller 1964). Only an anarchist, the liberal posits, would deny the rule of law's virtues (Bedau 1961: 659–60). Where, as in most liberal democracies, most citizens also contribute to law's enactment, we should for the most part abide the law (Cohen 1971: 5).

On this view, every political order should be expected to realize publicity, generality, clarity, prospectiveness, as well as consistency and constancy, in its laws. The idea of the rule of law demands fidelity not to law per se but instead to a legal system whose elements instantiate substantial legal virtues (clarity, publicity, generality). Only when law does so, the liberal believes, can government realistically provide a modicum of legal security and liberty. Without the rule of law, government is unlikely to act in a minimally consistent, predictable, and transparent manner. Absent legally constrained state action, it becomes difficult to see how political actors could ever enjoy personal let alone political freedom. Brutal dictatorships such as Nazi Germany or Stalinist Russia may have possessed "law" in some broad sense of binding government commands. Yet they did not achieve the "rule of law" in this more demanding sense (Fuller 1964; Neumann 1957).

In Rawls' formulation, every just order should rest on the rule of law, a notion he, like his liberal allies, discussed at length, and without which both legal regularity and equal liberty were deemed unachievable (1971: 239; also, Kornhauser 2015: 175–220). Fidelity to the law means respecting a fundamental ideal of "justice as regularity," an "ideal notion which laws" should be "expected to approximate" even though they sometimes fail to do so (1971: 236). When civil disobedients express fidelity to the law they implicitly require that officials guarantee

> that laws be known and expressly promulgated, that their meaning be clearly defined, that statutes be general both in statement and intent and not be used as a way of harming particular individuals ... that at least the more severe offenses be strictly construed ... For if, say, statutes are not clear in what they enjoin and forbid, the citizen does not know how he [sic] is to behave. (1971: 238)

Liberty's boundaries then become vague and uncertain, and government may act arbitrarily by treating like cases or situations in unlike ways (1971: 239). The rule of law – in the rudimentary yet indispensable sense of demanding clear, general, prospective legal rules, as well as independent courts – hardly provides airtight protection against injustice. Yet its virtues are not by any means negligible: no free and decent political order can do without them (1971: 236).

Disconnecting civil disobedience from its prior sectarian foundations, the liberal model hardly means an obsession with "hair-splitting legalistic details" (Sitze 2013: xix). On the contrary, it offers a supple reinterpretation of the nexus between political lawbreaking and respect for law. Unfortunately, its accomplishments come at a high price: civil disobedience's once ambitious political contours tend to get neutralized.

For Gandhi and King, as we have seen, conscientious lawbreaking contained forward-looking and even radical political implications, with lawbreakers pictured as contributing directly to a novel order where universal love, mutual respect, and nonviolence were more fully realized. Their liberal admirers, to be sure, sometimes pointed in a similar direction. For the philosopher Ronald Dworkin, disobedients courageously challenged hegemonic views of constitutional law, demanding of authorities that they reconsider settled positions. Principled lawbreakers demonstrated fidelity to the rule of law by providing reasoned legal reinterpretations, with their dramatic acts encouraging others – and ultimately government – to grant legal validity to alternative legal views. When successful, their previously heterodox interpretations could become influential. On this version of liberalism, civil disobedience prodded overdue constitutional correction and innovation (Dworkin 1977: 206–22).

Nonetheless, the liberal approach ultimately tended to acquire more cautious political traits. Civil disobedience, as noted, was generally conceived as appropriate to existing and supposedly "nearly just" (liberal and democratic) societies. It had nothing in common with radical calls for transformational political or social change. In Rawls' account, it served as a corrective to violations of basic civil and political but not social or economic rights. Legal fidelity was similarly reduced to a cramped allegiance to "the existing legal order as a whole" (Bay 1971 [1967]: 72), standing "constitutions of modern states" (Cohen 1972: 289), and the present "frame of established authority and the general legitimacy of the system of law" (Cohen 1966: 3), viewed in static terms. Nonviolent lawbreaking as embodying the "highest respect for the law" simply meant showing one's loyalty to the fundaments of a more-or-less sound extant legal and constitutional system, though not specific (unjust) laws in need of revision.[15]

Among his liberal admirers, King's view of fidelity to law as congruent with radical change, even to the point of getting "rid of the system," vanished. So too did his reading of the *Declaration of Independence* and the US Constitution as launching pads for broad political and social transformation. It is hard to imagine King, in any event, endorsing Rawls' view of the US and other "advanced" democracies as "nearly just," a category astute critics have deemed analytically imprecise and politically tendentious (Lyons 2013: 134–5; Sabl 2001).

When push comes to shove, major challenges to the community's shared views of justice, the consideration of basically novel types of rights or political participation, or prospects for far-reaching social and economic change, get pushed to the sidelines (Arato and Cohen 1992: 574–604). The liberal model's quiescent political drift, to be sure, arguably rested on unexamined diagnostic as well as core philosophical tenets. Too often, it simply mirrored the broad public consensus within North America and western Europe that theirs were "advanced" democracies with some blemishes and requiring modest reform, but hardly in need of systemic overhaul.[16] Predictably, liberals tethered civil disobedience to a circumscribed reformism that often veiled the prevalence of deeply rooted structural injustices and inequalities (based in class, race, and gender). For anyone hoping to pursue more radical political and social change, the liberal model seemed accordingly unsatisfactory.

Beyond liberalism?

Liberal civil disobedience takes major steps beyond its religious precursor. That earlier model's most appealing components are preserved without their controversial spiritual undergirding. Unfortunately, liberalism's tendency to weld them to a limited and probably overcautious vision of political reform risks neutering civil disobedience in ways that should trouble us. Rather than a legitimate mechanism for significant political and social change, civil disobedience risks becoming a stabilizing corrective to a status quo viewed as fundamentally sound.

Even as liberals were still energetically debating the details of their model, by the late 1960s and early 1970s younger activists and intellectuals had already abandoned the benign portrayal of existing society on which it implicitly built. Better attuned to King's radical views about the US and other liberal societies, they posed some astute critical questions. Why, for example, did political apathy remain pervasive? What were the hidden costs of liberalism's preoccupation with political stability? Why were so many young people nonetheless challenging the legitimacy of liberal society's key economic institutions (Habermas 1975 [1973]; Pateman 1970)? Inspired by increasingly widespread calls for extensive reform, they also set about trying to restate the idea of civil disobedience in a decidedly more democratic fashion.

3
Deepening Democracy

Concerns about the liberal model's limits generated a volley of critical responses during the 1970s and 1980s. Here we examine the democratic alternative to liberalism as sketched out by a diverse group of authors. Despite sizable political and philosophical disagreements, those embracing a more robust democratic model of civil disobedience consistently rejected complacent accounts of the liberal status quo as basically or "nearly just," building instead on a more critical diagnosis. In the democratic model, civil disobedience aims at maximizing meaningful deliberation and participation. Because democracy remains an open-ended historical project, with its institutions and laws always susceptible to sclerosis, civil disobedience represents an "unavoidable, integral part of a well-functioning democratic process" (Markovits 2005: 1902). It potentially unblocks the clogged arteries of the body politic, and when properly conducted revitalizes not only mass politics but also identifiably democratic – and not simply liberal – ideas of constitutionalism and law.

Writing in the shadows of global protests directed against the Vietnam War, the political theorist Hannah Arendt noted that liberal democracies such as the US faced a political crisis in which the "established institutions of a country fail to function properly" (1972 [1970a]: 101–2). Incidents of civil disobedience were undergoing a dramatic uptick because "the normal channels of change no longer function, and grievances will not be heard or acted upon" (1972 [1970a]: 74–5, 101–2). Civil disobedience had suddenly become widespread, Arendt insisted, because ordinary citizens were increasingly denied effective opportunities for shaping their common affairs. Normative accounts of how self-government *ought* to work seemed ever more remote from disheartening political realities (Singer 1973: 124). *Pace* hostile law-and-order conservatives, civil disobedience was not in fact contributing to endemic lawlessness. Instead, it was political elites who were abandoning regular institutional channels when politically convenient. Civil disobedience represented an appropriate and perhaps necessary response.[1]

With the liberal state more and more estranged from ordinary citizens, it was vital to figure out how politically motivated lawbreaking might best contribute to political and social change. Political and institutional deficits obstructed overdue social reform, necessitated by the liberal polity's failure to adapt sufficiently to rapidly changing conditions. According to proponents of the democratic model, society's worst ills "remain unassailable by [liberal] civil disobedience, and thus left to the ordinary weak ministrations of free speech and the electoral system, which have hardly been able to budge these problems" (Zinn 2002 [1968]: 36–7).

Peter Singer, a transitional figure in the debate, posited that when political rights and procedures had been violated, a proper public hearing denied alternative viewpoints, and a political majority had to be pushed to reconsider its positions, nonviolent civil disobedience might be legitimate. Civil disobedience, in short, could be directly justified on democratic grounds (1973: 63–91). For Carole Pateman, the liberal view of civil disobedience as public speech, conjoined with the standard demand that disobedients accept punishment, reduced it "to little more than the 'all-purpose threat' of the little girl in the English children's stories: 'if you don't do it I'll scream and scream until I make myself sick'" (1985 [1979]: 58). Politically motivated lawbreaking should instead be viewed as "one possible expression of the active citizenship" on which a future and more richly participatory democracy would directly rest (1985 [1979]: 162). Liberal civil disobedience neither did justice to the realities of grassroots lawbreaking "on the ground" nor provided a helpful guide for those hoping to pursue it. If democratization were to advance into the workplace and the family, a new conception of political disobedience would have to supplant it.

In the previous chapter I conceded that my ideal-typical recapitulation of the liberal view of civil disobedience potentially downplays key differences between and among its variants. A similar caveat is appropriate here. Some authors – most prominently, Arendt – whose contributions I place under the rubric of "democratic civil disobedience" would assuredly resist this categorization.[2] Even among those who would likely embrace it, we encounter rival (discourse-theoretical or deliberative, participatory, radical, and republican) theories of democracy. Those understandably interested in such philosophical disagreements will need to look elsewhere (Held 2006). I bracket them simply to highlight illuminating, yet easily overlooked, commonalities between and among an otherwise disparate group of writers, commonalities deriving from a shared quest to transcend liberal views of civil disobedience on the basis of more energetic commitments to self-government.

The liberal model, as noted in the preceding chapter, always contained democratic elements. Its proponents were liberal democrats (or, perhaps more accurately, democratic liberals); "liberalism" for them included representative democracy. Analogously, democratic theorists of civil disobedience build on the liberal legacy. Following the liberals, they generally distinguish civil from conscientious disobedience. Civil disobedience is again detached from its religious roots, with democrats generally skeptical of the idea that private morality or conscience suffices as a ground for politically motivated lawbreaking. Like Rawls and other liberals, they acknowledge modern pluralism and irrepressible moral and religious disagreement. Disobedience here is also primarily political, not moral or spiritual. Democrats typically take core liberal rights seriously, and acknowledge civil disobedience's proper role in aiding embattled minorities whose rights have been violated.

Debts to the liberal model notwithstanding, the democratic approach constitutes a decisive break. Even when it reproduces liberal components, they undergo decisive changes. For liberals, threats to liberty stem primarily from overreaching political majorities that menace basic rights. When a minority's core civil and political rights are systematically violated, and normal institutional mechanisms for redress fail, civil disobedience can help ignite corrective action. Civil disobedience, in the liberal view, remains in key ways democracy-limiting: it checks the excesses of (democratic) majority rule, restoring the proper balance between democracy (majority rule) and liberalism (the preservation of basic civil and political rights).[3] Not surprisingly, the liberal account often pushes self-government to the analytic sidelines, while implicitly relying on some of its pillars. Liberals speak regularly of the need for disobedients to act openly to sway publics consisting of fellow citizens. Yet they often say little about the proper contours of public action, or the necessary presuppositions of the free-wheeling deliberation essential to it.[4]

But what of lawbreaking that aims at more than securing individual liberties against overreaching majorities? When Vietnam War-era activists burned draft cards or undertook illegal sit-ins at military bases, for example, they were protesting a war never formally declared by the US Congress and lacking a proper democratic footing, with many momentous political decisions kept from the public eye. Those outside the US pursuing similarly motivated lawbreaking also claimed that their political leaders had complacently acquiesced in a US-dominated "free" order. The fact that the US could wage – and its allies slavishly support – an unjust war absent meaningful public input and despite massive opposition, raised unsettling questions for them as well about the liberal status quo.

Political lawbreaking, in sum, increasingly targeted democratic deficits, and especially the ways in which real-life practice contravened core democratic norms. By the early 1970s, civil disobedients around the globe were acting on a widespread perception that liberal representative democracy was no longer responding satisfactorily to popular grievances, and that more effective channels for active citizenship had to be created. Civil disobedience, on their view, represented such a channel.

Analogous anxieties soon inspired Jürgen Habermas, contemporary Germany's most formidable political thinker, to defend civil disobedience. Writing in the 1980s in the shadows of mass lawbreaking by European peace and anti-nuclear activists, Habermas worried that the Federal Republic's only "halfway functioning constitutional state" systematically blocked popular challenges to policy and law (Habermas 1985a [1979]: 11). Habermas came to view civil disobedience as democracy-enhancing, as a popular instrument for making sure that democracy is actively practiced and not just preached. Suspended between positive law and democratic legitimacy, civil disobedience could play a constructive role in protecting and potentially reconfiguring both democracy and constitutional government.

Because of their major contributions to the democratic approach, this chapter focuses on the theoretical heavy-weights Arendt and Habermas. Before doing so, however, it turns to the illuminating contributions of the radical US activist and historian, Howard Zinn, who anticipated some of its core traits. Zinn's version also helps pinpoint possible weaknesses. The remainder of the chapter then considers whether the democratic model can successfully circumvent them.

Zinn's challenge

Zinn was a life-long activist and frequent civil disobedient in many of the great US political battles of the 1960s, 1970s, and beyond. For Zinn, civil disobedience is a tool for ambitious democratic political and social change: "Democracy must improve itself constantly or decay" (2002 [1968]: 18). US democracy – the author's main preoccupation – represents an unfinished project in which popular groups assert power not only over the state but over everyday life (the workplace, for example).[5] More generally, "democracy is not just about counting up votes; it is a counting up of actions" (2002 [1968]: 25). Without grassroots extra-institutional action by the socially and politically excluded, the liberal state systematically favors the powerful and privileged. Real political and social change only follows popular mobilization and politically motivated lawbreaking. Civil disobedience is indispensable to democratic renewal since it forces well-situated power blocs to make concessions.

Existing liberal – and especially judicial – institutions impede democratization, partly because of the disproportionate influence of political and social elites, and partly because of the political machinery's sluggish operations. Neither the courts nor other key institutions ever initiate progressive change; they accept reform only when forced by popular movements to do so. A key contemporary dilemma is the temporal disconnect between our rapidly changing social universe and the laggard temporality of liberal institutions, which inevitably fall behind the fast pace of present-day social change.[6] Fortunately, civil disobedience can "quicken the pace of change," offering an effective way for disadvantaged groups to accomplish what ordinary, slow-moving institutions cannot achieve: dynamic, forward-looking democratic politics in sync with contemporary society's rapid-fire temporal dictates (2002 [1968]: 19).

To succeed, activists need new "techniques of civil disobedience which not only ruffle the complacency of the powerful ... but begin to replace the old institutions, the old leaders" (2002 [1968]: 108). Zinn sees no division between civil disobedience as a reformist and more revolutionary tool. With echoes of Gandhi and King, it represents an "attempt to bring about revolutionary social change without the enormous human toll of suicidal violence" (2002 [1968]: 109). Overlap with Gandhi and King notwithstanding, Zinn proposes a significantly broader definition:

> civil disobedience is the deliberate, discriminate violation of law for a social purpose. It becomes not only justifiable but necessary when a fundamental human right is at stake, and when legal channels are inadequate for securing that right. It may take the form of violating an obnoxious law, protesting an unjust condition, or symbolically enacting a desirable law or condition. It may or may not eventually be held legal ... but its aim is always to close the gap between law and justice, as an infinite process in the development of democracy. (2002 [1968]: 119)

His redefinition results in a loosening of many familiar preconditions. Although typically open or public, lawbreakers here can also circumvent public punishment, hide from authorities by going underground, and engage in acts whose details remain hidden from the public eye (by creating, for example, an "underground railroad" for those evading military service) (2002 [1968]: 112; 1990: 120–3). They are no longer limited, as in the orthodox liberal model, to addressing public or state authorities. Private institutions can be rightfully targeted, for example, by people protesting the "hot, stinking, crumbling, vermin-infested holes" in which they are forced to reside (2002 [1968]: 112). Because democratization potentially extends beyond the state, civil disobedience can legitimately take direct aim at unjust social and economic practices. Zinn refuses to tether civil disobedience to the violation of specific laws or policies, since deeply rooted social ills may have only a tangential relationship to individual statutes: "Poverty, for instance, is not represented by specific 'poverty' laws which the poor can violate in protest" (2002 [1968]: 37). By experimenting with socially useful but illegal practices or institutions, activists might pursue symbolic enactments of a prospective and more desirable law or condition (2002 [1968]: 119).

"Violence is in itself an evil," yet here nonviolence no longer prohibits destruction of property or material objects, since it can offer a useful way to dramatize one's cause and generate public discussion (2002 [1968]: 49). Even direct harm to persons may be necessary when "guarded, limited, [and] aimed carefully at the source of injustice" (2002 [1968]: 50). Zinn blurs the divide between nonviolent civil disobedience and violent resistance. Nor does anything about his redefinition prohibit obstructing public or private institutions and keeping them from performing their tasks (2002 [1968]: 33–4). Against liberals who worry that such acts sometimes occasion coercion or force, Zinn belittles liberalism for trivializing the widespread "violence to body and spirit," deriving from "ill-health, unemployment, humiliation, loneliness, a sense of impotence," generated by the everyday operations of liberal society (2002 [1968]: 19). Seeing violence as endemic to liberal society, and suggesting a more encompassing definition of violence than previous religious or liberal thinkers, he has few qualms about watering down the nonviolence requirement.[7]

Zinn's fiercest ire is saved for liberal jurists who insist that disobedients should accept legal penalties, and that by so doing they exhibit proper respect for law. King may have accepted penalties in Birmingham and elsewhere, Zinn admits, but was he right to do so? "Why should there not [instead] have been bitter, forceful complaint across the country against this set of oppressive acts?" (2002 [1968]: 29). If a law is oppressive, there are sound reasons for circumventing it and any resulting penalties (1990: 122). The real problem contemporary society faces is not excessive lawlessness but blind subservience to bad laws. Zinn rejects outright the idea of a "rule of law" and any notion of a basic obligation to law. "To exalt the rule of law as an absolute is the mark of totalitarianism" (2002 [1968]: 120). When jurists and philosophers talk of a highfalutin rule of law they provide an ideological disguise for the ugly realities of a political and social order plagued by unfair laws and arbitrary legal prerogative (1971; 1990: 110–14). Misleading appeals to the rule of law close our eyes to law's role in buttressing injustice. Civil disobedients, in any event, are under no obligation to express fidelity to law.

Despite some innovations, Zinn's model seems unsatisfactory. On the one hand, he provides a harsh account of the rule of law and the idea of a general obligation to law. On the other hand, he regularly appeals to a legal standard, an idea of human rights, a notion he attributes to Thomas Jefferson and the *Declaration of Independence*, and which he views as a normative compass to civil disobedients (1990: 109, 133; 2002 [1968]: 23). His rejection of the nexus between civil disobedience and respect for law proves less categorical than initially seems to be the case. He also regresses to the preliberal intuition that moral conscience can serve as a lodestar for lawbreaking, and that civil disobedience is fundamentally conscientious: "Why should not the individual 'pick and choose' according to conscience, according to a set of humane values beyond the law?" (2002 [1968]: 24). Civil disobedience again tends to become a moral obligation, though one no longer resting exclusively on divine inspiration. Unfortunately, Zinn never satisfactorily identifies where we might locate "humane values," or how a pluralistic society with deep moral and religious divisions could impartially negotiate among them.

Zinn's open-ended definition of civil disobedience (as a "deliberate, discriminate, violation of law for a vital social

purpose") is also worrisome. Public and open (yet sometimes hidden or secret), nonviolent (yet perhaps violent),
and direct lawbreaking – as well as episodes where activists symbolically anticipate novel laws or social changes, all
now fall under it (2002 [1968]: 119). Vexed by liberalism's
constrictive account, Zinn counters with a permissive redefinition that excludes relatively few political illegalities, with
the term taking on connotations that would have vexed not
just liberals but sometimes also Gandhi and King. A tendency
to privilege civil disobedience over ordinary political and
legal channels follows from his anarchist-inspired skepticism
about law and the state.[8] Yet Zinn simultaneously restrains
his anarchist instincts by conceding that law and policy can
be effectively shaped by social movements. If law and institutions sometimes embody the results of political victories
by the excluded and oppressed, they probably deserve some
minimal respect, Zinn's claims notwithstanding. At the end of
the day, in short, Zinn's version of the democratic approach
seems conflicted.

Civil disobedience, law, and the revolutionary spirit

Arendt also pursues a less restrictive definition of civil disobedience than most liberals, and her reflections sometimes
echo Zinn's. Yet she places them on firmer ground.

Arendt joins in criticizing the orthodox thesis that civil
disobedients should expect punishment, seeing in it vestiges
of a narrow and one-sidedly legalistic version of liberalism.[9]
For many liberal jurists, she points out, politically motivated
lawbreaking is basically analogous to individual criminal or
civil lawbreaking, deserving of punishment as a way of evincing the lawbreaker's obligations to the legal status quo. *Pace*
this view, for Arendt civil disobedience should neither be
viewed as a legal test of a statute's constitutionality nor as
possibly falling under existing constitutional protections (free
speech, for example). However well intentioned, liberal
lawyers who seek to subsume it under existing law occlude
civil disobedience's special political traits. They reduce it to

just another individual legal case to be dutifully subjected to the operations of an already functioning judicial machinery, in the process missing what makes it politically special.

Like Zinn, Arendt draws no clear line between revolution and civil disobedience. Though nonviolence represents one "generally accepted necessary condition," civil disobedience can open the door to sweeping change (1972 [1970a]: 77). A cramped liberal legalism, Arendt's main target, not only obscures the fact that civil disobedience can prove transformative but also that it is appropriately pursued by groups of active citizens, that it represents public action in concert by self-organized political minorities bound together by common views and not simply overlapping private interests (1972 [1970a]: 56). Acting openly and dramatizing matters of common concern, theirs is principally a political intervention, with their endeavors embodying a distinctive human capacity for political action, or what

> makes man [sic] a political being …; it enables him to get together with his peers, to act in concert, and to reach out for goals and enterprises that would never enter his mind … had he not been given this gift – to embark on something new … Since we all come into the world by virtue of birth, as new-comers and beginnings, we are able to start something new … No other faculty except language, neither reason nor consciousness, distinguishes us so radically from all animal species. (1972 [1970b]: 179)

Arendt acknowledges that civil disobedience often functions defensively to protect existing political channels from threats.[10] Yet it also can engender desirable innovations having potentially radical political ramifications (1972 [1970a]: 75–7).

Since citizen action rests on a logic fundamentally different from political violence, civil disobedience ideally remains nonviolent. Gandhi's startling victory over British colonialism proves that it can effectively defang potent regimes and generate massive change.[11] At the same time, Arendt considers it politically naïve to count universally on success from Gandhi's approach:

> If Gandhi's enormously powerful and successful strategy of nonviolent resistance had met with a different enemy – Stalin's

Russia, Hitler's Germany, even prewar Japan, instead of England – the outcome would not have been decolonization, but massacre and submission. (1972 [1970b]: 152)

Like liberals, Arendt rejects spiritual notions of nonviolence; she is skeptical as well that nonviolent lawbreaking can always do the requisite political work. She is noticeably less interested in discussing the pros and cons of nonviolence, however, than in highlighting what it tells us more generally about civil disobedience: it constitutes political action par excellence, admirable cooperative activity resting on the reciprocity and mutuality of equal citizenship, and therefore in principle incongruent with violence. Political action depends on horizontal relations between and among those who debate and act on matters of shared concern, whereas violence is essentially mute, instrumental, and conducive not to action in concert with peers but to shaping or fabricating objects for everyday use (1972 [1970b]; also, Bernstein 2013: 78–104). In contemporary society, she believes, too few possibilities for political action are available.

Such action manifests itself paradigmatically within voluntary associations, where people come together to work on matters of public concern, developing the political ties necessary to pursue common goals. Republican self-government, where political action thrives, correspondingly requires a rich variety of voluntary associations. Revealingly, Arendt describes those engaging in civil disobedience as constituting "nothing but the latest form of voluntary association," and thus "in tune with the oldest traditions" on which republicanism – in her view best exemplified by the US – was founded (1972 [1970a]: 96). Civil disobedients act together voluntarily, in the process giving expression to the original revolutionary spirit on which republican government rests.[12] Self-government represents an ongoing and probably always incomplete project, with civil disobedients depicted by Arendt as potentially coming together to augment and update existing political and legal practice. While maintaining fidelity to the republic's original spirit and aspirations, they adapt its laws and institutions, creatively reforming and amending them.

Like Zinn, Arendt finds a troublesome gap between "the unprecedented rate of change in our time" and political and legal institutions, with one consequence being a tendency for them to fall badly out of step (1972 [1970a]: 80). In sharp contrast to Zinn, she believes that no society can survive without the stability provided by "the legal systems that regulate our life in the world and our daily affairs with each other" (1972 [1970a]: 79). Social acceleration places law's stabilizing functions at risk; Arendt questions whether law can be properly synchronized with society's high-speed temporality via conventional institutional mechanisms. Law too often falls behind contemporary needs. The judiciary can perhaps codify and help stabilize political change when it has already occurred, "but the change itself is always the result of extra-legal action" (1972 [1970a]: 80). Only the civil rights movement's mass civil disobedience campaign, accordingly, eventually forced US citizens to tackle segregation's evils (1972 [1970a]: 80–1).

Given present-day social temporalities, civil disobedience alone provides citizens with the requisite opportunities to counter obsolescent legal norms and institutional practices. If public-minded citizens are going to have a real chance to update them, civil disobedience's distinctive merits need to be properly recognized. The best way to do so, Arendt tentatively suggests, would be by providing it with some sort of "constitutional niche," an institutional guarantee ensuring that disobedients' voices be "present and to be reckoned with in the daily business of government" (1972 [1970a]: 101).

This somewhat vague proposal has ignited controversy (Kalyvas 2008: 286–8; Kateb 1983: 141–4; Smith 2012). Given Arendt's worries about unsuitable legalistic accounts of civil disobedience, why advocate what seem to be institutional – and probably legal or constitutional – protections for it? Why legalize a practice whose virtues allegedly derive from its specifically political, extra-legal traits?

Despite her opposition to liberal legalism, Arendt reformulates the old idea that civil disobedience and respect for law go hand in hand. On her reconstruction, civil disobedients pay homage to an admirable conception of law and constitutional government. They do so in a different manner than either liberals or religious thinkers, however, had in mind.

As noted, Zinn occasionally resuscitates the older religious view of civil as conscientious disobedience. Arendt categorically rejects this position. Even more systematically than liberals who distinguish civil from conscientious law-breaking, she views conscience as basically incongruent with public-minded civil disobedience (1972 [1970a]: 58–68). Civil disobedience represents political but never moral action. When sensibly practiced, it constitutes sound politics, not a moral duty or obligation. Private morality and conscience are not only inadequate starting points for civil disobedience; they distort its core political attributes. Individuals who circumvent the law because of conscience do so for self-interested and even selfish reasons, Arendt declares, whereas civil disobedience entails action with others for the public good. In modernity conscience is necessarily private, subjective, and unreliable. Its existence can no longer be taken for granted (1972 [1970a]: 64–5). Some liberals try to quarantine conscience, Arendt concedes, yet they fail to do so satisfactorily.

Regrettably, Arendt probably goes too far here (Cooke 2017). Does it make sense to purge civil disobedience of *any* element of conscience? Whatever its limitations, conscience probably should remain part of the story. Arendt seems too cavalier in her reading of conscience as inherently self-centered and unavoidably anti-political. Why not, for example, instead concede that moral conscientiousness in civil disobedience merely means that activists are "at least for the while, and at least on one gravely important issue, more seriously moral than most other people" (Kateb 1983: 106)?[13]

Fortunately, Arendt's account of the nexus between politics and law proves more satisfying. The US founders, on her reading, rightly saw in constitution-making the "foremost and noblest of all revolutionary deeds" (1963: 158). They envisaged constitutionalism not as exclusively about limiting the state but also about supporting future possibilities for political action, as empowering later generations to exercise political freedom via legal and constitutional protections for participation and deliberation. They sought not just a limited government but one that invited political action in concert among and between political equals. Theirs was

> a constitution [aiming] to lay down the boundaries of the new political realm and to define the rules within it ... [T]hey had to found and build a new political space within which the

"passion for public freedom" or the "pursuit of public happiness" would receive free play for generations to come, so
that their own "revolutionary" spirit could survive the actual
end of the revolution. (1963: 126)

Optimally, constitutional government helps secure the survival of the original revolutionary spirit on which republican
government rests, allowing citizens to act together with their
peers in no less politically consequential ways.

Neither the present-day US political system nor others
elsewhere, however, presently provide sufficient channels for
political action. Arendt's enthusiasm for civil disobedience as
practiced by civil rights, anti-war, and student activists stems
from their exemplary political character, their "sheer courage,
an astounding will to action, and ... no less astounding
confidence in the possibility of change" (1972 [1970b]: 118).
Yet it also derives from her hope that they might revitalize a
more productive and mutually supportive nexus between
politics and law, one that transcends both legalistic liberalism
and the legal skepticism of radicals like Zinn. Civil disobedients recall a "never fully articulated concept of law" in which
law not only checks powers but empowers autonomous
citizen action (1972 [1970a]: 83). They implicitly pay heed
to an idea of law still deserving of our loyalties, with their
endeavors potentially exemplifying admirable legal and constitutional ideals (Smith 2009).[14]

Arendt theorizes that the US republic's framers aptly jet-
tisoned an unsatisfactory vertical notion of the social contract, in which law constituted a top-down command or
imperative, issued by a sovereign state standing above and
beyond a motley collection of previously isolated individuals
who created it. With Thomas Hobbes in mind, Arendt is
irritated by this model's starkly individualistic – and for her
basically unpolitical – starting point, as well as its idealization
of the contemporary realities of many state activities that
seem at most tangentially related to individual consent: this
model is "entirely fictitious; under the present circumstances,
at any rate, it has lost all plausibility" (1972 [1970a]: 89). In
its paradigmatic Hobbesian version, the dissolution of government necessarily means anarchy and violence, with individuals reverting to a horrific fictional "state of war" they

originally fled. The vertical contract simply cannot make sense of nonviolent civil disobedience, since lawbreaking always means disorder and probably chaos.

Fortunately, the US framers turned to a superior notion of a horizontal social contract, in which individuals prior to government's creation already constituted an egalitarian social community built on symmetrical ties. Inspired by John Locke, this model requires of individuals that they bind themselves together via reciprocal promises and agreements (Arendt 1963: 170). Discarding the vertical contract's hierarchical structure, it takes the idea of equal participation in public life seriously. Law relies not on obedience to a potentially omnipotent sovereign state but on deliberation among equals, and the "promises, covenants, and mutual pledges" they jointly generate (1963: 181). Support for law is never blind or unquestioning but instead predicated on lively political exchange – and the possible expression of dissenting views – within a pluralistic political community (1972 [1970b]: 140).

Arendt prefers this second model for many reasons. It acknowledges the right to dissent from and even break the law when it is made by political majorities. Significantly, it grounds the possibility of lawbreaking not primarily or exclusively because of liberal worries about majoritarian threats to individual rights, but rather because it sees government as subordinate to a more primordial political community resting on mutual promises and obligations. When political majorities – or state officials acting in their name – pursue illegal or unconstitutional action, in effect breaking their promises to their political peers, they betray their most sacrosanct political obligations. Citizens can then legitimately respond with their own extra-legal political acts – in other words, with civil disobedience.

For Arendt, civil disobedience can only be properly understood when viewed through the lens of this horizontal social contract. It permits us to appreciate lawbreakers not "as rebels and traitors ... against the letter" of the constitution but as embodying the "spirit of American laws" (1972 [1970a]: 76). Though acting beyond the law and thus extralegally, activists do so as part of organized, nonviolent movements, with their endeavors having nothing in common with the isolated individuals depicted in Hobbes' violent and lawless state of nature. They exemplify not only the horizontal contract's egalitarian presuppositions but also an idea of law where the right to disagree and dissent – if necessary, by responsible lawbreaking – remains indispensable.

Like Zinn, Arendt sometimes privileges civil disobedience over ordinary political and legal mechanisms. She does so because of her dreary view of the liberal status quo and deep reservations about modern representative democracy, some of which are surely overstated (Kateb 1983). Yet, in contradistinction to Zinn's approach, civil disobedients here still prospectively exemplify loyalty to noble legal and constitutional aspirations. They do so not primarily to demonstrate, as liberals posited, respect for the legal status quo or a notion of legality defined in terms of prospective, public, general norms. Nor do they bear divine witness, contributing in the process to a more divine legal order. Instead, they act publicly, nonviolently, and help "to protect or perfect the Constitution," conceived in dynamic terms because it is an unavoidably open-ended republican project (Kateb 1983: 21). As part of that unfinished project, citizens sometimes need to break the law to augment and adapt it in accordance with new political exigencies and rapidly changing social conditions. Like their revolutionary ancestors, they pursue illegal action, potentially for the sake of reconstructing constitutional basics, because effective self-government requires it.

How might we determine whether disobedients are in fact demonstrating proper fidelity to law, in Arendt's demanding sense? Her answer seems unclear, in part because of her reluctance to accept civil disobedience's standard test for legal fidelity (i.e., accepting legal penalties). Unfortunately, Arendt also undermines her own potentially fertile insights by tying them too strictly to the idiosyncrasies of US political experience.[15] She knows, of course, that civil disobedience has been practiced elsewhere, yet insists that the phenomenon is congenitally US-American. The notion of a horizontal contract, for example, supposedly makes up a core feature of a specifically US "spirit of the laws" (1972 [1970a]: 85–102). Conveniently, she makes only fleeting references to non-US examples, at times appearing to foreclose the prospect that activists elsewhere might successfully pursue civil disobedience for the sake of republican renewal by building on their own local legal traditions. This controversial claim rests on an overstated and probably untenable contrast between the allegedly exemplary US Revolution and its altogether unattractive French counterpart, whose pathologies Arendt views as having disastrously plagued democratic politics elsewhere (Arendt 1963). Because most liberal democracies rest on the flawed vertical social contract, she tendentiously asserts, they provide poor soil for civil disobedience. Only US-Americans, she seems to believe, are likely to prove lucky enough to achieve civil disobedience along the lines she sketches.

Civil disobedience: between legality and democratic legitimacy

During the 1970s and 1980s, anti-nuclear, environmental, and peace movements worldwide effectively disproved Arendt's claims for civil disobedience's uniquely American characteristics. Even in West Germany, then still viewed by skeptics as lacking deep democratic roots, civil disobedients garnered broad sympathy for protests opposing nuclear energy and NATO's installation of cruise and Pershing II missiles directed at the Soviets, a decision perceived by left-leaning west Europeans as militarily provocative and strategically destabilizing.[16] Like others there and elsewhere, activists illegally occupied sites for planned nuclear plants and reprocessing centers. Incensed by US President Ronald Reagan's harsh cold war rhetoric, they blockaded military bases, forming "human chains" to obstruct access. Though committed to strict ideas of nonviolence and inspired by iconic figures like King, activists faced draconian state responses in sync with what Arendt might have predicted: German officials treated disobedients as at best ordinary criminals and at worst violent rebels (Hughes 2014; Quint 2008). In contrast to Arendt's expectations, however, civil disobedience successfully galvanized public attention and helped build support for the largest demonstrations in West German history, with pollsters in the 1980s periodically corroborating the protestors' claim that they, and not government officials, spoke for a political majority.

Germany's most prominent intellectual, Jürgen Habermas, not only weighed in on the wide-ranging public debate but, in the process, reformulated the democratic model of civil disobedience.[17] His sophisticated rendition overcomes many previous weaknesses.

As Habermas pointed out, at stake in illegal protests against nuclear power and the arms race were not violations of civil rights like those that had motivated King and the US civil rights movement (1985b [1983]: 107–8). Instead, the government in Bonn was jamming through divisive security and technological policies, with minimal public or even parliamentary debate, "which strike deeply in the lives of each individual as well as the chance for survival of entire nations" (1985b [1983]: 109). Political elites conveniently chased democratically dubious short-cuts to promulgate policies on matters viewed by sizable constituencies as ill-advised and possibly life-threatening. In a more fully developed democracy, in contrast to Germany's unsatisfactory version, fundamental decisions would be made by extensive public debate and deliberation, with special attention to the normative prerequisites of majority rule. Threadbare parliamentary majorities would not be allowed to suffice in the context of truly consequential decisions.

Majority rule and democracy, Habermas correctly recalled, are by no means equivalent. Majority rule is a decision-making procedure resting on demanding presuppositions if its democratic accreditation is to obtain. Majority decisions derive their legitimacy from a broad process of free-wheeling deliberative exchange between free and equal citizens. They make sense only when today's outvoted political minorities have a realistic chance to become tomorrow's majorities, and when present decisions can be effectively reversed by prospective majorities. When those premises are abrogated, it becomes unclear why outvoted minorities should abide majority decisions: why accept permanent rule by an irremovable and implacable political majority (1985b [1983]: 110–11; 1985c [1984]: 138–9)?[18] Habermas sympathized with those arguing that the installation of a new generation of NATO first-strike nuclear missiles violated majority rule's prerequisites. Political elites actively circumvented and even discouraged meaningful public debate, rushing what effectively were permanent decisions having life-or-death consequences: "Yes, missiles might be installed and then dismantled," Habermas conceded (1985c [1984]: 139). Yet one could also reasonably conclude that their deployment aggrandized an already perilous arms race between the superpowers, with potentially irreversible consequences.

Activists, in short, were voicing apt criticisms of the liberal status quo's institutional and especially deliberative deficits. Their worries deserved a fair hearing. How then to secure it? Civil disobedience provided an answer. When issues are grave and ordinary channels blocked, civil disobedience can be justified, which is neither to say that it is always prudentially sensible, nor that it should rest directly on a legal or constitutional right.[19] Like Arendt, Habermas opposes efforts by liberal jurists to interpret civil disobedience as justified directly on statutory or constitutional grounds:

> [T]he undesirable effects of normalizing the extraordinary argues against the legalization of civil disobedience. If all personal risk is eliminated, the moral foundation of the illegal protest becomes questionable; its effectiveness as an appeal is damaged as well. (1985b [1983]: 106)

When activists are forced to recognize that they are engaging in personally risky illegalities, they are likely to weigh the costs carefully. This not only encourages a measure of responsibility but also provides skeptical publics with visible evidence of lawbreakers' moral and political seriousness.

Civil disobedience, on this view, operates in a gray zone between positive or existing laws and the foundations of democratic legitimacy, between existing law and democracy. Democratic legitimacy relies on the intuition that binding decisions should in principle derive from the uncoerced "agreement of all concerned" and ideally embody a common or generalizable good (1985b [1983]: 102). The law-based or constitutional state – for Habermas as for Arendt, an unavoidable component of modern self-government – correspondingly draws its normative energies from universally endorsable principles (for example, basic rights, due process, separation of powers), on which it always depends yet never perhaps perfectly instantiates. Even if the democratic constitutional state's underlying "universal principles remain constant … the historical circumstances to which they are applied change" (1985c [1984]: 135). Gaps between existing political and legal practices and their normative bases regularly surface. Historical experience counters the commonplace yet misleading view that existing political and legal practices can fully or perhaps even sufficiently realize the demanding norms and procedures on which they implicitly rest. Democracy and the constitutional state constitute a "constantly interrupted" (and nonlinear) "learning process [that] is by no means at an end today" (1985c [1984]: 135). The democratic constitutional state is a messy and conflict-laden historical experiment, always subject to correction and regularly in need of reform and revision.[20]

Constitutional democracy's own latent normative energies provide activists with plentiful resources for immanently criticizing existing practices. The ensuing political battles, Habermas notes, ideally come about via ordinary channels (most importantly, free elections). Yet historical experience here as well highlights a general problem: laws and institutions tend to immunize themselves from the demands of the oppressed and exploited. Terrible injustices can be embodied in existing laws and institutional practices. Modern constitutionalism's architects were cognizant of the harsh realities of "fallible human reason and corruptible human nature" and sought to design institutions accordingly (1985c [1984]: 135). Nonetheless, self-correcting institutional devices can still falter. Constitutional democracy thus faces the paradoxical task of having to protect and sustain a healthy "distrust of injustice that appears in legal form" without being able to legalize or institutionalize it fully since then it would likely prove vulnerable to the same dangers (1985b [1983]: 104). Democracy needs ways of checking the "systemic inertia of institutional politics" but cannot always give them a formal-legal or institutionalized status (1996 [1992]: 383).

Civil disobedience suggests a possible solution. Nonviolent activists who break the law take on the "plebiscitary role of the citizen in his directly sovereign capacity" (Habermas 1985b [1983]: 103). They "intercede directly in their role as sovereign," demanding that ordinary citizens, not political leaders hemmed in by ossified laws or rigid institutional practices, exercise power (1985c [1984]: 136). Citizens break the law because in their considered view it fails to meet constitutional democracy's own implicit normative standards. They act not as a revolutionary avant-garde, but as free and equal citizens of a pluralistic community addressing their peers on the base of the democratic constitutional state's implicit underpinnings. Acting illegally and thus "outside" the law, they aim to adapt and improve that order.

For Habermas, as for Arendt, civil disobedience represents illegal (or extra-legal) action essential not just to political but also to possible constitutional reform. Habermas similarly describes its tasks as defensive as well as innovative. Civil disobedience sometimes wards off troublesome government policies; it can also serve as a "pace-setter for long overdue corrections and innovations" (1985b [1983]: 104). Civil disobedients push against sclerotic or unjust laws and institutions, on occasion proving to "be the true patriotic champions of a constitution that is dynamically understood as an ongoing *project*" (2004: 9, original emphasis). Though acting illegally, they propel the unfinished project of constitutional democracy forward. By dramatizing injustices, they possibly contribute to a nonviolent but still radical reformism, in which the status quo's institutional decks are reshuffled in far-reaching and historically unprecedented ways. Looking back at modern political history, Habermas notes that

> it is easy to discover the blindness and prejudiced readings which framed the different national paths of contemporary democracies ... This is evident in such basic issues as freedom of speech, universal suffrage, freedom of association. If Kant excluded from the right to vote not only women and day laborers, but also independent workers this was hardly a simple conceptual mistake. The selective realization of general norms becomes evident only in the light of altered situations and historical circumstances. Harsher political struggles and long term social movements were needed for people to become aware of the unjust, selective realization of the law. (1985c [1984]: 135)

Civil disobedience helps bring incomplete realizations of basic democratic and constitutional principles to public attention. Acting beyond the law, while appealing to constitutional democracy's own implicit ideals, lawbreakers can ignite the requisite change.

Despite substantial overlap with Arendt, Habermas exhibits neither nostalgia for the American Revolution nor sympathy for her view of civil disobedience as US-based. He offers a robust normative account of democracy and has more to say about its complex relationship to law and constitutionalism (Habermas 1996 [1992]).[21] One consequence is that any modern democratic constitutional state embodies principles to which those considering civil disobedience should principally be able to appeal.

Like Zinn, Habermas views democratization as a broad political *and* social project.[22] But he rightly sees existing laws and institutions as embodying past struggles and building on latent normative resources having potentially radical implications. As a consequence, he avoids Zinn's anti-statism and anti-legalism. Partly for political-diagnostic and partly for conceptual reasons, Habermas' tests for civil disobedience also prove more demanding. A tough critic of existing liberal polities, Habermas does not view them, as Zinn and even Arendt probably did, as bankrupt. This is probably why he is more willing to preserve key components of the liberal template, while placing them on firmer democratic footing. If civil disobedience is to be viewed as structurally akin to expressions of unmediated popular sovereignty, "people's power" on the streets, it behooves us to show why and how it offers no blank check for irresponsible or willful action. It is one thing to assert that disobedients can be viewed as active participants in the democratic constitutional state as an ongoing project. Yet how can we be reasonably certain that civil disobedients are acting responsibly and taking this role seriously? Here again Habermas' answer proves illuminating.[23]

He revisits – while subtly revising – Rawls' definition of civil disobedience as public, conscientious, nonviolent, illegal action aimed at changing law and policy, by means of which lawbreakers show their basic fidelity to law.[24] Like Rawls, Habermas views moral conscience as a legitimate

yet necessarily incomplete basis for lawbreaking. He provides, unlike Arendt, room for conscientious appeals, while
agreeing with Rawls and others that such appeals do not
suffice given moral and religious pluralism (1987 [1986]:
66). Against both Arendt and Zinn, Habermas believes that
disobedients should face possible legal repercussions. Why?
Lawbreakers should be expected to distinguish their activities from violent revolution. Observers need some relatively
transparent way to ascertain whether political lawbreakers
take seriously their status as participants in the ongoing –
and still incomplete – project of constitutional democracy.
Significantly, Habermas also demands of legal authorities
that they not punitively equate disobedients with ordinary
criminals or violent rebels. Only by responding respectfully
and probably leniently can officials suitably acknowledge
civil disobedience's valuable political functions.

Civil disobedience requires, in sum, self-restraint from
both officials and lawbreakers. Officials are obliged to exercise restraint because it is simply wrong to conflate nonviolent
civil disobedience with criminality or violent resistance.
Whenever possible, prosecutors and judges should exercise
discretion to protestors' advantage. In turn, lawbreakers
should restrain themselves because they need to evince respect
for their political equals. Nonviolence means acting responsibly to safeguard others' physical and psychological integrity, since anything less would violate their status as moral
and political equals. Defending a somewhat looser definition
of violence than many liberals, Habermas licenses a wide
range of potentially confrontational – but, on his terms, still
identifiably nonviolent – protests.[25] Nonviolence leaves room
for militant protestors to impair third parties' freedom of
movement (via blockades or sit-ins), for example, and emo-
tional or psychic pressure when responsibly exercised (1985b
[1983]: 100–1).[26] In principle, it may prove consistent with
damage to property. Commenting on the "Plowshares Eight"
protest, in which Daniel and Philip Berrigan joined others in
trespassing onto a US nuclear weapons facility before damaging nuclear missile cones, Habermas cautiously observed:
"Perhaps tomorrow we will include in this tradition [i.e., civil
disobedience as practiced by King and others], with greater
self-evidence than is possible today, the Berrigan brothers and

all those who renounce civil obedience in order to achieve the legally binding proscription of all weapons of mass destruction" (Habermas 1985b [1983]: 107).[27]

At any rate, when activists engage in militant lawbreaking, they need to keep their act's primarily symbolic contours in mind: if they block access to a NATO base, for example, they are aiming primarily to further public debate, not in fact cripple NATO's day-to-day operations. In sharp contrast, violent lawbreakers implicitly claim special rights and privileged access to truth, neither of which Habermas views as consonant with political equality and the unfinished project of constitutional democracy.

Despite the Rawlsian packaging, Habermas fills it with richer democratic content. Civil disobedience, *contra* Rawls, is not fundamentally about correcting majoritarian violations of civil rights in an already basically or "nearly just" liberal polity. Instead, it allows active citizens to address *any* potentially grave or serious issues and sometimes push for broad change. His reservations about majority rule, like Arendt's, stem chiefly from its dangers to self-government and not individual rights per se. Legislation by narrow majorities, absent meaningful public debate, can potentially be violated because it may lack sufficient democratic legitimacy. The obligation to abide law is qualified and not categorical because laws and statutes sometimes contravene democratic legitimacy.

Following Rawls, Habermas describes civil disobedience as a final or last resort for dissenters. Simultaneously, civil disobedience remains historically unexceptional: the need for it "will arise over and over again because the realization of existing constitutional principles with universalistic content is a long-term process" (1985b [1983]: 104). Law and constitutionalism are directly wedded to democratization, conceived as a continuous, ongoing struggle against exclusion and oppression. When disobedients accept legal penalties for their acts, they symbolically express fidelity to the law and constitution, no longer understood chiefly as an ideal of formal legality or rigid constitutional status quo, but rather to constitutional democracy as an incomplete project. Habermas conceives of civil disobedience as categorically distinct from violent resistance and revolution, neither of which he considers suited to contemporary liberal societies (1987 [1986]: 66).[28] Within existing constitutional democracy, its many ills notwithstanding, there are necessary limits to political illegality. Nonetheless, with echoes of both Gandhi and King, for Habermas civil disobedience can still legitimately transcend the narrow confines of limited or cautious liberal reformism.

Beyond the state?

Democratic civil disobedience, especially in Habermas' impressive version, takes major steps toward overcoming its liberal predecessor's limitations. Civil disobedience is no longer confined to defending individual rights against over-reaching majorities but now more broadly guards and potentially enhances democracy. Because democracy represents an ongoing project, this view of civil disobedience is decidedly more forward-looking – and potentially transformative – than its liberal competitor. Civil disobedience does not simply correct for majoritarian misunderstandings of a static shared conception of justice, as in the influential Rawlsian model, but instead potentially helps initiate novel views of justice and rights, new opportunities for participation, and extensive social and economic change. Fidelity to law means demonstrating a good-faith effort to participate in constitutional democracy as a dynamic and incomplete shared enterprise. Civil disobedients can play a pivotal role in updating and reforming self-government and constitutional government.

Not surprisingly, the democratic model continues to inspire political activists, including some involved in recent Occupy protests (Yingling 2016). Components of it also helped energize democracy movements in authoritarian settings, such as those in 1989 that helped bring communism in central and eastern Europe to its knees.[29]

Its accomplishments notwithstanding, the democratic approach still shares one striking – and hitherto unexamined – assumption with its predecessors. For liberals the modern state legitimately possesses a "comprehensive scope" and "substantial regulative powers with respect to other institutions" (Rawls 1971: 236). Because it permanently impacts our life prospects more decisively than other institutions, politics ultimately concerns the question of how best to shape government and its laws (Rawls 1971: 222). Accordingly, civil disobedience should generally target state officials. More radical-minded democratic theorists of civil disobedience, to be sure, move toward abandoning this narrow view of civil disobedience. Nevertheless, they still tend to presuppose the existence of a state resting on a monopoly of legitimate violence, alone capable of guaranteeing internal peace and legal security for all citizens (Habermas 1985c [1984]: 134).[30]

In recent decades, precisely this statist premise has faced heightened critical scrutiny from philosophical – and sometimes politically active – anarchists, with far-reaching implications for civil disobedience. Not surprisingly, such voices have expressed antipathy to the longstanding quest to marry civil disobedience to some idea of respect for law. To that anarchist critique we now turn.

4
Anarchist Uprising

Previous chapters examined rival models of civil disobedience. Our approach here differs: we consider the most wide-ranging challenge to civil disobedience as conceived and practiced by activists and intellectuals extending from Gandhi to Habermas. Since the 1980s many writers on political disobedience have embraced theoretical or philosophical anarchism, with anarchist philosophical reflections offering an imposing critical retort to conventional ideas of civil disobedience. Political anarchism has also enjoyed a renaissance, with anarchist activists playing a pivotal role in recent social movements (for example, the global justice and Occupy movements).

Anarchists come in multiple shapes and sizes. All anarchists reject the modern state, viewing it as basically illegitimate and complicit in a wide range of social and material injustices. As per conventional scholarly wisdom, we distinguish political from philosophical anarchists.[1] The former includes its most audacious historical figures (for example, Mikhail Bakunin, Pjotr Kropotkin, and Emma Goldman) as well as present-day anarchists who take to the streets motivated by the goal of jettisoning the state in favor of some presumably superior non-statist social order, to be constructed on voluntary and consensual ties. Political anarchism comes in both communalist and radically individualistic forms. In the simplest terms: the political anarchist pursues militant illegal action to destroy the state and other institutions incongruent with her preference for spontaneously organized, self-governing communities. In contrast, philosophical anarchists "do not take the illegitimacy of states to entail a strong moral imperative to oppose or eliminate states; rather, they typically take state illegitimacy to remove any strong moral presumption in favor of obedience to, compliance with, or support for our own or other existing states" (Simmons 1996: 20). Philosophical anarchism also comes in both left-wing (anti-capitalist) and right-wing (free market or libertarian) varieties; it has myriad real-life implications. Nonetheless, the philosophical anarchist is generally preoccupied not with waging political battles aimed at actively constructing a non-statist social order, but instead with discrediting the modern Leviathan and its moral foundations. Unlike its political counterpart, philosophical anarchism partakes of the post-utopian spirit of the times: it embodies a principled enmity to the state without much faith in the prospect of constructing a novel alternative.

Anarchists of either a philosophical or political bent are free to appropriate the term "civil disobedience" as they wish; no single political or philosophical orientation, as we have seen, can claim a monopoly over it. However, I focus in this chapter on anarchism's objections to previous models. Though some of its proponents may disagree, anarchism is most fruitfully interpreted as a thoroughgoing critique of core intuitions shared by religious, liberal, and democratic accounts. If the anarchist critique succeeds, very little remains of civil disobedience as usually theorized. Both philosophical and political anarchism undermine civil disobedience's political and conceptual distinctiveness. If the idea of civil disobedience is to survive in some minimally coherent form, we need to be able to counter the anarchist critique. That is the main aim of this chapter.

Civil disobedience, of course, always meant different things for its religious, liberal, and democratic advocates. Yet the term was not an empty shell into which competing political traditions arbitrarily poured different contents. Key variations notwithstanding, their competing approaches rested on four broad commonalities.

First, they all viewed civil disobedience as aiming to generate changes within the state and to law. Both religious believers and democrats opposed liberal attempts to limit civil disobedience to acts against public or state officials. Yet like the liberals they expected that lawbreakers would generally focus on trying to sway government officials. Why? Outfitted with a monopoly on legitimate coercion, the state possesses ultimate authority and shapes society in ways other institutions cannot. Even when initiating new laws and sweeping reforms, civil disobedience accordingly presupposed the institutional primacy of state and law. It accepted the necessity of legality, or a law-based social order (and "rule of law"), along with some sort of sovereign government or "state," outfitted with effective enforcement powers and usually pictured as essential to law's successful operations.

Second, all models of civil disobedience envisaged it as a distinctive mode of lawbreaking best conceived as predicated on fidelity to law, or what King dubbed "the very highest respect for the law." As we have now learned, most writers linked this to calls for civil disobedients to accept criminal penalties; others greeted such demands more skeptically. What set civil disobedience apart from ordinary or criminal lawbreaking, at any rate, was a concomitant appeal to basic legal and constitutional ideals a desirable society should aspire to realize. Even as religious, liberal, and democratic thinkers offered sharply contrasting versions of this shared intuition, they consistently saw civil disobedience as a type of lawbreaking whose superior normative credentials depended upon demonstrating fidelity to law.

Third, previous models of civil disobedience rested on a triple-pronged normativity, in which separate yet interrelated moral, legal, and political appeals loomed large. The details here are messy, with competing models of civil disobedience offering diverging accounts of the three prongs and their interconnections, and some writers trying to downplay or even drop one or more of them. Nonetheless, we find a general tendency to interpret civil disobedience as building on three moral, political, and legal prongs. As Rawls' liberal approach paradigmatically suggested, civil disobedients appealed publicly to other citizens to change public policy (*political* appeal), their actions rested on the voice of conscience (*moral* appeal), and, even when committing political illegality, should be expected to demonstrate respect for law (*legal* appeal). Within a broad tradition extending from Gandhi to Arendt and Habermas, the three prongs were subject to countless combinations. Yet that tradition repeatedly offered narratives about civil disobedience's three (political, moral, and legal) faces, based on the sensible underlying premise that its normative contours had to be rich and suitably multifaceted. Civil disobedience, on the standard view, could not successfully stand on any single (political, moral, or legal) basis, but had to tap into a richer multi-tiered normativity.[2]

Fourth, religious, liberal, and democratic models sought to flesh out what initially and perhaps misleadingly appeared as a straightforward set of preconditions (civility, conscientiousness, nonviolence, and publicity). Competing political traditions, of course, provided conflicting interpretations. Lively controversy surfaced, for example, about how best to understand and practice nonviolence. Nonetheless, thinkers from Gandhi on were committed to providing plausible interpretations of a common set of standards for legitimate civil disobedience. Whatever their disagreements, their alternative approaches could still be plausibly viewed as presupposing a shared, albeit unavoidably contested, normative framework. They participated in a common conceptual language, even as they employed that language to make opposing claims.

By attacking all four commonalities, anarchists aim to torpedo civil disobedience's conceptual and political distinctiveness. Political anarchism's attack, however, rests on a series of untenable premises about state and law. Philosophical anarchism pursues a more impressive offensive. Because even that more subtle approach occludes key elements of civil disobedience, it too misfires. A certain latent tension characterizes the anarchist challenge. Anarchists oppose conventional accounts of civil disobedience, yet they sometimes end up traversing familiar conceptual and political territory. When they do so, the flames of their at first glance fiery critique start to flicker.

Political anarchism and direct action

The nineteenth-century French political thinker Pierre-Joseph Proudhon vividly expresses anarchism's enmity to the state:

To be GOVERNED is to be at every operation, at every trans-action, noted, registered, enrolled, taxed, stamped, measured, numbered, assessed, licensed, authorized, admonished, for-bidden, reformed, corrected, punished. It is under pretext of public utility, and in the name of the general interest, to be placed under contribution, trained, ransomed, exploited, monopolized, extorted, squeezed, mystified, robbed; then, at the slightest resistance, the first word of complaint, to be repressed, fined, despised, harassed, tracked, abused, clubbed, disarmed, choked, imprisoned, judged, condemned, shot, deported, sacrificed, sold, betrayed; and, to crown all, mocked, ridiculed, outraged, dishonored. That is government; that is its justice; that is its morality. (Quoted in Miller 1984: 6)

States represent congealed force or violence. The modern Leviathan exercises a terrifying series of coercive, exploita-tive, and punitive functions against its subjects (Miller 1984: 6–7; also, Carter 1971: 38–40; Horton 2010: 107–9; Ritter 1980: 61–88). The horrors of modern totalitarianism, on this account, reveal the state's true face. Even when it appears to behave benevolently, the state's iron fist soon smashes those who dare to question its privileged power position. In such moments, state power unveils its violent core, as the police and military are unleashed and emergency or exceptional powers, the modern state's legal essence, supplant the so-called rule of law (Newman 2012: 313). Arbitrary police and military rule then simply manifest themselves openly rather than covertly.

Law – and the so-called rule of law – make up instruments of coercive power. Law is not in fact a possible check on state violence, but merely its most insidious manifestation. Mis-leadingly suggesting that the state advances higher normative ideals (freedom or equality, for example), the law mystifies de facto relations of power. Legal formalities and the "letter of the law" typically get in the way of justice. The generality of law is nothing more than a device for homogenizing and pulverizing the state's subjects, whose individuality is neces-sarily violated by law's uniformity. When people obey legal rules for their own sake, "their rational faculties will not be exercised and their minds will remain in a slumber" (Newman 2012: 311). Reducing individuals to obedient robots and making them complicit in the state's coercive pathologies, fidelity to the law degrades us. What instead should count is the "moral sovereignty of the individual," always and everywhere obliterated by the state and law (Graeber 2009: 222). Resistance to the state and law, accordingly, represents a moral and political imperative.

Given its congenital anti-statism and anti-legalism, political anarchism can offer no principled defense of civil disobedience as conventionally viewed. As the anarchist writer Paul Goodman accurately observed:

> "Civil disobedience" is a misnomer for our kind of resistance. According to that concept, the law expresses the social sovereignty that we have ourselves conceded, and therefore we logically accept the penalties if we disobey, though we may have to disobey nevertheless ... As an anarchist, I think all government and much law are foolish. (1970: 137)

When anarchists join hands with other activists pursuing familiar types of civil disobedience, theirs is at best an alliance of convenience. Anarchists want to dispose of state and law, not change or reform them. Appealing to political officials to correct an injustice, along with the idea of breaking the law for the sake of preserving or realizing more fundamental legal ideals, is necessarily anathema to the anarchist. Anarchists reject the idea that politically motivated lawbreakers should face legal penalties; civil disobedience's longstanding legal prong vanishes.

For the anarchist, the requisite radical change necessarily occurs beyond law and state, not in accordance with them. Like many liberals, anarchists juxtapose radical or revolutionary change to reform, associating civil disobedience with the latter but rejecting it because of its presumably quiescent contours. They often ignore civil disobedience's common normative language, endorsing secret and conspiratorial lawbreaking, condoning violence, and exhibiting little concern with civility. David Graeber, a prominent contemporary anarchist, mocks the idea that lawbreaking should sway political equals and democratic publics, which he describes as "a largely imaginary community of white, middle class families that is, in the opinion of most anarchists, largely a creation of the media itself" (2009: 420). Even when defined minimally in terms of basic respect for political peers, civility is pushed to the wayside: for the anarchist, of course, political and legal equality is in part an illegitimate state construct. Graeber appears to condone secret or furtive lawbreaking, the selective destruction of property (though not violence against persons), and he rejects what he describes as a masochistic Gandhian ideal of self-sacrifice (2009). The "new language" of civil disobedience he finds among present-day anarchists, not surprisingly, seems remote from most previous ideas about it (Graeber 2002).

Graeber and other contemporary anarchists tend to want to have their cake and eat it as well. After systematically deconstructing civil disobedience, they then try to repossess it (Newman 2012: 315). Sacrificing useful analytic and political distinctions, their reworked version becomes synonymous with a vast range of politically and morally motivated illegalities. As the term gets overinflated, its specific conceptual contours fade.

Some previous anarchists were more disciplined in their reflections. They defended what they openly described as revolutionary direct action as a form of resistance. Despite the terminological overlap (King and many others also used the term "direct action"), anarchists had something different in mind.

Direct action has taken many different connotations in the history of political activism (Carter 1973). For King and other defenders of civil disobedience, for example, it referred paradigmatically to militant protest outside the usual institutional venues, with activists putting their bodies on the line, willing to withstand abuse. In the most generic sense, direct action refers to any political action bypassing ordinary political and legal channels in order "to directly ameliorate or eliminate an injustice, or to slow down or obstruct regular operations of an unjust order. Strikes, street demonstrations, and occupations" represent familiar varieties (Conway 2003: 509). Direct action, on this view, can be either legal or illegal. When meeting certain conditions (for example, conscientiousness, publicity, and so on), it potentially falls under recognizable models of civil disobedience. Yet it need not. A violent occupation of public or private property by armed activists where lives are lost, for example, would not typically be so characterized.

Political anarchism favors a specific variety of direct action, as perhaps best exemplified by the nineteenth-century idea "propaganda of the deed," where dramatic political activity, probably illegal and possibly violent, aims to excite mass attention and inspire a popular uprising. Here action ideally speaks for itself, conveying a direct and easily comprehensible message, with its confrontational attributes performing immediately symbolic services. Early Italian anarchists, for example, seized control of local farming communities they subsequently reorganized along anarchist lines, hoping that other peasant communities would follow their example (Miller 1984: 100–2). More recently, anarchists in 1970s and 1980s Amsterdam, Hamburg, and elsewhere protested housing policy not by petitioning parliaments or sitting in government offices, but instead by occupying or "squatting" buildings and transforming them into cooperatives built on communal and non-hierarchical ideals. They challenged irresponsible housing policies simply by acting as though the buildings were already commonly owned. Anarchist squatters hoped that their acts would inspire a broader revolt against not only irrational public policy but also private property and the liberal state.

When the police tried to clear squatters, violent clashes sometimes ensued. For anarchists, violence is an unfortunate yet sometimes unavoidable fact of political life if experiments in non-statist self-organization are to be defended. It represents justifiable self-defense against the statist Leviathan, the real nucleus of political violence.[3] Direct action, for the anarchist, can also be clandestine or secret. Publicity may prove valuable as an organizational and political tool, but not as moral witness or principled expression of respect for other citizens. Political anarchists, in fact, do not always seek dialogue or conversation with their legal peers in a state order they deem bankrupt. Nor do they show much interest in reaching some mutual understanding or moral reconciliation with foes. Rather, they aim for exemplary political action that motivates others to join in militant resistance. Bakunin contrasted anarchism's preference for inspirational deeds to mere ideas and "grand theoretical discourses" (quoted in Miller 1984: 98). Prefiguring a novel anarchist social order, direct action optimally provides palpable evidence of its virtues and viability. One insists "on acting as if one is already free," not by pleading with other citizens or officials to change policy, but instead by creating counter-institutions and practices operating beyond the tentacles of state power (Graeber 2009: 207; also, Goodway 2012).

To be sure, Gandhi, King, and others also envisioned civil disobedience as prefiguring a superior social order. Yet for them, doing so demanded strict nonviolence and some proof of the lawbreaker's respect for law, since any more divine prospective alternative would have to be nonviolent as well as law-based. For the anarchist, in contrast, the future ideally lacks state and law. Interestingly, some contemporary anarchists reject violence against persons on related grounds, interpreting it as incongruent with the consensual, non-hierarchical social world they hope to start building in the present.[4] When operating in a liberal democratic context they also typically make concessions to more familiar ideas of civil disobedience (Graeber 2002; 2009). One reason seems clear enough: if anarchists are to succeed in building a broad movement, they in fact need to persuade others. Because conventional modes of civil disobedience offer an effective device for doing so, anarchists may embrace them, especially if the non-anarchists, with whom they sometimes are forced to cooperate, favor them.[5] In this vein, many anarchists today endorse a "diversity of tactics" that pragmatically licenses nonviolent civil disobedience as well as more militant tactics (Conway 2003). Ultimately, however, it remains unclear whether such tactical eclecticism represents anything more than a temporary concession.

Political anarchism's built-in anti-statism and anti-legalism remain its Achilles' heel. Political anarchists have sometimes spearheaded innovative protests and revitalized moribund social movements. Even non-anarchists have been inspired by their courage. Anarchism also usefully reminds us of the modern state's repressive perils: I do not mean to discount anarchism's insights or political accomplishments.

Nonetheless, the anarchist theory of state and law remains badly one-sided. Modern states differ: some are indeed totalitarian, while others, however imperfectly and incompletely, buttress self-government and social justice. Political anarchism occludes the modern state's productive political and social uses, suggesting – with limited evidence – that they could be effectively performed by non-state institutional alternatives. Predictably, it also obscures law's vital protective functions, crudely viewing it merely as an instrument of domination favoring the privileged and powerful. "As compromised as the Rule of Law is and always has been," the radical but non-anarchist jurist Chase Madar correctly notes, "we would do wrong to discard it entirely" (2013: 123). More than mere liberal ideology or window-dressing for social injustice, the rule of law provides essential protections to the politically and socially vulnerable (Neumann 1957).

More fundamentally, democratic equality and liberty depend on fair procedures able to shape our common affairs. Democratic deliberation and participation only make sense if we can reasonably expect that our voices will result in some course of action that will prove effectual. At a minimum, we need institutions outfitted with effective coercive mechanisms to enforce binding decisions against powerful constituencies that sometimes prefer resisting them. Can we be sure that basic democratic rights and procedures can be preserved without state devices necessarily playing some role in doing so? Our right to free speech is only likely to prove secure, for example, if we can be sure that violators face some prospect of legal sanctions.

Anarchism, of course, seeks social justice and far-reaching material equality. Even in a more just and egalitarian society, however, we will need state and law. Under the conditions of modern pluralism, where competing conceptions of the good life inevitably lead to disagreement and conflict, legal institutions (for example, basic rights) play a crucial role in protecting those with unpopular views or preferences. Forms of institutionalization we historically have associated with the state remain crucial to law's efficacy. Legal enforcement will continue to depend, if only in the final instance, on coercive sanctions (Schauer 2015). Given pluralism and irrepressible political conflict, it seems starry-eyed to expect otherwise. Without unduly simplifying a complex matter, one justification for the state seems straightforward: self-government rests on rigorous (normative) ideas of basic equality and reciprocity. Any realistic effort to institutionalize those ideals requires not only binding but also enforceable general legal rules and rights. In order to preserve democracy, we hardly need the monstrous and violent Leviathan described by anarchist critics. Nonetheless, a functioning and sufficiently well-coordinated possibility of recourse to state coercion remains essential.

Because political anarchism's challenge to standard views of civil disobedience rests on tendentious ideas about state and law, it fails. Philosophical anarchists, however, have tried to overcome some of their political cousins' mistakes.

Philosophical anarchism: Back to Locke and Thoreau?

Philosophical anarchists do not offer up heated denunciations of the state or law, nor do they advocate taking to the streets to fight for a stateless utopia. In part because philosophical anarchists are, well, mostly academic philosophers, their perspective tends to be not only conceptually more rigorous but also politically more cautious. Nonetheless, philosophical anarchism poses a deep challenge to the ideas of civil disobedience discussed in previous chapters. Since the 1970s, philosophical anarchism has flourished among Anglophone political philosophers; among many who refuse to embrace the label, some of its key tenets are still endorsed.[6] If its critique of longstanding notions of civil disobedience holds water, then much of the theorizing recounted in previous chapters is no longer tenable.

Philosophical anarchism pursues a different strategy from its political cousin. Rather than beginning with a heavy-handed picture of the state as a violent monster, or one-sided views of law as nothing more than a weapon of the privileged, it tirelessly chips away at allegedly sacrosanct ideas about political and legal obligation. That is, it challenges the many ways in which mostly liberal theorists justify the intuition that citizens, particularly in basically decent or just societies, have some general or prima facie obligation to obey the law, even when doing so may seem morally deplorable, or the likely consequences counterproductive or harmful. Philosophical anarchists disagree about how best to conceive such a duty or obligation; on this and many other complex matters their analyses are nuanced and theoretically rich. Yet their main goal remains straightforward: they hope to discount the familiar intuition that law *qua* law deserves our loyalty or fidelity, that because some legal norm or rule has been promulgated we are obliged to follow it, and that pressing reasons typically demand of us that we abide the law. On their account, such a view of law is both philosophically unjustified and politically unattractive, since it breeds blind obedience rather than healthy skepticism about government.

Philosophical anarchists follow this alternative path by offering critical rebuttals to a wide range of attempts to generate robust notions of general political or legal obligation. They take on utilitarian accounts that ground such an obligation in ideas of utility or the general good, revisit ideas of "government by consent," and probe the writings of Rawls and other prominent liberal theorists to reconstruct possible justifications for the existence of a special moral relationship between citizens and their state (Egoumenides 2014; Feinberg 1979; Green 1988; Simmons 1979; Smith 1973). At the end of the day, they insist, all such justifications either fail on conceptual or philosophical grounds, or when they succeed cannot plausibly be fitted to the disconcerting realities of the modern state. All modern states are illegitimate not chiefly because they are violent Leviathans (though some philosophical anarchists also share this diagnosis), but instead because no political theory can be found successfully supporting the intuition that we have a general or prima facie obligation to obey them. Robbed of the aura of a general duty or obligation, the state simply becomes one powerful – and particularly dangerous – institution among others, to which we owe no special moral duties. We may on occasion opt to obey it, but should do so only on concrete, situation-specific moral or pragmatic grounds.

The idea of a fundamental incongruity between a normatively sound account of political obligation and the harsh facts of modern statehood has been developed most impressively by the libertarian thinker John Simmons, who has laid out the fundaments of an individualistic theory of political consent, inspired substantially by John Locke (1979; 1993). On this view, specifically political relationships – and the state itself – can only be grounded on voluntary, consensual acts or agreements. In Simmons' reworked Lockean social contract, no existing political order successfully lives up to its tough normative tests. All fall short: no existing liberal state can plausibly claim to take the idea of voluntary individual consent sufficiently seriously, with only very few of us – naturalized citizens perhaps – having freely chosen our government in the demanding manner Locke, when appropriately interpreted, had in mind.[7] With great rigor, Simmons makes mincemeat of a host of influential attempts to interpret the modern liberal state as somehow resting on a sound idea of individual consent, express or otherwise, concluding that though some states are less onerous than others, even relatively decent and just liberal democracies can be viewed as basically illegitimate. What follows is that citizens even in liberal states are under no strict obligation to obey the law. There may be moral or prudential grounds for obeying specific laws, or tolerating government activity in some areas, but no reason for interpreting the legal order as possessing a special normative status. The Leviathan, in short, has no clothes: it is naked power.

Building on his creative reconstruction of Locke's theory, Simmons argues that natural moral duties to respect the lives, liberty, health, or goods of other persons, and to refrain from committing serious crimes (murder, assault, rape, theft, fraud) should still lead us to follow the law when it instantiates them. People may not act "however they please" (1993: 262, also 1987). Legal prohibitions on murder should be heeded, for example, because they build directly on the Lockean idea of a natural moral duty not to harm others. When law expresses some morally justifiable positive duties and rights (to aid those in need, for example), or where an individual's violation of otherwise morally neutral laws endangers others, there may be solid ground for abiding the relevant statutes. Yet the reason for then doing so is that we have a moral responsibility not to harm or endanger other persons and their goods, not some make-believe general obligation to government and its laws.

For Simmons and other philosophical anarchists, discrediting the notion of a general or prima facie legal obligation paves the way for an attack on standard ideas about civil disobedience. In the conventional view, disobedients are expected to pass a strict series of tests in part because the onus is on them to justify lawbreaking. If no general legal obligation obtains, however, we can evaluate lawbreaking "in the same way we judge most other kinds of acts, that is, on the basis of their character and consequences" (Smith 1973: 972). Since political lawbreakers no longer need to worry about demonstrating fidelity to law, they need not accept legal punishment, at least if no undue harm accrues to others, and sound pragmatic reasons suggest that it makes sense to avoid doing so. What counts is simply the soundness of their moral and political goals, and whether the impact on others can be viewed as acceptable (Feinberg 1979: 57–8). When reflecting on whether to respect the law, "calculated compliance based on consequentialist reasoning" is what really matters (Green 1988: 254). Prospective lawbreakers should focus on the foreseeable moral and political consequences of their acts, with political disobedience in principle no different from other illegal actions justified on moral or pragmatic grounds – for example, violating traffic rules to avoid some greater harm. If we harmlessly ignore a stop sign to transport to the hospital a friend whose life is in danger, few would criticize our act. If instead we cause a fatal accident, and the friend's life turns out never to have been in danger, most would condemn it. Similarly, what counts in politically or morally motivated illegality is not that the actor evinces legal fidelity, or meets some demanding conditions (civility, publicity, nonviolence), but simply whether the act seems well intentioned and produces morally permissible results.

Writers from Gandhi to Arendt and Habermas similarly demanded of civil disobedients that they think hard about possible consequences. Yet they also expected more. Notwithstanding disagreements between political and philosophical anarchists, the tendency here again is to dissolve civil disobedience's shared conceptual traits.[8] Simmons returns to the nineteenth-century dissident Henry Thoreau to redefine civil disobedience broadly as deliberate, principled lawbreaking, usually limited to immediate aims or goals (Simmons 2005). Civil disobedience morphs into an open-ended category encapsulating what previous writers saw as separate categories of lawbreaking: it covers acts that can be either politically or morally motivated, nonviolent or violent, public or secret. In the process, Simmons and other philosophical anarchists sacrifice civil disobedience's common categorical language, redeploying it in ways that would seem idiosyncratic to most standard speakers.

In Thoreau's writings, Simmons finds appealing elements of a suitably individualistic theory of political consent, with parallels to Locke's, along with the requisite voluntarist hostility to state and law. Like Locke, Thoreau was a philosophical anarchist *avant la lettre* who recognized the illegitimacy of both state and law.[9] In 1846, Thoreau spent a night in jail for refusing to pay his poll tax, an incident that probably would have been forgotten had he not subsequently penned an eloquent moral and political justification. In contrast to political anarchists, however, Thoreau did not view his tax revolt as part of an effort to realize a stateless utopia. Nor did he conceive of resistance to lawful authority as a general imperative or obligation (Hanson 2017).[10] Yet, Simmons claims, he astutely anticipated the contemporary philosophical-anarchist insight that misplaced notions of legal obligation buttress correspondingly confused ideas about the need for lawbreaking to be public (or political), nonviolent, a last or final resort (following the exhaustion of normal channels), and requiring legal punishment. Once we deny the idea of a general political obligation and recognize the state's illegitimacy, Simmons believes, we can appreciate Thoreau's expansive account of civil disobedience, an account too often submerged or distorted by subsequent writers.[11] Civil disobedience need not be a political or public act aimed at persuading other citizens; it can also refer to conscientiously motivated attempts to frustrate evil or avoid complicity in wrongdoing. As Thoreau declared, "[t]he only obligation which I have a right to assume, is to do at any time what I think right" (1996: 2). Civil disobedience sometimes means ignoring or evading law, or even – as in Thoreau's endorsement of the abolitionist John Brown[12] – violent action. The nonviolence requirement is probably dispensable since violence is notoriously difficult to define; under some circumstances, violent acts can be justified. Civil disobedience is principled in character when practitioners possess cogent moral grounds for acting. They need not worry, in any event, about showing respect for the law or accepting legal penalties.

On this conceptual rebooting, longstanding conceptual and political distinctions – between civil and conscientious disobedience, nonviolent lawbreaking and violent resistance – fade into the background. Where then might we get good advice about when and how best to pursue lawbreaking? A Lockean conception of political authority as resting on voluntary individual consent, Simmons believes, provides useful strictures. Civil disobedience, even when broadly reconceived, does not mean "anything goes," since Locke's theory provides reasons for limiting the scope and character of illegal actions (1979: 193–4; 1987; 1993: 260–9).

By day's end, however, Simmons' libertarian model builds upon a tendentious brand of individualism. Thoreau, we might recall, was criticized by Arendt for reducing political life to the dictates of individual moral conscience. On her more critical reading, Thoreau's extreme individualism did a disservice to civil disobedience as joint action in concert among and between citizens (Arendt 1972 [1970a]). Thoreau, in fact, privileged moral conscience, interpreted in a highly individualistic and subjective manner, over shared political and social obligations (Rosenblum 1981: 98). Not surprisingly, Simmons seems eager to justify acts of individual resistance, in the process downplaying civil disobedience's civic contours as joint public action for the common good. Simmons admits that his Lockean-inspired account begins with a rejection of the contrasting philosophical position, found in Aristotle, Hegel, and others, that "we cannot understand persons, morality, or social interaction" along his own starkly individualistic lines, such that political life rests on a contingent choice between and among freestanding individuals (1993: 36). Controversial anarchist ideas about state and law, in effect, have probably already been built into his theory's extreme individualistic starting point. Individual autonomy is conceived from the outset to be such that it can never be properly squared with political or legal authority: government is illegitimate on the basis of a conceptual fiat.[13] The latent assumption that "individual moral judgment can be exercised in complete absence" of basic intersubjective social ties tends to function as a premise rather than a controversial thesis requiring a sustained defense (Pateman 1985 [1979]: 139).[14] Unavoidably, state and law are irrepressibly opposed to the individual, rather than potentially complementing and supporting him or her.

Philosophical anarchists also conveniently start from strict and probably misleading ideas of legal and political obligation. On their view, "political obligation purports to bind *all* citizens to *all* laws" (Green 1988: 228; emphasis added). It represents "a general obligation applying to *all* the law's subjects and to *all* the laws on *all* the occasions to which they apply" (Raz 2009 [1979]: 234; emphasis added). There is nothing wrong per se with this definition. Problems arise, however, when it serves to caricature standard notions of civil disobedience.

The activists and writers discussed in previous chapters did not in fact regularly prescribe this rigid account of obligation. Rather, they typically posited a qualified obligation to obey the law, regularly defending the possibility of more-or-less far-reaching lawbreaking. In fact, no political order probably needs a strict or universal sense of obligation to flourish (Greenawalt 1989: 20). When insisting that lawbreakers should express fidelity to the law, they did so neither because of some belief in a perfect or universal duty by *all* citizens to obey *every* law, nor because existing states in their eyes were fundamentally legitimate. Instead, their insight was that by demonstrating respect for law, activists could prefigure the more completely just order they wanted to create. King, for example, neither viewed the US as fundamentally legitimate nor its legal order as deserving of universal obedience. Nonetheless, he expected his disciples to evince respect for law because by doing so they could help construct a radically reformed polity more fully in sync with the unrealized ambitions of the *Declaration of Independence* and US Constitution. Arendt and Habermas pictured civil disobedience and respect for law as intimately interlinked, not because they considered contemporary liberal states perfectly legitimate or legally sound, but because lawbreakers should work toward perfecting the unfinished project of constitutional democracy.[15] For the liberal jurist Dworkin, civil disobedience's legal prong was about showing respect for dynamic constitutional principles, principles in need of more-or-less constant adaptation and reinterpretation.

Philosophical anarchism misses the legal prong's forward-looking connotations, treating it in a fashion many religious, liberal, and democratic writers would have a hard time recognizing as their own. Because philosophical anarchism does not in fact cleanly dispose of civil disobedience's legal traits, it proves less disruptive than initially appears to be the case. Not surprisingly perhaps, one encounters a certain tendency among philosophical anarchists to pull back from what initially looked like a frontal assault. Like many contemporary political anarchists who find themselves pragmatically joining forces with mainstream practitioners of civil disobedience, philosophical anarchists similarly revisit familiar territory.

After rejecting strict but misleading ideas of universal or general obligation, philosophical anarchists offer reassurances that they do not intend to open the door to mass lawbreaking. Why not? Even if there is no presumption to obey law *qua* law, "ninety percent of all illegal acts" are wrong on moral grounds and thus are unacceptable (Feinberg 1979: 57). Simmons offers a detailed account of why many laws should be obeyed because of moral duties we owe other persons. Even if it is mistaken to believe we have prima facie legal obligations, pressing moral reasons suggest that we should typically follow the law: "We will normally have good reasons for obeying the law, and for supporting some types of governments of which our own may be one" (1979: 194). Joseph Raz jettisons the idea of a strict legal obligation but expounds at length on why a basic respect for the law, "an attitude to law ... such that those who have it have a general reason to obey the law," can be justified (2009 [1979]: 250). Most people, he concedes, have grounds to obey the law most of the time (2009 [1979]: 242). For Leslie Green, "[o]ne should never disobey lightly, not because that would violate a prima-facie obligation to obey, but because public acts of disobedience may have serious consequences which it is always wrong to ignore" (1988: 254–5).

Philosophical anarchists implicitly acknowledge many reasons why those located especially in liberal democracies should follow the law. In reality, they often proffer a newfangled version of the old idea of a limited or qualified obligation

to obey law: their anti-legalism and anti-statism prove surprisingly cautious (Gans 1992: xi). If good reasons for typically obeying the law remain, then those who break it should
still probably also be expected to explain why their acts can
be squared with their basic legal obligations, or why "in a
reasonably just state any consideration in favor of disobedience has to overcome a presumption against it" (Raz 2009
[1979]: 262). Or, as Simmons concedes, "[i]t will usually be
best to press for *public recognition* of ... wrongs, sometimes
even by conspicuous disobedience, within the *legal frameworks* offered in our society" (1993: 268; emphasis added).
The civility requirement reappears here as well: lawbreakers need to demonstrate a "willingness to deliberate about
the character of injustice before disobeying" (Green 1988:
265). In a political community where reciprocity and social
solidarity are suitably valued, we may be forced to tolerate
minor or occasional injustices (Green 1988: 266). Philosophical anarchism, in effect, eventually repossesses familiar ideas
about civil disobedience.[16]

I do not mean to trivialize philosophical anarchism's challenge to standard views of civil disobedience. Nor do I intend
to simplify its impressive contributions to contemporary
debate. However, as we similarly saw in our discussion of
their political cousins, at the end of an exciting day spent
exploring other venues, philosophical anarchists tend to come
home. They too find themselves discussing how lawbreaking
can be viewed as legitimate, and when best for it to be civil,
public, open, and nonviolent. Despite their opposition to the
shared conceptual language of civil disobedience, they find
themselves speaking it. Philosophical anarchists ultimately
posit some notion of obedience or fidelity to law, in the process
reopening the door to the old idea of civil disobedience as
congruent with respect for the law. By admitting some room
for law, anarchists concede that some states, though never
perfectly legitimate, perform useful functions. Revealingly,
some philosophical anarchists end up devoting some attention to the perennial question of what an ideal state would
look like (Wolff 1970: 21–67). Others simply claim that some
states can be justified (when, for example, taking a form consistent with a Lockean account of basic moral duties) even
when not fully legitimate (Simmons 2001: 122–57). When all

is said and done, they seem eager to reclaim stock notions of civil disobedience, though their anti-statism and anti-legalism get in the way of them systematically doing so.

Surviving anarchism

At the start of this chapter I described an implicit set of thematic commonalities shared by most accounts of civil disobedience. Although anarchists fire many powerful shots at them, their assault falls short.

Conventional theories of civil disobedience are threatened not only by anarchism but even more so by real-life political and social trends, trends I describe in the next chapter as postnationalization and privatization. Standard models built on now tenuous premises not about state or law per se but instead about the primacy of the nation-state and its national laws. Whether the concept of civil disobedience still makes sense given dramatic recent changes to the nation-state and its legal order is the subject of the next chapter.

5
Postnationalization and Privatization

On November 30, 1999, thousands of nonviolent protestors, mostly from North America yet many from elsewhere as well, successfully blockaded World Trade Organization (WTO) ministerial talks in Seattle, bringing them briefly to a standstill. Activists hoped to raise public awareness of neoliberal globalization's ills and force the WTO to take social concerns on board. Many engaged in a "lockdown" that made it difficult for the police to remove them, since doing so meant arduously cutting through a series of pipes to avoid injuring protestors. Simultaneously, anarchist ("Black Bloc") groups damaged downtown storefronts of major multinationals like McDonald's, Nike, and Starbucks. In what since has come to be described as the "Battle of Seattle," Seattle's mayor declared a state of emergency, inviting an aggressive police crackdown. According to witnesses, the police indiscriminately lumped all activists, violent or otherwise, together and effectively put a stop to many peaceful protests (Perrine 2001). Within the diverse band of global activists converging in Seattle, a lively and sometimes heated debate emerged, dealing with familiar questions. When, if ever, should political lawbreakers condone the destruction of property? To what extent can or should anarchists and other groups effectively cooperate in pursuing civil disobedience (Conway 2003)?

Commentators who saw in Seattle the makings of a "global peoples' movement" opposing neoliberal globalization found some initial confirmation for their expectations in subsequent protests at the International Monetary Fund (IMF)/ World Bank meetings in Prague during 2000 and the G-8 meeting of the heads of rich industrialized states in Genoa in July 2001 (Bleyer 2000: 31). Activists hailing from different countries directed their grassroots energies at meetings of powerful global players, with some innovative forms of protest emerging. At the Genoa protests, for example, "White Overalls" activists covered their bodies in protective materials (foam rubber padding, shin pads, helmets) before moving provocatively into what the police defined as out-of-bounds areas prohibited to protestors. Espousing nonviolence, yet viewed as dangerous provocateurs by the police, the White Overalls invited police attacks to focus public attention on state repression (Della Porta et al. 2006: 134–5). Predictably, strategic and philosophical differences in Genoa and elsewhere generated tensions between anarchists and other activist groups.

Gathering under the slogan "We are the 99%," protestors who occupied New York's Zuccotti Park in 2011 rapidly inspired similar actions in over 80 countries. Occupy activists faced legal penalties for criminal trespassing and other politically motivated illegalities.[1] Significantly, many Occupy participants, anarchist or otherwise, did not chiefly or even primarily target state officials or bad public policy but instead bankers and a global capitalist economy viewed as culpable for runaway inequality.[2] They occupied public and private locales strategically selected to express their discontent. Zuccotti Park, for example, lies in Lower Manhattan's financial district. In the UK, Occupy established a camp outside St. Paul's Cathedral in the City, after its initial efforts to do so across from the stock exchange were blocked by a court ruling. German Occupy managed to set up camp directly opposite European Central Bank (ECB) headquarters in Frankfurt.[3]

Although commentators have noted differences between Occupy and earlier civil disobedience movements, it would be a mistake to overlook commonalities.[4] Many participants endorsed relatively strict ideas of nonviolence and viewed their acts through a well-worn lens. As one prominent Occupy Wall Street activist tellingly commented, protests should make "it completely clear why the laws are being violated and how the laws are being violated, so the public sees what our intent – that our intent isn't just to break laws for the sake of breaking laws, or to cause chaos or hurt regular people, but to get to the heart of how the one percent, how the elite in this country enforce their unpopular policies" (quoted in Del Signore 2012). Occupy Wall Street activists refused to heed eviction notices from Zuccotti Park, with some participants illegally occupying foreclosed homes as a way of protesting unfair bank mortgages. While doing so, they tried to communicate that they were neither acting irresponsibly nor condoning lawlessness.

Aiming to mobilize nascent global public opinion against state authorities, Gandhi and King similarly sought to build international support. During the Vietnam War and other contexts, disobedients appealed to international law (and especially core legal principles declared at the Nuremberg Trials). Many proponents of civil disobedience, as we discussed in previous chapters, have also defended it when directed not just against public but also private authorities. Such continuities notwithstanding, the novelties remain significant. Civil disobedience today increasingly constitutes a response to what I describe as postnationalization and privatization. Political authority is presently undergoing far-reaching postnationalization, with even the most powerful nation-states sharing authority with major global institutions (for example, the UN, WTO, or IMF), intergovernmental organizations, international agencies and regimes, regionally based supranational institutions (most notably, the European Union), and privileged private actors. Simultaneously, the state's organizational structure is experiencing extensive privatization, with the actual day-to-day exercise of political authority dependent on private businesses, outsourcing, contracting out, and novel organizational structures inconsonant with traditional notions of top-down, hierarchical public administration.

Global justice proponents, Occupy, and other recent social movements more and more address issues with a postnational or global scope, oftentimes relying on the cooperative efforts of activists from different countries (Della Porta et al. 2006: 134–49; Douzinas 2013: 6, 50, 89–106; Gould-Wartofsky 2015; Schock 2015: 90–1). They target both public and private decision-making sites sometimes located "beyond the nation-state," drawing their ranks from cross-border constituencies. Admittedly, they employ the term "civil disobedience" loosely; their usages might surprise Gandhi, King, and others. As a starting point for analysis, however, it seems appropriate to take seriously what many global activists are saying, and they in fact are frequently placing their endeavors under the rubric of civil disobedience. Still, activists clearly face some sizable hurdles in reproducing traditional (religious, liberal, democratic) templates for civil disobedience. This chapter suggests that postnationalization and privatization can help explain why.

Do recent changes in the structure of political authority require us to rethink conventional views of civil disobedience?[5] If so, what – if any – revisions are called for? Here I revisit Rawls' influential liberal account of civil disobedience. The Anglophone debate on civil disobedience in the 1960s and 1970s was complex and wide-ranging; Rawls was only one among many impressive voices, many of whom were directly inspired by King and the US civil rights movement. Nonetheless, the stunning success of his *A Theory of Justice* (1971) meant that the Rawlsian defense of civil disobedience, warts and all, soon took on a canonical stature, for both liberals and those skeptical of liberalism. His model, of course, has long been subjected to a barrage of criticisms; I have already endorsed some of those criticisms. Yet in deference to the usual convention among scholars of civil disobedience, this chapter focuses on Rawls. Though I cannot sufficiently document this claim here, some and perhaps many of the arguments I direct against, and sometimes cautiously in defense of, Rawls also apply to competing ideas about civil disobedience.

To formulate my criticisms, I turn to an illuminating body of empirical research about state transformation to analyze a set of revealing implicit presuppositions about state and society. Oftentimes missed by philosophical critics, those assumptions not only proved more contingent than Rawls and other liberals in the 1960s and early 1970s grasped, but now seem empirically obsolete. By reconsidering the Rawlsian model's original political and social framing we can better grasp its weaknesses. We can also perhaps better understand why so many forms of politically motivated lawbreaking now clash with the Rawlsian model: postnationalization and privatization pose serious challenges to it.

Nonetheless, the story hardly buttresses the easy conclusion that Rawls' view should be discarded *in toto*. When properly reconceived, some of its basic features remain pertinent. Admittedly, this modest conclusion is unlikely to satisfy either orthodox Rawlsians or their harshest critics. Yet I believe that it can be successfully defended.

Revisiting Rawls

Rawls viewed civil disobedience as a means for political minorities to communicate to majorities a competing interpretation of the community's underlying sense of justice. The disobedient "declares that in one's considered opinion the principles of social cooperation among free and equal men [sic] are not being respected," and that the majority has ignored or violated the polity's shared ideas about justice (1971: 364). Civil disobedience represents a symbolically assertive, yet politically defensive, signal to majorities that they have irresponsibly infringed on principles of justice they share with those being mistreated.

Because it contradicts our usual legal obligations, disobedients are expected to communicate a basic fidelity to the law so as to prove "to the majority that the act is indeed politically conscientious and sincere, and that it is intended to address the public sense of justice" (1971: 366–7). This can be accomplished through nonviolence and a willingness to accept legal consequences. Civil disobedience should also remain exceptional or unusual because in "nearly just" societies outvoted minorities should generally be able to identify ordinary institutional channels for redress. Even in such basically just social orders, however, grave injustices sometimes occur, and civil disobedience may then prove appropriate (1971: 351, 363). When dissenters challenge only flagrant injustices, and not those potentially countered by ordinary political and institutional means, civil disobedience can be viewed as potentially legitimate.

Although civil disobedience demands proof of moral seriousness, appeals to private morality or religion do not suffice. Instead, disobedients should speak a common or shared language of political justice. Lest one worry that this demand clashes with the dictates of modern pluralism, Rawls conceded that there can

> be considerable differences in citizens' conceptions of justice provided that these conceptions lead to similar political judgments. And this is possible, since different premises can yield the same conclusion. In this case there exists what we may refer to as overlapping rather than strict consensus. (1971: 387–8)

An overlapping rather than perfect consensus about justice could still provide the requisite normative basis for prospective disobedients. Sometimes the best evidence for the existence of such an overlapping consensus, Rawls suggested, was the authorities' refusal to suppress or punish illegal protests. "Ruthless tactics that might be contemplated in other societies are not entertained" because the majority has perhaps implicitly acknowledged the soundness of the disobedient's cause (1971: 387).

Looking back from the vantage point of four decades of accelerated globalization, we can see how the Rawlsian account rested on certain implicit premises about state and society. When Rawls demanded of disobedients that they address a broader public, the "public" he had in mind was the national public of (existing) constitutional democracies, which he took to be the central site for the realization of the shared sense of justice to which disobedients were expected to appeal. More generally, Rawls' theory implicitly followed the strictures of what Nancy Fraser has described as the "Westphalian political frame" (2009: 76–99). The national public Rawls envisioned entailed a shared liberal and pluralistic political culture. Disobedients were obliged to appeal to common political principles of justice because modern pluralism limited the persuasive force of traditional moral and religious appeals. The political give-and-take between lawbreakers and powerful political majorities also presupposed a shared linguistic and communicative infrastructure (for example, a nationally centered mass media). Nonviolence was exercised in relation to one's fellow nationals because it was their mistaken views about justice one had to correct, and it was they to whom disobedients owed proof of their moral seriousness. Disobedients sought corrections from errant majorities that had come to dominate policy making over a state apparatus exercising "final and coercive authority over a certain territory" (1971: 222). Policy changes sought by conscientious lawbreakers were, of course, intended for the national levels. Fidelity to the law meant fidelity to the legal order of specific "nearly just" (nation-state) constitutional democracies. Legal penalties were to be meted out by national political authorities.

Tellingly, Rawls' exposition directly reproduced the Westphalian premise of a strict divide between domestic and international affairs (Beitz 1979; Pogge 1988: 211–80). Rawls thought it made sense to distinguish civil disobedience from conscientious objection; he outlined many grounds for drawing a line between them. Yet one reason for the delineation was geographical: civil disobedience concerned domestic affairs, whereas conscientious refusal entailed the extension of "the theory of justice to the law of nations" (1971: 377). His model's implicit Westphalian framing also included once commonplace ideas about the state's institutional primacy, and especially the expectation that a state is "capable in principle of regulating its inhabitants' affairs and solving their problems" (Fraser 2009: 79). Rawls was no apologist for the postwar welfare state status quo or existing regulated capitalism. Yet he sometimes endorsed relatively conventional postwar assumptions about state and society, assumptions widely shared by left-liberals and social democrats in Europe, North America, and elsewhere. Rawls envisioned a basically just order as one where a robust state sector would correct for a market economy (1971: 258–83). The "nearly just" society he had in mind was one where public authorities could effectively tame otherwise divisive economic and social conflicts since they possessed "substantial regulative powers with respect to other institutions" (1971: 236).

Those premises undergirded Rawls' view that civil disobedience should be limited to infringements of civil and political rights. To be sure, core philosophical claims about the lexical primacy of the first principle of justice (that is, the idea of equal liberty) also played a major role in his analysis (1971: 302–3). Yet his position conveniently reproduced the widespread postwar faith that state authorities, acting via an array of interventionist and regulatory measures, would succeed in reducing economic injustice and civilizing capitalism. Under a more-or-less well-functioning liberal polity we can realistically expect public authorities to keep social injustice "from getting out of hand" (1971: 373). Social and economic policy is best left to legislatures, where pragmatic considerations about efficiency and welfare tend to predominate. Unlike principled and easily communicated disputes about civil and political rights, appeals to the public's conception of justice are unlikely to prove sufficiently clear or persuasive in social and economic policy. Consequently, "they should not normally be protested by civil disobedience" (1971: 372). Like other liberals writing about civil disobedience in the 1960s and early 1970s, Rawls tended to look askance at civil disobedience in the context of distributive justice and when directed primarily at private institutions.

Postnationalization and privatization

These premises about state and society no longer unreservedly obtain. The relevant empirical literature is complicated; it would be misleading to posit a neat scholarly consensus about the main changes or their underlying causes. However, the literature tends to point in two relatively clear directions (Genschel and Zangl 2008; Hurrelmann et al. 2007).

First, nation-states now share decision-making authority with many institutional actors on the international scene. The actors take myriad forms. They include regional organizations (like the EU or the North American Free Trade Agreement [NAFTA]), powerful international organizations (the WTO or IMF), as well as more familiar global political bodies (the UN). To be sure, nation-states remain crucial sites for authoritative decision making; fashionable talk about global governance sometimes masks that abiding reality. Yet they no longer enjoy the virtual monopoly on political decision making Rawls presupposed and which in empirical reality was perhaps approximated among many OECD states during the 1960s.[6] The "final authority" Rawls associated with nation-states tends increasingly to be situated in a complex multi-layered system where national decision makers remain central yet no longer always dominant players. Empirical evidence, in short, suggests a heightened role for international and postnational decision-making sites to a degree Rawls and his contemporaries generally failed to anticipate.

Here we can speak of an internationalization or *postnationalization of decision-making authority*, or what we might cautiously describe as a nascent post-Westphalian institutional constellation. In any event, "stateness" as a *decision-making complex* is presently co-produced by a complex mix of political authorities both within and beyond the nation-state. No overarching global or world state, possessing a centralized monopoly over legitimate coercion, presently exists. Nonetheless, some key state functions are being exercised, albeit incompletely and oftentimes haphazardly, by nation-states operating in conjunction with a messy array of international institutions.[7]

Second, there have been dramatic changes in the state's administrative structure and *organizational capacities* since the 1970s. Despite neoliberalism, states are in fact oftentimes involved in more areas of social existence than during the heyday of the postwar interventionist and welfare state. Yet they decreasingly rely on classical top-down public-bureaucratic mechanisms when doing so. This trend manifests itself in many ways. Privatization is widespread (Freeman and Minow 2009; Zohlhöfer and Ohringer 2006); outsourcing and contracting are ubiquitous; regulation often depends on novel public-private cooperation (Schuppert 2010). These changes directly impact even those functions conventionally associated with the "hard" kernel of state sovereignty: "in many countries private security personnel now outnumber their public counterparts" (Abrahamsen and Williams 2011: 1). The massive growth of state surveillance activities in recent years, for example, has been abetted by burgeoning private intelligence and security firms heavily dependent on lucrative government contracts (Shorrock 2008). Even when the state apparatus remains directly involved in specific regulatory tasks, that apparatus has been reorganized in accordance with new organizational ideals (e.g., "governance" or "new public management") that have generated dramatic administrative restructurings.

Here we can speak of a de-statization or *privatization* of political authority. "Stateness" as an *organizational complex* is being co-produced in conventional public-bureaucratic and novel private and quasi-private institutional sites, many of which mesh poorly with traditional ideas about public administration. Internationalization and privatization sometimes coalesce: some forms of international business dispute resolution, for example, rely heavily on what are essentially private adjudicators (Cutler 2003).

One immediate consequence of these shifts deserves special attention. Whatever the precise causal mechanisms, the structural shifts at hand seem related to a noticeable fraying of the nation-state such that it decreasingly seems capable of successfully managing social and economic affairs along the lines Rawls and other postwar left-liberals and social democrats hoped. Despite national variations, for most developed OECD countries the general trends remain striking: the welfare state social net fails to protect many social groups; material inequality has increased drastically; state regulators have not been able to ward off devastating economic disturbances and crises (for example, the 2008 financial crisis). The nation-state too often appears inadequate when it comes to managing our globalizing and increasingly high-speed capitalism. Nor have effective postnational regulatory mechanisms filled the resulting gaps. Nobody should romanticize the "golden age" of the postwar welfare and interventionist states. Yet some fundamental – and basically troublesome – shifts have occurred. Whatever the specific causes, the existing political order too often seems inept when it comes to grappling with contemporary capitalism's pathologies.

Novel threats to Rawlsian civil disobedience

What then do these broad structural shifts suggest about Rawls' liberal model? The story is messy. To be sure, the Rawlsian framework can occasionally help us make sense of challenges faced today by those contemplating civil disobedience. However, shifts in state/society relations tend to stretch his model to the limits. In some ways, it no longer seems relevant.

1. The internationalization and postnationalization of decision making strains the assumption that civil disobedients, publics (and political majorities) to which they appeal, and the relevant political authorities overlap within the borders of a single territorially bound polity. Since many key decisions are still made by national institutions and directly impact specific national constituencies, the Westphalian frame remains pertinent. Yet prospective conscientious lawbreakers face complicated questions the Rawlsian framework conveniently submerged because of its Westphalian framing, a framing which decreasingly meshes with the complex and multi-layered character of contemporary political decision making. To whom (local, national, or postnational addressees) should the disobedient's appeal be directed? Which political majorities need to be swayed, and at which level of decision making are they located?[8] From which political authorities should one seek redress? What are the relevant (national or global) laws or policies that require change, or the shared principles of justice on which one's appeal should rest? Which laws are crucial when expressing fundamental fidelity to the law? The emerging system's complexity and resulting lack of transparency make it difficult for activists to find answers, let alone develop a persuasive political appeal. Admittedly, previous civil disobedients faced parallel questions: Gandhi and King also strategized about how to propel local political battles into the global limelight. Nonetheless, those today pursuing civil disobedience confront them in exceptionally complex

and pressing ways, in part for reasons I try to outline in what follows.

2. If the disputed law or policy can be attributed to international or postnational authorities, for example, or if linked, as is commonly the case, to a multiplicity of decision-making sites, prospective disobedients will need to do something Rawls never really considered, namely move beyond the usual local preoccupations and address publics and political authorities "beyond the state." Yet empirical research suggests that this is extraordinarily difficult. Even those activists who successfully focus on postnational issues tend to remain embedded in domestic politics, with their efforts oftentimes proving fragile and short-lived. Relatively few activists have been able to bridge national gaps and come together across borders in pursuit of an identifiably shared postnational agenda (Schock 2015: 140–57; Tarrow 2005).[9] Although recent Occupy activists, for example, developed cross-border ties and spoke directly to common concerns about global inequality, their efforts soon dissipated (Gould-Wartofsky 2015). Of course, there are some exceptions: global justice activists, including many who engaged in nonviolent civil disobedience, and also recent anti-austerity protestors in Greece, Spain, and elsewhere, have effectively targeted postnational authorities (the G-8, WTO, and EU) and have brought public attention to controversial policies having cross-border ramifications. The global justice movement successfully forged activists from different countries around a coherent agenda and was identifiably transnational in character, despite significant linguistic variations and differences in political culture. It also creatively updated civil disobedience's arsenal of tactics (Della Porta et al. 2006). At any rate, activists today are clearly cognizant of the daunting challenges at hand, with their internal debates sometimes implicitly tackling the toughest questions. They argue, for example, about how best to frame their appeals given political authority's multi-tiered contours, or where ideally (that is, at the local, national, or postnational level) to focus their organizational energies. Despite their oftentimes admirable efforts, our decentered and multi-layered

postnational system impairs the formulation of coherent let alone easily communicable justifications for civil disobedience. Even when disobedients manage to do this, it remains unclear whether their efforts can result in changes to law or policy along the lines Rawls envisioned: too many of the key decision makers are insulated from public opinion and the familiar political mechanisms operative, however inadequately, in "nearly just" liberal democracies. Neither the WTO nor the European "troika" (European Commission, European Central Bank, and IMF), for example, seems to pay the same political price or face the same repercussions risked by elected national officials when ignoring mass civil disobedience. Global justice and anti-austerity movements have so far probably only had a marginal impact on policy making at the postnational level.

3. Despite its conceptual limits, Rawls' framework provides some resources for explaining why this is so. Postnationalization of decision making means that key decisions are increasingly being made at sites that arguably fail to meet basic democratic tests of legitimacy. I will not revisit the familiar question of whether it makes sense to democratize international organizations or even the EU, and if so, how best to do so. I merely recall the crucial Rawlsian proviso that civil disobedience presupposes the existence of a "nearly just" society in which familiar liberal and democratic mechanisms typically function. It remains an open question whether our emerging global system could even pass some minimal interpretation of the "nearly just" standard. On many occasions nation-states are expected to abide rules promulgated "from above" by institutions (the IMF, for example, or WTO) whose democratic credentials remain dubious.[10] This is important for two reasons. First, Rawls insisted that prospective disobedients should first exhaust ordinary political channels. In our emerging post-Westphalian universe, however, the relevant channels often lack transparency or remain badly underdeveloped. Second, Rawls conceded that, absent a reasonably just democratic system, more militant forms of resistance and even violent revolution, where protestors evade legal penalties and other tests

associated with nonviolent civil disobedience, might in principle prove legitimate (1971: 365–8).[11] Revealingly, though their role has probably been overstated, small groups of global activists have in fact sometimes abandoned strict nonviolence, opting to pursue messier and more militant forms of political illegality. Global justice protestors, for example, were widely criticized for "clashing with the police, setting fire to cars, and smashing windows" (Della Porta et al. 2006: 147). European anti-austerity protests have comprised some violence as well (Hatzopoulos and Patelis 2013). If in fact postnationalization has undermined rather than refurbished the accountability of key decision makers, Rawls might still have been forced to acknowledge the possible legitimacy of such actions. (Of course, their possible legitimacy hardly guarantees either their appropriateness or effectiveness. When poorly conceived or timed, such actions can easily prove counterproductive.)

4.   The fact that the emerging postnational political order perhaps fails the "nearly just" test has further implications. Rawls envisioned civil disobedience as a defensive action targeting majorities that had infringed on a pre-existing conception of justice already ensconced in social and political institutions. It helped stabilize basically just constitutional systems (1971: 384). Absent liberal democracy, protest in principle could take not only a more militant but also a more forward-looking and fundamentally constructive approach. Interestingly, some recent movements targeting postnational or global institutions and policies appear to do just that. Although their political rhetoric sometimes sounds defensive,[12] they demand basic and potentially transformative reforms, with many of them suggesting the need for a far-reaching democratization of global institutions (Della Porta et al. 2006: 203–5; Smith 2007), or an EU in which economic policy is no longer dominated by the European Central Bank or powerful member states (Douzinas 2013). Even when engaging in what otherwise look like familiar forms of nonviolent civil disobedience, their actions can hardly be considered politically or institutionally defensive (Green 2002). For understandable reasons, the movements in

question do not believe that we presently possess a shared postnational order or overarching view of global justice worth defending.

5. Rawls worried that absent a shared and publicly recognized conception of justice, civil disobedience would inevitably fail and the ruling "majority may simply be aroused to more repressive measures" (1971: 387). Postnationalization exacerbates this danger. The notion of an overlapping consensus was introduced partly in order to explain how pluralistic political communities might provide the requisite normative terrain on which disobedients could act. Can we identify something along these lines in the postnational arena (in the EU, for example, or elsewhere) such that prospective disobedients could identify a sufficiently robust common normative basis on which to sway political opponents? Given the conditions of what Alessandro Ferrara (2014) aptly describes as global hyperpluralism, the answer is hardly self-evident.

6. Postnationalization challenges the institutional primacy of the state and thus its exclusive capacity to satisfy its inhabitants' basic social and economic needs. This tendency is compounded by the privatization and de-statization of the state's organizational capacities. In principle, privatization might bolster rather than undermine the state's monopoly over decision making and with it also the state's capacity for effective intervention and regulation, as long as public authorities can exercise proper oversight and core political functions remain in public hands. However, empirical evidence suggests that these basic tests are often left unmet: the rage for privatization means that a growing number of previously public functions, including those pertaining to basic security, are being outsourced to private and quasi-private entities enjoying substantial leeway and subject to merely cursory oversight by public authorities (Metzger 2009). Even scholars otherwise sympathetic to privatization have acknowledged the dangers (Verkuil 2007). Admittedly, Rawls' view of the state as possessing comprehensive scope and primacy vis-à-vis private institutions was an idealization even during the heyday of the postwar welfare state and regulated capitalism. Today it seems

increasingly detached from empirical reality. Accordingly, it no longer seems clear that civil disobedience should target only public but not private authorities. Where poorly regulated private corporations affect life prospects in a manner at least as consequential as government, they become fair game for political lawbreaking. When the state ceases to be institutionally supreme in the fashion presupposed by Rawls (and many others), public officials no longer "manage" the private sphere. Instead, political functions are increasingly placed directly into private hands, and then it probably makes sense for disobedients to take aim at non-state institutions.

7. Even when not directly targeting private corporations engaging in what traditionally have been considered public or state activities, many protestors and closely related civil disobedients (e.g., in Occupy, or recent European anti-austerity activists) are focusing their energies on egregious forms of economic injustice.[13] Though this trend conflicts with the Rawlsian model, its underlying sources are clear enough. Given postnationalization and privatization, OECD states no longer can prevent economic injustices from "getting out of hand." Rawls' postwar faith that liberal nation-states would be able successfully to oversee the economy seems unrealistic. In the eyes of many contemporary activists, the most shocking injustices are basically economic (for example, rising material inequality and increasing economic insecurity). Nor do they seem to share Rawls' worry that economic appeals are necessarily any less clear than appeals to civil and political rights.

8. Some writers have creatively relied partly on Rawls to analyze the possibility of politically motivated lawbreaking by states, or "international civil disobedience." Unfortunately, they perhaps reproduce the conventional but outdated view of the nation-state as the predominant institutional player on the global scene (Goodin 2005; Miller 2015).[14] Moreover, the move to depict "states" as conscientious, nonviolent lawbreakers is normatively dubious. Does it make sense to label the messy and multi-headed institutional complexes we call "states" conscientious moral actors? By doing so, we risk attributing

to states a unified moral agency and capacity for systematic moral reflection they probably lack. Given its arsenal of destructive instruments, it also seems implausible to associate state activity in the international arena, especially when it involves lawbreaking, with principled nonviolence.

What remains? Rawlsian civil disobedience today

My analysis so far corroborates the critical view that the Rawlsian definition of civil disobedience as a "public, nonviolent, conscientious yet political act contrary to law usually done with the aim of bringing about a change in the law" seems increasingly irrelevant (Rawls 1971: 364). Its skeptical assessment of civil disobedience when targeting private actors (for example, banks or corporations), its view of civil disobedience as fundamentally defensive, and its hostility to militant forms of (potentially "uncivil") disobedience – each tenet is rendered suspect by postnationalization and privatization. Our evolving political order invites novel types of political lawbreaking, some of which Rawls never anticipated and probably would have criticized. Yet some of them, even on his theoretical terms, now seem potentially legitimate.

These findings potentially provide fodder for those arguing that we should simply jettison the liberal for a revised postliberal model of civil disobedience more attuned to the messy and sometimes "uncivil" forms politically motivated illegality presently takes.[15] By doing so, critics posit, we can successfully overcome the liberal model and its many limits while simultaneously permitting activists to benefit from the normative prestige the idea of civil disobedience continues to enjoy. Why should only iconic lawbreakers like Gandhi or King but not recent disobedients enjoy such benefits (Sauter 2014: 19–38)?

Much can be said in favor of this position. I argued previously that a robust democratic model of civil disobedience, when properly conceived, might successfully overcome liberalism's limitations. It could only do so successfully, I also suggested, by building constructively on liberalism's accomplishments. In the same spirit, I believe that a sensible response to the Rawlsian approach's flaws should be reconstructive and not one-sidedly deconstructive.

Nothing in the analysis here, for example, discredits the Rawlsian (or standard liberal) view of civil disobedience as public and communicative, that is, as an act aimed at persuading political peers and (eventually) the relevant political authorities to change policy, even if postnationalization and privatization manifestly complicate matters. The complex normative commitment to publicity sometimes gets interpreted too narrowly, a pattern Rawls and many others unhelpfully set by asserting that disobedients should provide "fair notice" of their impending protests to public authorities, a view which even on orthodox Rawlsian grounds seems unnecessary (1971: 366). Political movements always depend on elements of confidentiality, privacy, and even secrecy: we should reject mechanical or overly stringent accounts of publicity. When less strictly construed, publicity remains constitutive of civil disobedience.

Nor does my analysis threaten the rudiments of Rawls' intuitions about the necessarily circumscribed role of conscience. He thought it made sense for disobedients to provide evidence of their moral seriousness in order to impress on others their sincerity, and also because it was crucial to demonstrate that lawbreaking rested on "a sufficient moral basis" (1971: 367). Here we face thorny philosophical issues concerning Rawls' ideas about morality and religion in public life and, more generally, the public/private divide. I do not intend to endorse Rawls' views *in toto*; they require more critical scrutiny (Cooke 2016). Yet Rawls was probably right to highlight the circumscribed place of moral and religious appeals in pluralistic societies where conscience cannot speak in one voice or even in a sufficiently robust shared moral language. Given intensified globalization, Rawls' insights about the limitations of conscience-based justifications for civil disobedience remain relevant. The prospect of a viable "legal system in which conscientious belief that the law is unjust is accepted" as an adequate basis for noncompliance seems even more troublesome today, given global "hyperpluralism," than in Rawls' day (1971: 367). Under contemporary conditions, a legal order where moral conscience sufficed to justify disobedience would necessarily render respect for the law episodic. As Rawls rightly grasped, however, any decent or just order requires the rule of law, where authorities are expected to follow clear, public, prospective, general rules alone capable of proffering a reliable and predictable framework for social cooperation. A legal "system" in which noncompliance became widespread would simply be inconsonant with this worthwhile aspiration (1971: 235–43).

Nor has anything I claimed been directed in principle against Rawls' view of nonviolence as an expression of basic respect for those with whom disobedients disagree but to whom they owe evidence of their sincerity and must convince through persuasion. "To engage in violent acts likely to injure and to hurt is incompatible with civil disobedience as a mode of address" directed at political actors whom one needs to bring over to one's side (1971: 366).[16] All that has been demonstrated is that on Rawls' terms, given the key premise of "near justice," even he might now be forced to concede the possible legitimacy of more militant or even revolutionary lawbreaking.[17] Nonetheless, he could also reasonably oppose embracing open-ended definitions of civil disobedience that risk occluding vital empirical and normative distinctions.[18]

What then of the crucial idea that legitimate as well as effective lawbreaking should evince what King famously described as the "very highest respect for the law" (1991 [1963]: 74)? Like King, Rawls endorsed the seemingly paradoxical thesis that nonviolent lawbreaking was sometimes necessary to preserve the law, that it should be viewed as "disobedience to law within the limits of fidelity to the law" (1971: 366). He also suggested, again following King, that fidelity to the law was best demonstrated by the civil disobedient's willingness to accept legal consequences.

Rawls' position here again initially seems anachronistic. He insisted on disobedients evincing respect for law because they were expected to appeal to a shared and already extant view of justice. That notion of justice, he suggested, had to be publicly recognized and was essential to the relevant nation-state-based constitutional order (1971: 386–9). He also claimed that in "nearly just" communities we should typically follow the law even when it is unjust because "civility imposes a due acceptance of the defects of institutions and a certain restraint in taking advantage of them" (1971: 355). Only flagrant injustices should trigger civil disobedience.

Amid postnationalization and privatization these arguments no longer readily obtain. If, as noted above, ours is hardly a nearly just but instead an increasingly undemocratic, unfair postnational order, where institutions like the WTO or ECB possess significant autonomy, it is no longer clear why politically motivated lawbreakers targeting postnational decision makers should be expected to show respect for law. Why should transnational or global-minded activists express their loyalty to a deeply flawed postnational legal system? Rather, as many of them plausibly demand, we urgently need to create a superior, more just postnational order.

Nonetheless, it would still be wrong to discard this component of the Rawlsian model. Political decision making today is not simply postnational but also decentered and multi-tiered. When activists targeting global-level policies do so within political contexts where authorities respect basic rights and the rule of law, they enjoy massive advantages vis-à-vis activists operating in authoritarian contexts. Even if it no longer makes sense to characterize key traits of our post-Westphalian system as meshing with Rawlsian notions of "near justice," it is no less misleading to downplay the vital importance of preserving basic rights and the rule of law where protestors can effectively take to the streets and non-violently break the law. It remains vital for disobedients to communicate to those whom they hope to sway a shared commitment to protecting law-based government. As King, Rawls, and countless others grasped, the best way to do so is by showing that civil disobedience remains consonant with a broader commitment to law.[19]

Rawls was also right to insist that every just order must rest on the rule of law, an "ideal notion which laws" should be "expected to approximate," even though they sometimes fail to do so even in liberal societies (1971: 236). When politically oriented lawbreakers express fidelity to the law they implicitly appeal to a normative ideal demanding of power holders that they realize the necessary legal presuppositions of a free and decent order. This element of Rawls' theory of civil disobedience remains pertinent as well. Too often, powerful postnational and private decision makers make a mockery of basic legal virtues, especially when doing so potentially benefits the politically and socially vulnerable. Global players often prefer unchecked legal discretion to strict rules, particularly when the rules provide a possible check on their activities.[20] Disobedients who hope to challenge this and other disturbing trends should evince fidelity to the rule of law as *an ideal power holders should be expected to heed.* Fidelity to the law in this context anticipates the possibility of a reformed and significantly improved order in which emerging postnational constitutional and legal rules might in fact prove more fully worthy of our respect. By expressing fidelity to the law, politically motivated lawbreakers contribute toward creating such an order. Their actions, though illegal, prefigure its existence. They then directly symbolize their role as midwives to the new global political and legal order we need if the powerful and privileged are finally going to be forced to play by the same rules as everyone else.[21]

Admittedly, powerful global players often preach and sometimes even practice the "rule of law" when doing so serves their own interests. The rule of law, on its own, hardly guarantees democracy or social justice. Nonetheless, the "greatest assault on the Rule of Law" still generally stems from those "who hold themselves above the law and have the power in fact to stay above it." If only because of its indispensable protective functions, "[a]s compromised as the Rule of Law is and always has been we would do wrong to discard it entirely" (Madar 2013: 123–4). Any prospective improved and reformed postnational political order will need to rest on the rule of law, if it is to embody justice and prove worthy of our respect. Even in the shadows of postnationalization and privatization, civil disobedience should remain "disobedience to law within the limits of fidelity to the law."

Postnationalization and privatization may leave us with a bare-bones version of Rawls' liberal model of civil disobedience. Nonetheless, bare bones remain better than no bones. Some might also dispute whether the remaining bones look enough like the original. Yet Rawls surely would be able to see in them the skeletal remains of the influential account he formulated in his landmark *A Theory of Justice.*

6

Digitalization

Digital disobedience, defined here as "politically motivated online lawbreaking," seems to be spreading like wildfire.[1] The term covers a wide range of activities. They include: DDoS (Distributed Denial of Service) actions, where activists repeatedly access websites as a way of disabling them for political purposes; "hacktivism," in which hackers break into computer servers as an entry for shaming targeted organizations and their practices; leaking and whistleblowing by individuals (for example, Chelsea Manning or Edward Snowden), or groups such as Anonymous and WikiLeaks, where confidential or classified electronically stored data is leaked to the press or public.[2]

Not surprisingly perhaps, digital activists and their defenders are resorting to the familiar language of "civil disobedience" to describe their actions. Government officials rarely take the bait. Instead, prosecutors and judges are insisting on a clear delineation of (allegedly) criminal and morally unacceptable digital lawbreaking from civil disobedience as practiced by King and other iconic figures. Since conventional physical or "on-the-street" civil disobedience occasionally enjoys some measure of political and legal respectability, for digital activists the stakes are high.[3] Consistent with this trend, digital disobedients are facing draconian criminal penalties. The late Aaron Swartz, for example, was charged under the 1986 US Computer Fraud and Abuse Act (CFAA) chiefly for trying to make JSTOR academic articles easily accessible to a broad public. Swartz faced multiple felony charges, up to $1 million in fines and 35 years in prison, before tragically taking his own life. In another case, Jeremy Hammond, a Chicago activist who hacked a private intelligence firm with a sordid history of spying on social movements, was convicted of computer fraud in November 2013 under the CFAA and is now serving a ten-year sentence in a US federal prison. In January 2015 Barrett Brown, an activist and journalist with links to Anonymous, received a 63-month sentence and was fined $890,000. According to Brown's vocal defenders, his most egregious criminal act was copying a link to the hacked materials Hammond had previously uploaded to the web.[4] More prominently, Manning was successfully prosecuted under the US Espionage Act and initially given a 35-year sentence, before President Obama eventually commuted it. Snowden is still being pursued under the same statute and remains in Russian exile.

Although the official response in the US has been particularly harsh, governments elsewhere are penalizing digital disobedience as well. For example, Ryan "Kayla" Ackroyd, a UK citizen, was sentenced to 30 months in jail in May 2013 by British courts for hacking a variety of public and private sites.[5] Even where authorities have demonstrated more leniency, recent legislative changes may prevent their successors from following in their footsteps. In 2001, for example, 13,000 Germans participated in a DDoS action protesting Lufthansa's deportation of immigrants, a protest that ultimately forced Lufthansa to end its involvement in the program (Sauter 2014: 5). Although Andreas Thomas Vogel, a key participant, was initially fined and given a 90-day prison sentence by a local court, a higher court overturned the verdict in recognition of his contributions to public debate. A controversial 2007 anti-hacking law passed by the *Bundestag*, however, now clearly prohibits DDoS of this type.

Despite their efforts to gain some legitimacy for their actions, digital disobedients worldwide face an uphill battle. They encounter not only enmity from government officials but also widespread skepticism from publics not quite sure what to make of them.

Commentators have criticized the punitive treatment of digital disobedience, arguing that it does conceptual violence to the phenomenon at hand and, even worse, potential violence to the activists (Sauter 2014: 138–57). Nonetheless, they tend to neglect a fundamental question: how should we interpret the nexus between digital disobedience and the law? Does digital disobedience represent, as US officials now regularly assert, a criminal and indeed full-fledged assault on the rule of law? Or does it instead, at least potentially, constitute politically motivated lawbreaking based in principle on what King famously described in his "Letter from Birmingham City Jail" as the "very highest respect for the law" (1991 [1963]: 74)? Might it evince, as Rawls noted in his influential discussion, "disobedience to the law within the limits of fidelity to law" (1971: 366)? For King and for many inspired by him, conscientious acts of political illegality were legitimate only when appealing to some fundamental ideal of law. Should we perhaps interpret digital disobedience as nothing more than modernized civil disobedience, better suited than its familiar "on-the-street" forerunners to our digital age?

Digital disobedients and their sympathizers have not always been sufficiently clear in their views of the law. One often encounters decidedly anti-legal strands among their ranks. Nonetheless, some of their actions can in fact be interpreted as supportive and not destructive of the rule of law. State officials aggressively pursuing digital disobedients, along with the legally dubious surveillance policies they defend, often constitute the main threat to law-based government. My efforts here to interpret digital disobedience as a form of political lawbreaking consonant with the idea of "highest respect for the law" notwithstanding, we should hesitate before rushing to group its manifold manifestations under the rubric of civil disobedience. Doing so risks distorting the novelties at hand while fitting digital disobedients with a suit they may not always want to wear.

Digital disobedience, surveillance, and the rule of law

A tendentious view of law is being mobilized by state authorities to justify a repressive legal response that, in fact, makes a mockery of the rule of law. When Jeremy Hammond was sentenced, for example, US District Court Justice Loretta Preska explained the harsh sentence she handed down by declaring that nothing less was required by our shared commitment to "respect for the rule of law." As she continued, "these are not the actions of Martin Luther King, of Nelson Mandela ... or even Daniel Ellsberg."[6] Facing protestors demanding that he explain his Administration's prosecution of Chelsea Manning, Barack Obama in April 2011 responded: "We are a nation of laws. We don't let individuals make decisions about how the law operates. He [meaning Manning] broke the law" (quoted in Greenberg 2012: 44–5). In a chilling 2013 interview, Donald Trump referred to Snowden as a "terrible traitor, and you know what we used to do in the good old days, when we were a strong country – you know what we used to do to traitors, right?," more or less openly calling for his execution (quoted in Chumley 2013).

What should we make of this view that the venerable idea of the "rule of law" demands the aggressive criminal prosecution of digital disobedients? The immediate weakness of this position is that it ignores the rule of law's minimal but essential normative substance. The rule of law, to be sure, is a complex and contested concept (Tamanaha 2004). On the standard view, however, it requires that every legal order aim to realize publicity, generality, clarity, prospectiveness, consistency, and constancy. The rule of law is also typically defined as requiring independent courts free from partisan political pressures. In this familiar account, whose philosophical foundations can be found in classical writers as diverse as Locke, Rousseau, and Hegel, the rule of law demands of government that its actions always rest on laws embodying substantial doses of specific legal virtues (for example, clarity, publicity, generality). Absent the rule of law, we cannot expect individuals to enjoy a minimum of personal security or political freedom. Even when its contributions to justice and equal liberty may seem limited, they are "not by any means negligible" (Rawls 1971: 236). Not surprisingly, thinkers from a wide range of philosophical and political orientations, including republicans and neo-Marxists, have defended it (Neumann 1957; Pettit 1997: 174–7).

Why is this relevant? The statutes under which digital disobedients are being prosecuted – in the US, the Espionage Act
and CFAA – make a mockery of basic rule-of-law aspirations. Both statutes are filled with vague legal standards
inviting massive legal and especially prosecutorial discretion.
As Harold Edgar and Benno Schmidt (1973) documented
in an eye-opening critical discussion, the Espionage Act's
messy and occasionally incomprehensible language outfits the
executive with arbitrary power over a vast array of activities
concerning the poorly defined arena of "national security,"
and it is arguably unconstitutional. Not surprisingly, it has
generally served as a clumsy instrument of political repression (Stone 2004: 173). Similarly, the Electronic Frontier
Foundation and other US-based civil libertarian groups have
documented how the CFAA criminalizes commonplace Internet usage (for example, checking personal email on workplace computers), potentially making it a federal crime to
access an unauthorized computer, but without sufficiently
laying out what "authorization" means. Mindboggling in its
open-endedness, the CFAA characterizes "computer fraud
and abuse" to include attempts to obtain national security
information, violate or threaten to damage a broad array
of (vaguely specified) "protected" computers, compromise
confidentiality or traffic in passwords, as well as access computers to defraud and obtain something of value. It offers a
vivid example of how sloppy legal craftsmanship can produce
draconian consequences probably unintended even by those
who promulgated the statute.[7]

In the traditional view of the rule of law, generality in law
is interpreted as requiring like rules for like cases: similar or
at least analogous situations are treated in similar or at least
analogous legal ways. Treating morally conscientious and
politically motivated digital lawbreaking as computer fraud
or espionage leaves much to be desired from this conventional
legal perspective. Judge Preska may be right: a hacktivist
like Hammond is a very different political creature from
Martin Luther King, Jr. Yet he is hardly a "crook" using
computers to rip people off for personal or private gain, or
a fraudster engaging in deception or stealing trade secrets for
profit. Only under a contorted understanding of "fraud and
abuse," namely one in which digital disobedience's political

motivations are simply ignored, could one possibly place recent hacktivist acts under its rubric.

Nor are Manning and Snowden spies, despite the US government's aggressive deployment of the Espionage Act against them. They neither sought to obtain information about national security to imperil the United States, nor promoted the success of enemies abroad. Rather, their actions represent examples of what Holloway Sparks calls "dissident citizenship": they challenge "prevailing arrangements of power by means of oppositional democratic practices that augment or replace [ordinary] institutionalized channels of democratic opposition when those channels are inadequate," as both Manning and Snowden believe to be the case (1997: 75). Angered by what they diagnosed as a lack of minimal public oversight of key surveillance and foreign policies, their lawbreaking was clearly meant to be democracy-enabling. It was necessary, they asserted, because major threats to the democratic process required correction. Simultaneously, both shared a characteristically liberal concern with the sanctity of basic individual rights (to privacy, for example) egregiously violated by officials. They have also argued, at times persuasively, that the US and its foreign allies have systematically violated their own domestic and international laws (Madar 2013; Scheuerman 2014b).[8]

Disingenuous prosecutorial strategies allow officials to downplay digital disobedience's distinctive normative traits, and especially its goal of generating public discussion about possibly illegal acts by government itself. To be sure, we need to guard against employing the category "civil disobedience" in an overly expansive fashion; digital lawbreaking's defenders sometimes employ the term loosely to cover activities that mesh poorly with the usual models.[9] At the same time, digital disobedience occasionally overlaps with Rawls' famous definition of civil disobedience as "disobedience to the law within the limits of fidelity to law." Some digital activists are breaking the law to highlight official illegalities so egregious that they deem them a just cause for their own relatively minor illegalities.

Something fundamental about the law is at stake. In his noteworthy *The Morality of Law*, Lon Fuller made the key point that fidelity to the rule of law (or, in his terms, "legality") was congruent with the pursuit of different and indeed potentially opposing political and moral aspirations. Legality, in short, is consonant with modern pluralism. Yet it still implicitly rests on an underlying notion of human dignity or respect. Fuller thought there was a straightforward way in which we could grasp this point: when a government tries to force people to follow an unpublished, secret, or retroactive statute, and thus in effect to do the impossible, or when it demands that they constantly alter their behavior according to the arbitrary and ever-changing whims of power holders, it communicates its indifference to them. When it systematically violates the rule of law, it reduces citizens to mere objects of state power; it demonstrates a basic lack of respect for people as independent agents capable of effectively planning their own lives. By insisting that state action rest on clear, public, general, and relatively constant norms, rule of law-based government instead expresses its respect for them as agents worthy of some minimal recognition or dignity (1964: 162–7). At the core of every political system instantiating the rule of law we can identify an implicit normative commitment to treating those on which it is binding in some minimally respectful and dignified fashion.

Admittedly, as a legal category "dignity" can mask "a great deal of disagreement and sheer confusion" (Rosen 2012: 67). In some jurisdictions appeals to it have produced regressive jurisprudence requiring citizens to conform to dubious standards of proper or "dignified" behavior. Yet Fuller need not lead us down that path. His core claim remains sound: a commitment to some notion of basic dignity entails making sure that the politically well-situated – and especially state officials – "should be required to express respect for the ordinary citizen, not citizens for the powerful" (Rosen 2012: 75). One instrument for doing so is making sure that the state and its activities remain strictly bound to the rule of law.

Contemporary digital disobedients are understandably outraged by growing evidence of massive and indeed histori-cally unprecedented surveillance, undertaken by both state and corporate authorities, and made possible by new tech-nologies. Though they have not always formulated their worries with the requisite clarity, their anger suggests that *their* actions, and not those of the government officials aggressively prosecuting them, potentially show a deep and abiding respect for the rule of law. What some digital activists have instinctively grasped is that, effectively unchecked, state surveillance is inconsistent with the rule of law's normative commitment to making sure that the state treats everybody with respect and some measure of dignity. Revealingly, the legal infrastructure undergirding recent surveillance policies turns out to be astonishingly shoddy. As Snowden has accurately observed, the main justifications that the US government has provided for its domestic spying are Section 215 of the USA Patriot Act (2001) and Section 702 of the Foreign Intelligence Surveillance Act (1978). One legal expert has confirmed that it "strains credulity to believe that there was any basis" in them for controversial US surveillance activities (Cate 2015: 27).

Ubiquitous public and private surveillance threatens to destroy the basic elements of our moral personhood. A form of what George Kateb describes as "painless oppression, of barely sensed degradation," the contemporary surveillance regime systematically violates once impermeable personal boundaries (2006: 98). Where my every move is carefully registered by powerful public or private interests, with detailed information about my actions and preferences stored more-or-less indefinitely, not just my right to privacy but my very dignity is under attack. Surveillance means that

> one is treated simply as an ambiguous or pathological specimen to be observed ... One is placed under constant suspicion just by being placed under constant watchfulness and subjected to the implicit interrogation that exists when the accumulated information on oneself is seen as a set of integrated answers that add up to a helpless, an unauthored, autobiography. Such a loss of innocence ... is so massive that the insult involved constitutes an assault on the personhood or human status of every individual. (2006: 97)

Unsurprisingly given the implicit links between legality and dignity, an increasingly all-encompassing surveillance regime makes a mockery of the former, as do hypocritical attempts by public officials to ward off overdue critical scrutiny.

Unchecked surveillance reverses the basic relationship between the individual and government on which the rule of law partly depends. Legality demands that state action be clear and public, so that individuals can plan their affairs accordingly, and that they can, at least in principle, learn what their government is doing so that they can change laws when appropriate. The rule of law does not, of course, require that individuals be transparent to the state (Bobbio 1987: 79–97). When instead the state and its corporate allies secretly spy to destroy privacy and anonymity, and then brazenly persecute those bringing their acts to public light, the rule of law is under attack.

Digital lawbreaking as civil disobedience?

One result of this cynical official legal position is that some digital disobedients appear to be internalizing a correspondingly one-sided view of law. The real threat to the rule of law does not, to be sure, stem from activists but instead from powerfully situated political and economic figures "who hold themselves above the law and have the power in fact to stay above it" (Madar 2013: 123–4). Nonetheless, it is hard to miss currents of anarchist, libertarian, and other anti-statist and anti-legal sentiments among digital activists, for whom – not surprisingly – the rule of law increasingly appears as a mere veneer for state repression. As an Anonymous activist posted in a revealing September 2010 statement, "[w]e are not concerned with legality ... Those who decide our laws are the same people who decided that public copyright harassment, erosion of civil liberties and abominations of censorship ... are good and just things to enforce upon the populace" (quoted in Coleman 2014: 113). Though understandable given the state's draconian response, this view risks reproducing precisely the position it purports to transcend. Reducing the multifaceted idea of the rule of law to authoritarian legalism, it ignores its normative core and essential protective functions. It misses the fact that the rule of law can help check repressive state endeavors, and that every decent political and social order accordingly needs it.

This troublesome tendency operates to counter the otherwise prescient appreciation among digital disobedients that surveillance rests on government lawlessness and undermines the idea of a community in which the rule of law effectively restrains not just the weak and vulnerable but also the powerful and privileged. One reason digital disobedients have sometimes had a hard time articulating their own implicitly legalistic intuitions is that they have come to view the rule of law in analogously authoritarian terms.

A second and related consequence is a certain tendency to embrace an open-ended view of civil disobedience in which some familiar components get deflated. One reason behind this move, we already observed, is political and strategic: defenders of digital disobedience hope that it can accrue some benefits that presently accrue to "on-the-street" civil disobedience. Another is conceptual: some forms of digital disobedience cohere poorly with standard views of civil disobedience. In Rawls' famous definition, civil disobedience refers to a "public, nonviolent, conscientious yet political act contrary to the law usually done with the aim of bringing about a change in the law or policies of the government" (1971: 364). Like most others in his generation, Rawls believed that civilly-minded lawbreakers should be ready to accept criminal penalties for their actions. However, his model's strict publicity conditions are possibly contravened by attempts to maintain the anonymity and confidentiality of leakers and whistleblowers (for example, Anonymous). Many digital disobedients are also reluctant to accept legal consequences for their acts, an understandable stance given the harsh penalties they face, but one which might have distressed Rawls and others.

Among those arguing for a broader definition of civil disobedience, Molly Sauter worries that the privileged status of the US civil rights movement in thinking about civil disobedience has engendered an "ahistorical myopia" that delegitimizes novel but legitimate forms of digital activism (2014: 26). Her answer to the tensions between digital disobedience and an inherited notion of civil disobedience is to broaden the latter to include many varieties of the former.

This approach faces major hurdles. By classifying myriad forms of digital disobedience under the category of civil disobedience, we stretch the term unduly and deny it some minimally coherent contours. Those struggling to tackle the genuine challenges posed by digital disobedience may end up lacking sufficiently nuanced conceptual tools for doing so. We downplay key elements conventionally associated with civil disobedience at the cost of sowing confusion. Useful differences between and among civil disobedience (as usually conceived), conscientious objection, leaking or whistleblowing, and violent resistance or revolution may get blurred or lost.[10] The high price we potentially pay is that they will not be able to recognize genuine novelties. Though digital disobedience includes some elements familiar from our conventional categories, it does not always fall neatly into the usual conceptual boxes.

My reading of a complicated scenario is that some, though certainly not all, digital disobedients have tried to follow "classical" recipes for civil disobedience, or at least have subscribed to some of their key features. Even Anonymous, for example, arguably remains committed to features of the standard publicity condition. While insisting on personal anonymity, its leaks are often public: the group has frequently made eloquent public statements in defense of its actions, which are obviously intended to have far-reaching political impact. Admittedly, in striking contradistinction to some previous civil disobedients (for example, Gandhi or King), Anonymous' members resist efforts for the group to gain a clearly recognizable public "face" or representative, in part because of worries about the ways in which protest movements often become dominated by media-savvy but also authoritarian leaders. The normative commitment to publicity within civil disobedience, as elsewhere, is unavoidably complicated. On one reading, Anonymous and other "secret" whistleblowers can be interpreted as expressing implicit fidelity to a modest interpretation of the publicity test. The publicity test never has – and never should – force disobedients to make themselves or their reflections perfectly transparent.

Similarly, even when recent digital lawbreakers circumvent criminal penalties they occasionally proffer principled legal rationales. In this spirit, Snowden has regularly outlined why his endeavors, and not those of the US government, demonstrate respect for law. He has never denied the possibility in principle of facing legal penalties, and in fact has said that he would be willing to accept jail time in exchange for a chance to return home (Peterson 2015). On Snowden's view, however, fidelity to the law would not be properly attested by submitting to the irregularities of the Espionage Act, a statute incongruent with core components of the rule of law. As Snowden rightly intuits, accepting penalties only makes sense if disobedients can count on legal proceedings embodying basic legal virtues. When disobedients face a situation where there is "no right of public trial, and no possibility of using punishment for publicity purposes, or if punishments were made draconian in order to prevent dissenters from publicizing their views," evasion is sometimes permissible (Singer 1973: 83–4). If criminal proceedings rest on vague and easily abused legal categories, suffer from excessive politicization so as to impair the possibility of a fair trial, and regularly mete out draconian sentences, by circumventing them the disobedient potentially avoids complicity in legality's destruction.

As Snowden also seems to concede, it then becomes incumbent on lawbreakers to offer some alternative proof of their respect for law. Not coincidentally, he has outlined detailed defenses of his actions by appealing to statutory, constitutional, and international law. He views NSA spying as illegal and unconstitutional, interpreting it as incongruent with the Fourth and Fifth Amendments to the US Constitution, the Universal Declaration of Human Rights, and many other international norms and agreements, about which he has spoken at great length. US surveillance policy, he also regularly infers, conflicts with a more basic notion of the rule of law. Accordingly, he has lambasted the secrecy of the US Foreign Intelligence Surveillance (FISA) Court, and he worries about "the federation of secret law, unequal pardon, and irresistible executive power" plaguing the relevant US legislation and jurisprudence (quoted in Greenwald et al. 2013). In striking contrast to the open and public character of his actions, the secrecy in which US surveillance has been shrouded corrupts "the most basic notion of justice – that it must be seen to be done. The immoral cannot be made moral through use of secret laws" (Snowden 2013). As Snowden appreciates, publicity, clarity, and constancy are fundamental to any decent system of legal order, whereas secret laws and courts provide an easy cover for arbitrary and irresponsible state action. By giving up a well-paying job and pleasant life in Hawaii, and now in legal limbo and likely to remain for the foreseeable future on the run from US authorities, Snowden has also paid a high personal price for his actions (Scheuerman 2014b).

In contrast, digital disobedients disdainful of the law rob themselves of powerful tools. Not able to justify their concrete illegalities as part of a broader quest to uphold legality, they may prove unable to justify their actions in the eyes of skeptical publics. By allowing repressive state officials to monopolize the language of law, they deny themselves effective normative resources and abandon fertile discursive and political terrain to opponents.

To be clear: my aim is not to defend the purity of "classical" civil disobedience as practiced by King or others in order to privilege it vis-à-vis novel forms of digital lawbreaking. Yet conflating digital with more conventional forms of civil disobedience risks distorting key differences.

Beyond civil disobedience?

Let us briefly revisit Jeremy Hammond's case. Hammond cooperated with Anonymous activists in 2011 to hack computer networks at Strategic Forecasting, Inc. (Stratfor), a private intelligence-gathering firm working on behalf of governments and other private firms. The leaks revealed, for example, that large corporations (including Dow Chemical and Coca-Cola) had hired Stratfor to spy on activists whom they feared might be interfering with their activities. (Dow Chemical had commissioned Stratfor to monitor activist groups that were publicizing its failures relating to the disastrous 1984 explosion at Union Carbide, a firm now owned by Dow Chemical.) Revealingly, many hacktivists, like Hammond, are targeting private contractors that are profiting not only from the public but also the private sector's growing taste for surveillance. As part of his actions against Stratfor, Hammond leaked credit card numbers from its servers (and used the numbers to try to make payments to the Bradley Manning Support Group),[11] defaced the company website, wiped the client database clean, and destroyed its email server. Those involved with the action issued various statements about their motivations, but what seems to have driven Hammond was a basic frustration with public ignorance about far-reaching secret surveillance: "I did this because I believe people have a right to know what governments and corporations are doing behind closed doors. I did what I believe is right" (quoted in Ludlow 2013).

To justify his actions and gain reduced criminal penalties, Hammond and his attorneys categorized his activities as civil disobedience. Judge Preska, as noted, was unpersuaded. Preska's own brand of authoritarian legalism, I have argued, is untenable. Nonetheless, one can appreciate why she and others might be skeptical about readily classifying Hammond's acts as civil disobedience.

Yet, why limit acceptable forms of politically motivated lawbreaking to civil disobedience? Why not concede that some types of digital disobedience transcend its contours, as conventionally defined, yet nonetheless remain potentially legitimate? If this intuition can hold up, it might then be incumbent on prosecutors, judges, and others to treat cases such as Hammond's in a more tolerant and liberal-minded spirit. Digital lawbreakers might sometimes be able to count on less repressive treatment at the hands of state officials. Judges and juries would have sound reasons for reducing or mitigating penalties against them.

Postnationalization and privatization open the door to messy and sometimes militant political lawbreaking that transcends standard models of civil disobedience. Digital disobedience is closely related to these broader trends. Many digital disobedients see their actions as potentially addressing not just their national consociates but also broader global publics. The Internet's partially deterritorialized character also raises tough questions about the appropriateness, or even effectiveness, of nation-state-centered attempts to control or regulate it. Some striking examples of politically motivated lawbreaking operate in the gray zone between state and private authorities. Snowden, for example was employed as a private contractor under the auspices of the US government, and claims that he and his colleagues were effectively allowed to engage in legally dubious forms of surveillance. Hammond's actions have directly targeted private corporations.

Michael Walzer, as we have already noted, provocatively argued that illegal protests against private firms, when those firms performed quasi-official functions, should *not* always be forced to meet the exacting tests civil disobedients typically face. Looking back to the historic labor upheavals of the 1930s, Walzer observed that many of the political illegalities committed by radicalized workers would not have satisfied the same tough requirements which, by the late 1960s, many had come to associate with civil disobedience. Labor actions such as the sit-down strike at Flint, Michigan, and elsewhere were hardly exemplars of "civility"; they often relied on secrecy and even violence. Nonetheless, Walzer thought they were legitimate, even if they perhaps could "not be called civil disobedience at all" (Walzer 1970 [1969]: 24). His key insight was that when challenging private corporations, standards for lawbreaking should be laxer than those for protests directly targeting the liberal state, where citizens generally possess some influence. Employees impacted by autocratic corporate decisions are often denied even those. Though "corporations collect taxes on behalf of the state, maintain standards required by the state, spend state money, and above all enforce a great variety of rules and regulations," unorganized workers subject to their authority may possess few if any legal vehicles to check them (Walzer 1970 [1969]: 26). Why then categorically oppose workers' preference for more militant and prospectively messier forms of lawbreaking?

I do not mean to equate hacktivists comfortably sitting in front of their computer screens with exploited workers who put their bodies on the line to achieve a measure of economic well-being. One might legitimately point out that digital disobedience, in many cases, does not involve taking commensurate risks or perhaps even much courage. Yet, the fact remains that digital disobedients are now sometimes directing their ire against private corporations engaging in quasi-governmental functions such as espionage. Even when private firms do so at the behest of the democratic state, the chains of legitimacy linking their activities to citizens and even their elected representatives seem fragile and perhaps broken (Shorrock 2008). The state's regulation of such activities remains shockingly underdeveloped. In this context, unconventional forms of illegal protest may in principle be legitimate given the circumscribed and perhaps nonexistent oversight of corporate espionage presently exercised by normal democratic mechanisms. Since those engaging in surveillance also have a vested interest in keeping their activities veiled, it is not even clear how citizens might learn about "what governments and corporations are doing behind closed doors" absent politically based illegal acts.

Whether such actions are likely to prove constructive or sensible, to be sure, is always a complicated matter of political judgment. My view is that nonviolence, vis-à-vis persons, remains a *sine qua non*, especially in the context of more-or-less functioning democracies.[12] Helpfully, principled nonviolence also rests on sound pragmatic grounds: social scientific research suggests, as Gandhi and King astutely intuited, that it generally offers impressive political and strategic advantages (Chenoweth and Stephan 2013). Of course, tough questions remain about how best to understand nonviolence, a controversial matter about which significant disagreement remains. Anyone seriously considering political lawbreaking, based on familiar ideas about civil disobedience or otherwise, obviously needs to take a sober look at the inherent dangers and risks. They should also be expected to act responsibly and thus to minimize any foreseeable damage to innocent parties. There are many pressing reasons, discussed at length in previous chapters, why they typically should try to follow longstanding (religious, liberal, and democratic) models of civil disobedience. In some situations, however, alternative modes of illegal activism may prove both necessary and appropriate.

To be sure, many acts of digital disobedience still target government activities. Their most important historical precursors are perhaps actions such as the 1971 break-in at Media, Pennsylvania, where New Leftists – angered by what they rightly intuited was widespread surveillance and harassment of activists – broke into a Federal Bureau of Investigation (FBI) office and then proceeded to leak an astonishing array of documents vindicating their worst fears. Operating conspiratorially and secretly, burglarizing a federal office under the cover of darkness, and keeping their personal identities secret, their actions surely could not be described as "civil disobedience" in any familiar sense of the term. Faced with the probability of draconian criminal penalties and a massive nationwide manhunt, activists successfully circumvented legal sanctions and kept their involvement secret for decades. Their decision to do so, not surprisingly, came at a huge personal cost: sometimes forced to take on new identities, participants had to cut ties to families and friends. Some of them remained "on the run" for decades because of fears that federal authorities might catch up with them (Medsger 2014).

Crucially, the Media activists, or self-named "Citizens' Commission to Investigate the FBI," always remained non-violent. The group also publicly defended and explained its actions, and made the leaked documents available to journalists. It not only opposed FBI illegalities, but its actions seem to have been predicated on a prescient intuition that politically motivated illegality was imperative if the rule of law was ultimately to be upheld in the face of a lawless J. Edgar Hoover and rogue FBI. As one of the activists commented, "We *are* a nation of laws, and for good reasons. Most of us take that very seriously. Deciding when to break the law is not a trivial decision or a light decision" (quoted in Medsger 2014: 428). Like many present-day digital disobedients, the Media activists believed that the only way to bring overdue public attention to legally dubious state surveillance was by stealing and then leaking stolen documents. Absent their efforts, the FBI would probably never have faced serious calls for reform in the 1970s.

Observers can legitimately disagree about how best to classify politically motivated illegalities of this type, though some version of the concept of "whistleblowing" offers potential advantages. Many present-day digital disobedients, like their forerunners in Media, aim to expose "serious government wrongdoing or programs and policies that ought to be known and deliberated about" (Delmas 2015: 101). They break the law only after determining, with some justification, that normal legal or political channels are unlikely to prove effective in bringing serious matters to public light. Finally, they have frequently exercised due care "so as to minimize the harms that could potentially ensue" (Delmas 2015: 101).

Whistleblowers already possess some basic, though inadequate legal protections, another reason why it may be sensible to try to place at least some types of digital disobedience under its rubric.[13]

Regardless of how we categorize specific acts of digital disobedience, a decent political and legal order is obliged to acknowledge their potentially vital contributions to democracy and the rule of law. Some types of digital lawbreaking, I have argued, can in fact plausibly be characterized as akin or closely related to civil disobedience. Even some others, where things look messier, deserve more respectful and probably lenient treatment from state officials. Digital disobedience's contributions to democracy and the rule of law, in striking juxtaposition to those of state officials who have tried to squelch it, remain auspicious.

7

Tilting at Windmills?

Civil disobedience remains an integral part of contemporary protest politics. Despite a trend toward supplanting it with more open-ended terminological rivals (for example, "resistance"), activists and their defenders still find the term useful, even when deploying it in novel ways. Coined perhaps by Thoreau's editor, and then transfigured by Gandhi, King, and others, the concept has long possessed global valence. Not surprisingly, the theoretical debate about it continues unabated.

We now examine the most recent contributions to that debate. I do not provide a full survey, in part because others have already fruitfully done so (Delmas 2016). But I hope to identify some ambivalent trends that could be taken as corroborating the inference, legitimately drawn from previous chapters, that civil disobedience's conceptual bases are under strain. Anarchism and major social processes (digitalization, postnationalization, privatization) challenge religious, liberal, and democratic models of civil disobedience. Present-day philosophical debate tends to do so as well. Recent thinkers have directed powerful criticisms at conventional ideas about civil disobedience. Yet, they risk throwing the baby out with the bathwater. Their criticisms tend to depend on highly selective accounts of a multifaceted conceptual history this volume has tried to recall.

The ghost of John Rawls

Perhaps the most striking feature of contemporary thinking about civil disobedience is its preoccupation with the liberal and especially Rawlsian model (Delmas 2016). Few writers on civil disobedience today fail to take a shot at the ghost of the late Rawls, with a substantial body of prior thinking about civil disobedience getting reduced to the account found in *A Theory of Justice* (1971).[1] Typically, commentators begin by emphasizing Rawls' impact. Tony Milligan finds an "uneasy [Rawlsian] consensus" on civil disobedience, "even among those [activists] who may never have heard of Rawls" (2013: 26). Raffaele Laudani similarly describes Rawls' views as canonical (2013: 112). Numerous authors target Rawls and an orthodox view of civil disobedience presumably indebted to him.[2] For a broad swath of scholarly opinion, Rawls and his views constitute a troublesome "other" that needs to be fought off before the advance to more sophisticated theories of civil disobedience can proceed.

Rawls' clout notwithstanding, this preoccupation offers a convenient rhetorical strategy. It allows critics to unleash a series of partly persuasive rebuttals, as though Rawls' theory of civil disobedience constituted *the* paradigmatic example of some (allegedly) orthodox model of civil disobedience. In a first step, critics reduce core traits of civil disobedience to their specifically liberal and Rawlsian renditions. In a second step, they discard those components, doing so chiefly because their critique starts from tendentious presuppositions. For example, many writers now reject the intuition, found among religious, liberal, and democratic thinkers, of a nexus between civil disobedience and respect for law. In the process, they abandon the triple-pronged (moral, political, and legal) normativity on which conventional ideas about civil disobedience have regularly built. They do so by means of a controversial exegetical move: Rawls gets uncritically taken as the paradigmatic example of "legalistic" models of civil disobedience. With the liberal (Rawlsian) model and the legal prong conveniently married, by discarding his flawed views we supposedly can dump his obnoxious legal partner as well. By so proceeding, critics inadvertently downplay other potentially more durable marriages between "legalism" and civil disobedience. Religious or democratic variants of those ideas critics have married to liberalism tend to get pushed to the wayside.

To be sure, many criticisms being voiced echo those discussed in previous chapters. Critics aptly worry, for example, about the democratic deficits of Rawls' model. As they accurately recall, civil disobedience can help repair major impairments to democratic politics, not just rights violations by majorities, by deepening deliberation and participation. It checks what the deliberative democrat William Smith, building on Habermas, aptly dubs "deliberative inertia," where political views about "problems that have demonstrable and urgent import" have been unfairly marginalized (2013: 70). In Daniel Markovits' imposing republican model, civil disobedience's function is to undermine political complacency by focusing attention on issues that may never have been meaningfully discussed in the first place, or where a necessary reconsideration of existing policy has been stymied by institutional stasis or powerful privileged interests. The principal dilemma sometimes is that a "policy was never approved by the democratic sovereign at all but instead arose in some other way, as through a slow and unattended transformation of an initially very different policy" (2005: 1933). For Robin Celikates, a radical democrat, civil disobedience dramatizes the fundamental contrast between constituent and constituted powers, functioning as a "dynamizing counterweight" by means of which popular sovereignty counters "the rigidifying tendencies of state institutions" (2013: 223). Civil disobedience allows "we the people" to act beyond and outside law and state. Etienne Balibar, an inspiration for Celikates, similarly views it as resting on horizontal, communally minded free association, committed to the general interest, that challenges and sometimes temporarily abolishes hierarchical, vertical state authority (Balibar 2014: 176, 289).

Others accurately note that the so-called orthodox (and Rawlsian) view seems more and more out of sync with the empirical facts of political lawbreaking. When anti-globalization protestors do battle with the police, or hacktivists secretly break into privately owned computers, their acts do not readily fall under standard rubrics. Nor does covert "animal rescue" by animal rights activists, or ecosabotage where militants engage in tree spiking or other controversial activities (Welchman 2001). Lawbreaking that aims primarily to unsettle deeply ingrained attitudes about gender and sexuality probably transcend conventional models as well (Hill 2013). When gay and lesbian ACT UP activists hector political leaders, disrupt church services, or shout barbs at straights, they push the limits of what some might deem acceptable "civil" disobedience (Brouwer 2001). Similarly, feminists worry about the exclusionary contours of standard liberal ideas of civility, which they criticize for presupposing a mythical, implicitly gendered, homogeneous public (Zerilli 2014: 116).

The misfit between civil disobedience, as usually conceived, and actual political lawbreaking is real; I have tried to address some of its sources in previous chapters. The solution, however, lies not in synchronizing our conceptual constructs with empirical realities, or by means of more practice-based ideational models directly attuned to real-life examples (Celikates 2016b: 986; Welchman 2001: 105). However appealing, this methodological move risks accommodating our concepts to such a diversity of conflicting political phenomena that by day's end they will no longer prove able to offer adequate normative or analytic guidance. Civil disobedience then potentially refers to a broad swath of political illegalities; useful categorical distinctions may go out the window.[3] Empirical facts, of course, never speak directly to us: we depend on ideational constructs, from the very outset of our inquiries, to frame them. Our concepts should both capture social realities and offer a solid basis for making helpful normative and political distinctions. An unavoidably evaluative concept like civil disobedience will always stand in tension with at least some empirical facts.[4]

Unfortunately, recent critics who criticize standard concepts of civil disobedience tend to reinvent the wheel, sometimes replacing it with a new one less fungible than its predecessor.

Bernard Harcourt, for example, declares that civil disobedience has always presupposed "the legitimacy of the political structure and of our political institutions," a view endorsed by liberals but not Gandhi, King, or many others (2012: 33). He inaccurately interprets the idea of respect for law as necessarily entailing fidelity to the political and legal status quo (2012: 34). Having reduced variegated defenses of civil disobedience's legal prong to its most politically quiescent rendition, he proposes a new paradigm for civil disobedience. That approach, though enlivened by some productive Foucauldian insights, ultimately reproduces many familiar ideas.

Similarly, Celikates wants to discard the standard liberal (and especially Rawlsian) tests of publicity and nonviolence. What frustrates him is an overly narrow – and probably dispensable – interpretation of the publicity standard as requiring of disobedients that they provide "the authorities fair notice in advance" of their actions (2013: 213; 2016a: 38). In part vexed by the fact that the nonviolence standard conflates violence against persons with violence against things, Celikates is also skeptical of conventional notions of nonviolence (2016a: 41–2). Like his liberal opponents, however, he probably preserves some version of nonviolence vis-à-vis persons (2010: 294–7). He abandons civil disobedience's legal prong, finding in it complacent support for the legal and political status quo (2010: 283–6; 2013: 216; 2016a: 38–9). Conveniently, he ignores its politically more ambitious variants. His view of law as a seemingly "irremediably hostile force" means that he cannot really take it seriously, even when doing so might support his own praiseworthy efforts to formulate a radical democratic alternative (Cooke 2016: 1001).[5]

Costas Douzinas abandons the term civil disobedience altogether, trading it in for a "right to resistance," interpreted as "both taking up and transcending" previous liberal and democratic ideas, which he views as inadequate to contemporary challenges (2013: 96). The right to resistance initially appears to rely on a traditional natural law "idea of a law higher than state law." Yet Douzinas, like Rawls and many others, doubts that natural law can be effectively refurbished today: it "has all the cognitive and theoretical difficulties of the belief in God's law" (2013: 90). Despite this shared launching pad, he wants nothing to do with liberalism: "The intolerance at the core of liberalism cannot be easily hidden" (2013: 93). At day's end, however, his proposed tests for legitimate resistance reproduce some old – and identifiably liberal – tropes. Protestors should be ready to not only accept legal penalties but also meet what in fact are relatively strict generality and publicity tests. Echoing Rawls and other liberals, Douzinas believes the failure to do so leaves us with mere "moralizing," not principled, legitimate political lawbreaking:

> The first test is the willing acceptance of the risk and possibility (nowadays probability) of punishment. The second brings the specific grievance or demand under the control of a moral principle ... [C]an the good or principle, the disobedient obeys, be addressed to everyone and anyone? Can it be universalized? ... [This] is a tough, anxiety-producing moral test; if absent, it is replaced by empty moralizing. (2013: 99)

For his part, Milligan jettisons Rawls' definition for a presumably more flexible civility-centered alternative. Criticizing the Rawlsian model for requiring disobedients openly to communicate their grievances, he believes that it reduces nonviolent lawbreaking to public speech (2013: 18). Its dialogical focus unfairly delegitimizes lawbreaking where communication and public dialogue are marginal, as when protests aim chiefly to disrupt or obstruct some activity. In his new model, however, disobedients are still expected to evince

> (i) respect for others or ... the recognition that other humans are *fellow humans*, i.e. members of the same moral community; (ii) the rejection of hate speech; (iii) the avoidance of acts which are driven by hatred; (iv) the largely successful commitment to *try* to avoid violence and threats of violence ...; (v) the avoidance of cruelty; and finally (vi) the recognition of a duty of care or an avoidance of the reckless endangerment of others. (2013: 36)

Even if we ignore the fact that such conditions seem unlikely to be met in a self-evident, non-communicative manner, but instead will require some articulate public defense, this new approach seems no less demanding or potentially restrictive than its liberal target. On one plausible exegesis, for example, stipulations to show a "duty of care" and respect for others as "members of the same moral community" might prove just as taxing as the Rawlsian original.

Kimberley Brownlee's *Conscience and Conviction: The Case for Civil Disobedience* (2012a), the most significant philosophical contribution to the recent literature, reinterprets civil disobedience as "a *conscientious* communicative breach of law motivated by steadfast, sincere, and serious, though possibly mistaken, moral commitment" (2012a: 23, original emphasis), also criticizing Rawlsian tests of publicity and nonviolence. Brownlee worries that the nonviolence standard generates confusion: violence can refer to "a range of acts and events that *risk* but do not necessarily cause damage or injury, such as catapulting stuffed animals at the police" (2012a: 21, original emphasis). As for the publicity test, some civil disobedients may initially need to keep their actions covert.

Here as well, it remains unclear whether the author has successfully moved beyond conventional notions. In place of the nonviolence standard, Brownlee underscores "the presumptively more salient issue of harm" (2012a: 22). Yet, the concept of harm, since John Stuart Mill made it a liberal-philosophical mainstay, has arguably suffered from as many ambiguities as ideas of violence. As for Brownlee's abandonment of the publicity test, she herself notes that initially covert acts of disobedience "may nonetheless [ultimately] be open and communicative when followed by an acknowledgement of the act and reasons for taking it" (2012a: 23). In fact, it is hard to imagine how "conscientious communicative breaches of the law," undertaken with an expectation of triggering changes to policy, might operate without openness or publicity, though Brownlee is surely right to doubt that every facet of civil disobedience should do so.

My aim, it should be clear, is not to salvage the orthodox liberal or Rawlsian view, which indeed suffers from serious problems. Instead, my point is simply that in their eagerness to fight off Rawls' ghost, critics discard core traits of civil disobedience that deserve a fairer hearing. They face a harder time transcending conventional views than they want to recognize. Reducing a wide-ranging debate about civil disobedience to its liberal or Rawlsian version, and then proceeding hurriedly to dispense with it, they throw the baby out with the bathwater. Whatever the limitations of his efforts, Rawls tried to follow King in viewing civil disobedience as potentially expressing our "very highest respect for the law." Tellingly, those now discounting his theory tend to neglect this appealing idea as well.

Anti-legalism

Deep skepticism about the law now seems widespread even among those who do not openly subscribe to political or philosophical anarchism. Contemporary theorists energetically reinterpret the intellectual history of civil disobedience by systematically scrubbing it of the legal prong (Lyons 2013). Others downplay law's place by means of revised definitions.[6]

The story, not surprisingly, is a complicated one. Yet one inspiration behind the present anti-legal mood appears straightforward enough: blame for the earlier model's perceived limitations regularly gets placed at its legal doorsteps. Interpreting legal appeals as an ideological veneer for state violence, or an invitation for pedantic legalistic hairsplitting, anti-legalism builds in part on heavy-handed legal skepticism (Lovell 2009: 47–8; Sitze 2013: xix). Another source is a tendentious anti-statism that views state and law as unequivocal threats to self-government rather than potential enabling conditions.

In the final instance, however, anti-legalism's main fount is probably the inaccurate claim that "highest respect for the law" irrevocably entails loyalty to the legal and constitutional status quo or "legitimacy of the judicial order" in its existing form (Milligan 2013: 99). Even as contemporary theorists claim to supersede liberal models, they reproduce its politically cautious ideas about the law. Present-day critics regularly deploy King against liberals, but they neglect his own provocative insights about the nexus between law and potentially radical change (Celikates 2013: 216–17; Lyons 2013: 112–29). They obfuscate the legal prong's potentially forward-looking and politically dynamic contours.

In a political universe where respect for law is widely shared, this legal prong still possesses noteworthy normative and political credentials. King, and many inspired by him, were right to highlight civil disobedience's intimate links to the rule of law. When "openly, lovingly" violating the law, as King observed, disobedients directly reproduce core fundaments of any normatively legitimate or just system of law (1991 [1963]: 74). They give immediate expression to a future-oriented aspiration for a reformed legal and political order. The open and public character of their acts mirrors the familiar rule-of-law demand for openness, clarity, and publicity in the law. By "lovingly" breaking the law, they embody a commitment to realizing a legal order based more directly than the unjust status quo on reciprocity and mutuality. King correspondingly defined a just law as "a code that a majority compels a minority to follow that it is willing to follow itself. This is sameness made legal" (1991 [1963]: 74). Only laws embodying generality typically contribute to justice and deserve our respect. By accepting the possibility of legal penalties, disobedients concede that they in principle are subject to the same legal rules as everyone else, even if present iniquities require them, regrettably, to break unjust laws.

Given modern pluralism, many conscientious moral appeals seem unavoidably subjective and unsatisfactory; controversial political arguments can appear no less so. In contrast, law consists of shared rules and principles, about which people inevitably disagree, but are still publicly announced and promulgated. If a political order takes the ideal of the rule of law seriously, it typically rests on clear, public, general, and prospective laws. As a relatively accessible shared code, law constitutes a collaborative source of normativity many moral and political appeals can neither match nor supplant. In political orders based on the rule of law, not surprisingly, political discourse tends irrepressibly to take "legalistic" forms. Intellectuals since Alexis de Tocqueville have noted this trend, and some communitarians may lament it, but it is vital to recognize that it implicitly highlights one of law's distinctive virtues, virtues that remain essential if illegal protest is to rest on more than a narrow sectarian basis. By speaking the language of law, disobedients productively transform controversial moral and political claims into broader and implicitly general normative appeals.

In principle, though of course not always in reality, law in a democratic society rests on the general agreement of its citizens, each of whom has contributed to its promulgation.

Law in principle belongs to all of us: it rests on complex processes of public contestation where everyone participates. Of course, specific laws can remain controversial or unjust; the political process that produced them may be flawed. Yet the mere fact of legal enactment or promulgation perhaps implies that the political community has managed to agree on a binding public rule even in the face of extensive disagreement (Waldron 1999). Binding law represents "a triumph of peaceful deliberation and respectful cooperation" in the context of modern pluralism (Whittington 2000: 693). In contrast to many contentious moral or political appeals, law takes pluralism and disagreement seriously, while acknowledging that we need shared binding rules to flourish. When the legal order successfully embodies basic legal virtues (publicity, clarity, generality, prospectiveness), it invites a potentially inclusive public conversation concerning those matters about which, if only for the time being, we possess certain binding norms.

The disenchantment of overarching moral worldviews, in conjunction with the pluralization of religious and moral perspectives, means that traditional notions of natural law can no longer plausibly claim universal validity. What survives is a principled commitment to "the generality of law, the equality of men [sic], the prohibition of individual legislative decisions, the impossibility of retroactive legislation, especially in penal law, and an independent judiciary" (Neumann 1957: 90). The rule of law, on this interpretation, represents natural law's bequest to a pluralistic and disenchanted moral universe. Though occasionally it may seem like a "thin and unsatisfactory" inheritance, since the rule of law should not be equated with democracy or social justice, it performs an indispensable role in preserving the presuppositions of any free and decent order (Neumann 1957: 4). We abandon it at great risk.

Admittedly, in racially and socially unjust communities, or in authoritarian states, this view of law may seem naïve (Celikates 2016b). Given ominous anti-liberal and anti-democratic trends in existing liberal democracies, even there it increasingly appears unrealistic. Yet even when the rule of law is only incompletely realized, some modicum of legal security has probably been secured. By guaranteeing that state action is public, the rule of law helps open the door, however tentatively, to political contestation and debate. Though history includes examples of legalistic authoritarianism, the rule of law typically helps counter dictatorship and oppression. Racist and authoritarian regimes generally prefer to decimate it (Fraenkel 2017 [1941]; Fuller 1964; Neumann 1957). When political systems sacrifice legal virtues to cover up dubious or repressive action, appeals to the rule of law offer an effective launching pad for critique. Even in the context of rampant injustice, legal appeals, when properly tied to militant protests, can spawn reform. By belittling civil disobedience's legal prong, contemporary theorists undermine civil disobedience's conceptual foundations and rob protestors of a vital line of defense.

Even as she offers a brilliant account of the role conscientious motivation plays in civil disobedience, Brownlee succumbs to the general tendency to devalue civil disobedience's legal prong. One source of the shift is the author's embrace of a starkly positivist jurisprudence that systematically disadvantages it vis-à-vis morally conscientious lawbreaking. Brownlee claims that the "procedural norms of generality and predictability," crucial to the codification of formalized legal structures and "often grouped together under the heading 'rule of law,' are compatible with a substantively unjust system." Such standard rule-of-law virtues should be considered subordinate to "the substantive, context-sensitive, and non-codifiable moral responsibilities of underlying moral roles" (2012a: 96). Restated in the simplest terms: since the rule of law can be congruent with terrible injustices, no principled grounds for favoring fidelity to the law over conscientious moral action can be identified.

The problem here is a controversial assessment of the rule of law that robs it of any normative substance, a position even legal positivism's sympathizers sometimes deem excessive (Waldron 2011).[7] The author's skepticism about law's normative resources surfaces elsewhere as well. In opposition to the view I recalled above, which emphasizes law's normative and political advantages vis-à-vis conscience, for Brownlee

[t]he law is only *the most blunt* manifestation of the social rules and moral norms that govern a reasonably good society,

and the law is not the final arbiter on the content and force
of those rules and norms. (2012a: 23; original emphasis)

Brownlee tends to depict the law as a burdensome and sometimes onerous restriction on morally conscientious action.
She worries about exaggerating its epistemic merits, proffering a deeply skeptical view of legislative politics to undercut
lawmaking's merits and familiar reasons for a qualified deference to law (2012a: 158, 175–6). She offers an unflattering
assessment of real-life democratic legislation, in order to contrast it unfavorably with a demanding – and highly idealized
– vision of morally conscientious protest. To be sure, Brownlee interprets civil disobedience as potentially enriching "the
deliberative democratic process" (2012a: 116). However,
because she views the crucial lawmaking element of that
process so harshly, a tendency to discount the law slips into
her account. The many reasons why respect for the law makes
sense when it is public, general, prospective, and derives from
an imperfect yet still inclusive, free-wheeling, deliberative
exchange get pushed aside.

Not surprisingly, Brownlee concludes that civil disobedients have a defeasible "moral right not to be punished"
(2012a: 240). The conventional demand that nonviolent lawbreakers accept legal consequences for their actions should
be questioned: society should "look to non-punitive, restora-
tive ways" to engage them (2012a: 251).

There are, in fact, sound reasons why civil disobedience should not always result in criminal sanctions. Absent
any whiff of anti-legalism, previous writers (e.g., Arendt,
Dworkin, Habermas) reached similar conclusions. In principle, a more fine-tuned approach to the legal treatment of civil
disobedience need not conflict with the disobedient's attempt
to prove fidelity to the law. Disobedients should generally
face only those legal repercussions that avoid the moral con-
demnation and opprobrium associated with criminal punishment. When conscientious and politically responsible, their
actions are qualitatively different from ordinary criminality;
the law may be justified in relying on sanctions that better
acknowledge their distinctive traits. Certain legal penalties
(for example, fines), but not an array of conventional punishments that stigmatize conscientious lawbreakers, are often

suitable (Lefkowitz 2007; Smith 2013: 94–8). Unfortunately, Brownlee probably goes too far. By systematically favoring a moral right to civil disobedience over the law, she ultimately cannot explain why "conscientious communicative breaches of law" rest potentially not merely on "steadfast, sincere, and serious, though possibly mistaken, moral commitments" but also a principled fidelity to law (2012a: 23–4).

Practical ramifications

Let me conclude by briefly responding to one likely rejoinder to my defense of civil disobedience's longstanding – yet increasingly controversial – legal prong. On one critical view, that endeavor is simply out of sync with contemporary realities: it cannot effectively buttress dissidents who seek to bring about meaningful political change. A key justification for abandoning civil disobedience's legal prong, after all, is precisely its misfit with contemporary political and social movements. Who today really believes that far-reaching change can be advanced via stodgy appeals to the rule of law?

Some contemporary examples perhaps suggest otherwise.

Edward Snowden's whistleblowing, which arguably meets some core conditions for legitimate civil disobedience, relies heavily on appeals to standing law and an implicit notion of the rule of law.[8] In a public statement delivered at the Moscow Airport in July 2013, he criticized surveillance policies by appealing to the US Constitution (and especially the Fourth and Fifth Amendments, requiring due process and prohibiting unreasonable searches and seizures), international human rights law, and the Nuremberg principle that

> individuals have international duties which transcend the national obligations of obedience. Therefore individual citizens have the duty to violate domestic laws to prevent crimes against peace and humanity from occurring. (2013)

Snowden has also pilloried the secret US Foreign Intelligence Surveillance Court for failing to exercise minimal judicial oversight, and he sees his illegal acts as necessary to refurbish existing constitutional (and international) law, generate overdue reform, and help better instantiate legal virtues associated with the rule of law. From his perspective, it is the US government that has systematically abandoned the rule of law, whereas his actions have helped bring its egregious illegalities to public light.

Fair-minded observers can reasonably disagree about why and how Snowden has ignited a massive worldwide public debate. Yet a strong argument can be made that part of his astounding appeal stems from his apt recourse to civil disobedience's legal prong. His example may also suggest that it remains valuable even in the context of postnationalization. Snowden's appeals to international law and the principle of legality transcend national borders; they have hit a raw nerve with people around the world. His cause has become a rallying cry for emerging global publics and political initiatives outraged by intrusive surveillances policies not just in the US or UK but elsewhere as well.

What then of the possible relevance of this approach for other settings?

Anti-austerity protests in Greece, Spain, and elsewhere provide a second recent example. Jonathan White (2015) uses the apt phrase "emergency Europe" to describe how recent EU elite-level political rhetoric regularly asserts the existence of a panoply of urgent exceptional and even existential threats to legitimize controversial measures "contravening established procedures and norms" as necessary, unavoidable, and thereby intrinsically rational. One consequence is a growing dependence on legally dubious top-down executive measures along with a disturbing tendency to demote normal deliberative and lawmaking channels. Within Greece, for example, the EU bailout and anti-austerity measures were arguably passed in violation of the rule of law:

> The loan and memorandum agreements imposed taxation increases and savage salary and pension cuts before they reached Parliament, which was reduced to the role of rubberstamping a *fait accompli*. The law implementing the agreement was adopted with a simple majority despite constitutional provisions requiring a three-fifths majority ... The complex memorandum imposing the austerity measures was passed

under "guillotine" procedures with minimal debate. The law gives *carte blanche* to ministers to issue executive decrees which can cover all aspects of economic and social policy, repeal pre-existing laws and sign further binding agreements giving away parts of national sovereignty without Parliamentary approval. (Douzinas 2013: 46)

The Greeks and others have faced a deplorable scenario where "all major aspects of legality have been weakened. Rule is replaced by regulation, normativity by normalization, legislation by executive action, principle by discretion" (Douzinas 2013: 44).

Not surprisingly, most protests have targeted specific injustices and the controversial national as well as EU-wide policies behind them. Yet, given the austerity measures' hardly coincidental sacrifice of basic legal virtues, it also makes sense for opponents to pursue nonviolent disobedience that vividly communicates their "highest respect for the law." If austerity is to be tempered or reversed, critics need to show potential sympathizers that it not only represents bad substantive policy but also a direct assault on longstanding rule of law ideals to which the EU, as well as its member states, claim loyalty. Activists need to take seriously the possibility that their lawbreaking should vividly express fidelity to the law and fundamental legal ideals at the heart of European democracy, ideals which have faced considerable pressure since the start of the crisis, and which, in some cases, have been systematically undermined. Here, as in many other scenarios, attacks on the rule of law and bad public policy often go hand in hand. A viable response will need to counter both the concrete harms at hand and the broader and potentially even more consequential attack on law-based government.

The familiar – but now increasingly neglected – idea of civil disobedience as congruent with the rule of law still provides impressive conceptual and political firepower. Those rushing today to discard it would do well to take note.

Conclusion

Civil disobedience now

This volume's introduction closed by asking whether the concept of civil disobedience helps us make sense of Black Lives Matter (BLM) and global migration. After a lengthy detour, we can now better appreciate how that initial, open-ended question might be productively reformulated: does lawbreaking as practiced by BLM, and illegal border crossing by migrants, correspond to elements of any of the four (religious, liberal, democratic, or anarchist) models of civil disobedience we have evaluated?

Even when so restated, the question remains complicated; legitimately conflicting answers seem possible. My hope is that those of you who have patiently followed this book's main claims are now better situated to provide your own answers. My brief comments here are hardly intended to be the final or even penultimate word. Much more remains to be said, and my wish is for readers to do so. As a starting point for discussion, I tentatively offer the following brief reflections.

Those critics, including President Trump, who accuse BLM of recklessly undermining "law and order" ignore the thoughtful moral and political concerns behind its protests. They unfairly reduce its powerful critique of racialized policing and criminal justice to garden-variety criminality. Even if one disagrees with BLM, it simply does not suffice to conflate its anti-racist lawbreaking with thuggery.

Nonetheless, I worry that BLM has made itself susceptible to opportunistic criticism by failing to reflect sufficiently on how its goals should shape its activities, including civil disobedience. An older generation is right to observe that BLM breaks with key facets of King's vision. However, the religious-spiritual model preferred by that generation suffers from many flaws; there is no reason it should serve as a privileged measuring rod. The source of the problem lies elsewhere.

At times, BLM's instincts seem anarchist and correspondingly anti-legal, not surprisingly given "its generation's experiences with a punitive state. A distrust of public institutions has generated an anti-statist thrust among many activists" (Biondi 2016). However understandable, this anti-statist tendency hinders the movement from effectively articulating some version of the very idea of civil disobedience as lawbreaking for the sake of law, as evidenced by its susceptibility to politically tone-deaf slogans targeting police officers (for example, "Pigs in a blanket! Fry 'em like bacon!").[1] At other times, BLM embraces elements of the liberal model of civil disobedience. Those involved in its "Campaign Zero," for example, offer a detailed defense of desirable political and legal reforms. They arguably interpret its nonviolent lawbreaking as implicitly consonant with respect for the rule of law and constitutional government, both of which potentially undercut official racism and police arbitrariness.[2] At yet other times, key movement figures such as Opal Tometi justify its "really courageous acts of nonviolent civil disobedience that are just taking this country by storm" as an appropriate response to "a crisis of our democracy" ravaging working-class black and other minority communities (quoted in Garber 2015). She and others appear to endorse identifiably democratic notions of civil disobedience.

Political movements are always messy; it should come as no surprise that BLM embodies competing ideas about civil disobedience. Still, its loose and decentralized organization, however politically advantageous, aggrandizes the fragmented character not only of its public message but also its version of civil disobedience.[3]

What then of global migration, now reshaping political identities everywhere, and possibly one trigger for a xenophobic political backlash in Europe, North America, and elsewhere?

As William Smith rightly points out, it seems odd to view border crossing in itself as conscientious public action aimed at shifting public opinion, in sync with either liberal or democratic models. Illegal migrants do not typically seem interested in communicating to others why they apparently view national borders as illegitimate. They refuse to comply with entry and immigration laws for a wide variety of reasons, many of which appear unrelated to standard justifications for civil disobedience. They rarely provide a moral or legal justification for their endeavors, nor do they accept the legal repercussions (Smith 2015). There may be sound moral, legal, and political reasons for loosening national borders. Yet placing illegal migration under the rubric of civil disobedience probably confuses the complicated issues at hand.[4]

Things look different, however, when undocumented migrants, like so-called DREAMers in the US, come forward publicly to reveal their "illegal" status, openly risking deportation for the sake of reshaping public opinion and generating reform of immigration laws.[5] Young Latino DREAMers have occupied the offices of Senator John McCain and other prominent politicians and blocked buses transporting undocumented "aliens" to and from deportation centers (Volpp 2014). One might legitimately debate how best to interpret their politically motivated illegalities; they also embody competing views of civil disobedience. However, there is no question that young Latino political activists are employing its shared conceptual language.

Civil disobedience for authoritarians and racists?

While presenting my ideas, I frequently encountered some version of the following questions: what of lawbreaking conducted by those disrespectful of basic rights, democracy, or even fundamental ideals of human equality? In our efforts to defend civil disobedience, might we inadvertently outfit racists and authoritarians, including neo-fascists, with a tool for dismantling democracy?

With authoritarian populists taking sizable political strides, these concerns demand a proper hearing. Neo-fascists, racists, and xenophobes have recently engaged in illegal acts that they and some observers have characterized as civil disobedience.

Civil disobedience is not, to be sure, just for the "good guys" (e.g., Gandhi or King) in history. The liberal and democratic models, notably, correctly presuppose modern pluralism, and with it the acknowledgment that no moral or political actor can claim privileged access to truth. No one possesses infallible advance wisdom about a proposed law or policy: only free-wheeling public debate and exchange, alongside the rough-and-tumble of political contestation, allow us to decide provisionally which views are deserving of binding legal status. And only subsequently will we be able to judge whether the results have met expectations. Since civil disobedience represents one part of that broader political process, we cannot determine definitively ahead of time whether the cause or idea behind it deserves our allegiance. Civil disobedience, particularly for liberals and democrats, represents an appeal to one's political peers, and like other political appeals, it may or may not turn out to be sound. Denying some views or groups a priori the possibility of pursuing civil disobedience, like efforts to rob them of basic political and especially communicative liberties, ignores pluralism and the core ideals of a political community premised on realizing freedom and equality for all members.

Many acts of civil disobedience, in fact, have been conducted by unpalatable figures. Not just those countering injustice or advancing democracy, but also those pursuing less uplifting causes, will continue to practice it. In a community that aspires to be free and decent, we should remain mindful of the dangers of repressively shunting unpopular positions aside. We need to provide ample space for civil disobedience not only for those with whom we might sympathize but also for those we dislike and perhaps abhor. When lawbreaking follows one of the main (religious, liberal, democratic) models, it typically deserves some measure, however begrudging, of respect, even when we vehemently disagree with protestors and their cause.[6] By following standard models, lawbreakers partake of a common normative language everyone should be able to understand. When doing so, lawbreakers implicitly communicate basic respect for their political opponents. Those hoping to stall their (possibly odd or even alarming) agendas should be expected to reciprocate. State authorities, correspondingly, should also respond respectfully and, in many cases, with leniency.

This does not mean that anything goes. It remains difficult to imagine how authoritarians or racists could ever meet core conditions of legitimate civil disobedience, even if their tactics occasionally mimic its usual forms. Authoritarians necessarily belittle the underlying premise of liberal and democratic models, namely, the idea of government and society as a cooperative endeavor between and among free and equal persons. Any notion of civil disobedience as a device for shaping public opinion is necessarily anathema to dictatorship's advocates. They believe in manufacturing public opinion from above via manipulation and propaganda, not in permitting it to crystallize via grassroots contestation among political equals. It remains no less difficult to grasp how a principled authoritarian could abide the religious or anarchist models. The religious model's democratic credentials, I argued above, occasionally left something to be desired. Nonetheless, both Gandhi and King endorsed a range of moral and religious ideals requiring, at a minimum, that government treat everyone "lovingly" or respectfully. Propagandistic claims to the contrary, dictatorships fail to do so. Both men also fought bravely to extend, not deny, basic rights to the excluded and oppressed. As for anarchism, its bogeyman has always been a "strong" centralized, hierarchical, and unaccountable state – in other words, precisely what authoritarians want.

The notion of racist, let alone fascist, civil disobedience is even less coherent. Racists and fascists challenge the fundamental idea of respect for human beings *qua* human beings, a notion implicitly shared by *all* models of civil disobedience discussed in this volume. When angry mobs attack buses transporting refugees or immigrants, chanting hateful racially charged, xenophobic epithets, or destroy temporary housing for migrants, their acts have nothing to do with civil disobedience.[7] On the contrary, they represent a direct assault on everything the competing religious, liberal, democratic, and anarchist political traditions jointly value.

Notes

Introduction

1 In an interview with Fox News on July 18, 2016, presidential candidate Trump accused BLM of encouraging violence against police officers, referring to videos of protestors chanting anti-police slogans ("What do we want? Dead cops"). A few days earlier, Fox News commentator Todd Starnes charged BLM with fomenting violence and anarchy, pointedly reminding its militants that "the rule of law matters" (2016).

2 The quotations come from a statement, "11 Major Misconceptions About the Black Lives Matter Movement" (Black Lives Matter 2015), posted on the group's website (http://blacklives matter.com).

3 As I write, however, Republican state legislatures in the US are debating the possibility of additional criminal penalties for those engaging in civil disobedience (by blocking highways, for example), in part as a crackdown on BLM.

4 Most examples of civil disobedience mentioned in this volume are drawn from the US and western Europe; my approach might be accused of Euro- or, even worse, US-centrism. However, I rely on these examples only because I know them best, not because I believe they should be imitated by others elsewhere, or that they prove more illuminating or valuable than non-western examples. I do not frankly know whether an alternative discussion, relying on a more representative global sample, would alter my overall conceptual story. I doubt, in any event, that the conceptual frameworks for civil disobedience analyzed throughout this book can be easily written off

as congenitally US-American or European and thus perhaps irrelevant elsewhere. Our story, in fact, begins with Mahatma Gandhi: every subsequent account of civil disobedience, if only implicitly, starts with Gandhi and his ideas, which underwent an astonishing global dispersion. From the very outset, ideas about civil disobedience have traversed national borders, as have the competing models analyzed in this volume.

5 There are good reasons why social scientists prefer the term "resistance," as useful empirical research shows. Some employ this broader category to paint a multicolored portrait of resistance, in which civil disobedience is only one of its many colors (Chenoweth and Stephan 2013; Roberts and Garton Ash 2011; Schock 2005; 2015). Within normative theory, however, the move sometimes obliterate key distinctions, as does the closely related tendency to jettison the term "civil disobedience" for the more generic "disobedience" (Caygill 2013; Laudani 2013). To be sure, the anarchist preference for "resistance" rests on specific theoretical and political shifts requiring careful consideration (see chapter 4).

6 As I write, US political moderates and liberals (participating in legal demonstrations), left-liberals and radicals (some engaging in nonviolent civil disobedience), and anarchists (including those who damage property and fight with police) speak of "resistance" to the Trump Administration. Whatever its virtues as an umbrella term, "resistance" here – as in other contexts – masks the reality of competing political views, strategies, and tactics (Scheuerman 2017).

7 One methodological caveat is probably in order: the competing models analyzed below represent ideal-types, meaning that they are indispensable for making sense of social reality, yet also stand in a complicated relationship to any concrete social setting. For example, many real-life examples of civil disobedience cannot be interpreted as falling completely under any individual (religious, liberal, democratic, anarchist) rubric; they seem, on many occasions, to combine elements from more than one. Nevertheless, we still require ideal-typical models to understand them and their (potentially conflicting) traits.

8 My decision to start with Gandhi will perhaps irritate some historically minded readers. Did not Socrates engage in civil disobedience? What about the nineteenth-century US dissident, Henry Thoreau, widely credited with having invented the term? Though I cannot sufficiently defend this claim here, I believe it is mistaken to read modern notions of civil disobedience back into classical antiquity: "The Greeks did not go on protest marches; Socrates never staged a sit-in" (Kraut 1984:

75). Thoreau's place in our story is more complicated (Hanson 2017); I address it in chapter 6.

9   For example, Holloway Sparks (1997) provides an impressive feminist-inflected analysis of Rosa Parks and other modern women civil disobedients. Yet her basic approach remains at its core (radical) democratic.

10   Of course, we know that over the course of history even seemingly simple, straightforward terms can take on new and unexpected meanings. Yet I do not aspire here to offer a timeless, trans-historical conceptual overview of civil disobedience, but instead one that I hope will prove useful in the present and foreseeable future.

1.   Divine Witness

1   On nineteenth-century US precursors, see Perry (2013).

2   Gandhi initially spoke of "passive resistance" and then, later, "civil resistance." He doubted that Thoreau's view of law-breaking rested sufficiently on a principled commitment to nonviolence, an idea he instead probably borrowed from Leo Tolstoy, whose followers played a crucial role in shaping Gandhi's views of Thoreau (Gandhi 1986a: 102–3). Despite his worries about the term "civil disobedience," he frequently used it. Like many others, Gandhi was wrong to attribute the term's invention to Thoreau: the original title for Thoreau's influential famous 1849 essay was in fact "Resistance to Civil Government," posthumously changed by an editor perhaps worried by its more radical political connotations (Thoreau 1996: 1–22).

3   Gandhi suggested a distinction between defensive and aggressive civil disobedience, with the former referring to reluctant or involuntary disobedience to laws so onerous and disrespectful of basic dignity that they must be violated, and the latter to laws willfully broken to challenge political authorities and bring about shifts to law and policy (Zashin 1972: 154–5).

4   Gandhi did not limit civil disobedience, as some liberals would (see chapter 2), to matters of (political) justice as opposed to issues of economic distribution or justice, in part because he never accepted a conventional liberal separation of state from society (or economy). Satyagraha potentially involved – as in the Ahmedabad labor dispute, where textile workers fought for higher wages – economic matters (Bondurant 1958).

5   See, among many others, Bondurant (1958), Brown (1977), Dalton (1993), Parekh (1989), and Terchek (1998).

6   David Lyons rejects the claim that Gandhi acknowledged "a moral presumption favoring obedience to law" (2013: 140). He provides little textual support for this view. Similarly, Etienne Balibar (2012) downplays Gandhi's legalist inclinations.

7   Gandhi occasionally denied that civil disobedience in fact constituted lawbreaking, since when properly conducted it reflected the law of divine conscience (Haksar 2003: 409).

8   Gandhi endorsed Thoreau's view "that government is the best which governs the least" (quoted in Gandhi 1986a [1936]: 413). Although he sometimes comes close to embracing anarchism, other strands in his political thinking, including his deep respect for law, predominate.

9   A claim, interestingly, buttressed by recent social scientific research suggesting that nonviolence leads to substantial "security force defections" (Chenoweth and Stephan 2013: 50).

10 See Chakrabarty (2013), Kapur (1992), Kosek (2008), Perry (2013: 181–246), Scalmer (2011), Weber (2004: 165–74), and Zashin (1972: 149–94). Gregg (1970 [1959]) and Shridharani (1972 [1939]) played major roles in translating Gandhi into a US-American idiom.

11 The gender subtext is, of course, striking. Both Gandhi and King shared many, though perhaps not all, of the standard patriarchal and sexist premises of the day.

12 Critics of King (Storing 1991 [1969]) who accused him of blurring the divide between liberal reform and revolutionary change were indeed onto something. However, this constitutes a potential strength, not weakness, to his approach.

13 Tommie Shelby captures the implicit logic of this political approach: "given the proven difficulty of establishing and maintaining just institutions in the modern world, preserving the reasonably just components of an overall unjust system while pushing insistently for broader reforms may ultimately be a better strategy than abrupt radical [or revolutionary] reconstruction" (2016: 225).

14 The transfer was made easier, to be sure, by the Tolstoyan (and Christian) features of Gandhi's complex theology (Tolstoy 1967).

15 The Jewish thinker Martin Buber also makes an appearance here (King 1991 [1963]: 73). More below on King's attempt to appeal to non-Christians.

16 For an opposing view, see Lyons (2013).

17 For an illuminating discussion, see Kramnick and Moore (2005).

18 For some examples, see Scalmer (2011) and Sharp (1973).

19   On Gandhi's charismatic appeal, see Rudolph and Rudolph (1967) and Balibar (2012).

20   On the New Left, in a similar vein, see Isserman (1987: 159–68).

21   To be sure, King rejected a naïve view of history suggesting that absent militant political action, "the very flow of time ... will inevitably cure all ills" (King 1991 [1963]: 76). Yet religious grounds ultimately motivated his view that the "arc of the moral universe" tends to bend toward justice.

22   Early US Catholic 1970s "pro-life" activists, for example, had been deeply involved in the civil rights and 1960s anti-war movements (Risen and Thomas 1998).

23   For a survey of these reasons, see Stevick (1969).

24   Consider, for example, the militant Catholic pacifist Daniel Berrigan, who burned draft records to subvert the Vietnam War and then tried to escape arrest (2009: 138–44).

2.   Liberalism and Its Limits

1   For useful historical accounts, see Carter (1973), Foley (2003), and Perry (2013: 212–83).

2   The list of figures participating in the liberal debate (e.g., Christian Bay, Hugo Adam Bedau, Carl Cohen, Marshall Cohen, Ronald Dworkin, Kent Greenawalt, Jeffrie Murphy, John Rawls, Joseph Raz, Bertrand Russell, Peter Singer, Michael Walzer, Richard Wasserstrom) reads like a *Who's Who?* of 1960s and 1970s Anglophone political philosophy. Some – most famously, Russell, the CND's most prominent representative – also participated in civil disobedience. The still unwritten intellectual history would probably start with a 1961 symposium, undertaken in the shadows of US civil rights protests, on "Political Obligation and Civil Disobedience," at an American Philosophical Association meeting (Bedau 1961; Welchman 2001).

3   See chapter 7. My discussion here relies extensively on Rawls' (now) canonical (1969 [1966]); 1971: 363–91) account of civil disobedience, though I refer to other liberals to supplement it.

4   See, in a related vein, Bedau's discussion of Thoreau (1991 [1970]).

5   This simple but key feature of civil disobedience gets obscured, I fear, by Ingeborg Maus' otherwise provocative critique, in which she interprets civil disobedience as a historically retrograde quest to reestablish medieval European notions of a (legal) "right to resistance" (Maus 1992: 32–42, 230–4). As we will see, the vast majority of defenses

of civil disobedience (1) define it as entailing illegal protest and (2) reject any notion of a legal or constitutional right to it. Moreover, important approaches (see chapter 3) clearly view it as much more than a device for conserving the legal or constitutional status quo.

6   For early challenges to this view, see Singer (1973); also Zinn (2002 [1968]).

7   As noted in chapter 1, Gandhi and King suggested that nonviolent civil disobedience might productively funnel political anger otherwise likely to generate destructive political violence. However, they did not view it as performing a mere "ventilating" function within the contours of a basically just or sound liberal order whose stability needed to be assured.

8   Rawls, somewhat oddly, claims that broad public appeals concerning social and economic questions are unlikely to be "sufficiently clear" (Rawls 1971: 372).

9   Gandhi controversially claimed that civil disobedience might have productively aided Jews under Nazism. On nonviolence's successes against authoritarianism, see Schock (2005).

10   A point neglected by critics who highlight – and sometimes exaggerate – liberalism's restrictions (Laudani 2013: 112–16).

11   For a more critical take than my own on liberal ideas of nonviolence, see Smart (1991 [1978]: 202–6). Excellent surveys of the tough conceptual issues are provided by May (2015) and Vinthagen (2015).

12   For a contemporary critique of commonplace conceptual conflations, see Arendt (1972 [1970b]).

13   Liberalism leans toward embracing what C.A.J. Coady characterizes as a narrow or "restrictive" definition of violence (1986).

14   For this reason, some liberals, in contrast to Gandhi, allow for legitimate self-defense: if disobedients are physically assaulted, they may have grounds to defend themselves (Zashin 1972: 118).

15   Early on, Carter (1973: 94–117) identified this position's institutionally complacent implications.

16   Even on identifiably Rawlsian terms, the harsh facts of racism probably justify an interpretation of the US as "fundamentally unjust," as exceeding "the limits of intolerable injustice" (Shelby 2007: 151).

3. Deepening Democracy

1   Arendt worried about the disturbing growth of secret executive decision making (1972 [1971]). On the dialectic between

executive extra-legality and grassroots civil disobedience, see Scheuerman (2016).

2   Arendt distinguished democracy, which she tended to conflate with a crude political majoritarianism (and viewed skeptically), from republicanism, which she embraced. Her preference for the latter rests in part on the controversial postulate that active citizenship and deliberation "will never be the life of the many," and that a political community where they thrive conflicts with core traits of modern mass democracy (Arendt 1963: 275). For our purposes, we can provisionally bracket Arendt's criticisms of democracy. Her occasional conflation of democracy with majority rule, as we will see, is implicitly countered by Habermas.

3   My attempt to distill the ideal-typical outlines of democratic disobedience builds on previous efforts to do so by Arato and Cohen (1992) and Markovits (2005).

4   In contrast, both Arendt (1958) and Jürgen Habermas (1989 [1962]), major contributors to the democratic model discussed below, devote significant attention to such matters.

5   Despite Zinn's US-American focus, his ideas can be fruitfully interpreted as contributing to a more general democratic model.

6   Zinn and other democrats occasionally anticipate what Hartmut Rosa and I have described as "social acceleration" (Rosa and Scheuerman 2009; Scheuerman 2004).

7   Zinn does not mention "structural violence" (Galtung 1969). Yet, like some who endorse broad definitions of violence, he sees it (1) as a multifaceted phenomenon (having, for example, psychological or spiritual components) and (2) as rooted in the basic institutions (or structures) of contemporary society. One problem inadvertently generated by excessively broad views for theorists of civil disobedience is that they make it difficult to hold on to some politically fungible idea of nonviolence; broad definitions tend to see violence everywhere and anywhere. Not surprisingly, most theorists of civil disobedience have struggled to keep some distance from them.

8   Sometimes Zinn described his political position as anarchist, sometimes democratic-socialist. Problems that appear in his account, predictably, resurface among anarchists (see chapter 4).

9   Arendt seems to have been unfamiliar with the most impressive liberal contributions (for example, Rawls'), and she simply overlooks core liberal insights.

10   Her discussion sometimes seems preoccupied with civil disobedience as a counterweight to illegal and unconstitutional overreaching by the executive branch (1972 [1970a]).

11   See Arendt's illuminating November 1952 comments (2016: 273).

12   For discussions, see Bernstein (2009), Kalyvas (2008: 283–91), and Smith (2012). On a skeptical note, Maus (1992: 231–4). More generally, the classical discussions of Arendt by Benhabib (2002) and Isaac (1992).

13   Arendt seems inconsistent: the 1960s student activists she praises for engaging in (essentially political) civil disobedience are elsewhere lauded for their "moral considerations" (1972 [1970b]: 130).

14   A key point perhaps downplayed by Petherbridge (2016).

15   In Arendt's account, civil disobedience's role in directly attacking social and economic injustice also seems unclear, though Arato and Cohen interpret her as sympathetic to efforts to do so (1992: 598).

16   In December 1979, German Chancellor Helmut Schmidt moved forward with the deployment of new intermediate-range nuclear missiles, despite opposition from within his own Social Democratic Party (SPD). In March, 1983 a new German government, led by the conservative (Christian Democratic Union) Chancellor Helmut Kohl voted (282 to 226) to install them. They were stationed in Germany in November 1983. On the ensuing German debate on civil disobedience see Laker (1986).

17   For insightful analyses, see Arato and Cohen (1992: 599–604); Cidam (2017); Smith (2008); Specter (2010: 151–70); Velasco (2016); White and Farr (2012).

18   Here Habermas borrowed heavily from Guggenberger and Offe (1984). For a critical discussion, see Scheuerman (1995).

19   Writing similarly about 1980s anti-nuclear movements, a more skeptical Ronald Dworkin argued that civil disobedience should address matters of fundamental constitutional principle but not disagreements about public policy (1985: 104–18). Habermas occasionally echoes Dworkin's concern that civil disobedience risks getting overextended if employed whenever disagreements about policy surface. Yet he implicitly challenges any categorical distinction between constitutional principle and policy (for example, when he suggests that nuclear and security policy raises fundamental matters relating to political and constitutional identity). Habermas is probably right to challenge this distinction, which seems overly rigid.

20   On internal tensions within the argument, see Thomassen (2007).

21   Habermas defends a refashioned Kantian version of the social contract to interpret the normative contours of modern democracy and law. Arendt rejects this possibility, equating Kant's

(and Rousseau's earlier) version of the contract with Hobbes' (1972 [1970a]: 84). Interestingly, however, elements of Habermas' reworked Kantianism mirror Arendt's (Lockean) "horizontal" social contract.

22   Nothing here prohibits civil disobedience directed against social and economic injustice. Since on Habermas' diagnosis the boundaries between public and private institutions have blurred in welfare state capitalism, he cannot endorse the orthodox liberal view that civil disobedience should typically be limited to securing basic civil and political rights and appeals to state or public authorities (1975 [1973]; 1989 [1962]; 1996 [1992]).

23   I am less worried than Smith (2008) that Habermas' defense of civil disobedience remains too open-ended.

24   Habermas' employment of Rawls leads some to conflate their positions (Celikates 2016a).

25   In a discussion of Arendt's views of power, Habermas speaks of "structural violence," according to which political (and other) institutions systematically block "communications in which convictions effective for legitimation are formed and passed on," without those subjected to such blockages even being aware of their forced or coerced character (1986 [1976]: 88).

26   His analysis here, as on other key points, relies heavily on Frankenberg (1984) and occasionally Dreier (1983: 62–3). The protest actions Habermas defends as nonviolent were classified, in sharp contrast, by conservative West German judges as *Nötigung* [violent coercion].

27   The protest occurred in King of Prussia, Pennsylvania, on September 9, 1980. It garnered worldwide publicity.

28   Of course, below some threshold self-described liberal polities might no longer deserve to be viewed as such; more militant or radical lawbreaking might then be legitimate (see chapter 5). Habermas never seems to consider this possibility, probably because he considers it irrelevant to "halfway" functioning democratic and constitutional states such as the German Federal Republic.

29   See Ulrich Preuss' (1995) Arendt-inflected account of the upheavals in eastern Europe.

30   Though Arendt (1972 [1970b]) can plausibly be read as rejecting precisely this definition of the state.

4. Anarchist Uprising

1   Some commentators question whether the distinction holds water, arguing that philosophical anarchism (because of its

deep hostility to state and law) necessarily collapses into some variant of its political cousin (Harris 1991; Senor 1987). Contemporary "postanarchism" is best viewed as a novel type of political anarchism: a self-described political standpoint aiming for radical transformation, it represents a revival of classical (political) anarchism, now deepened and enriched by postmodernist and poststructuralist theoretical currents (Newman 2011; 2016).

2   For a similar theoretical move, see Cooke (2016), who provides a more ambitious philosophical grounding for civil disobedience's triple-pronged normativity.

3   Some anarchists (Georges Sorel, for example) celebrated political violence. For recent postanarchists, state violence requires a potentially violent popular response, but one that "seeks the abolition of violence itself" (Newman 2016: 72).

4   They remain willing to pursue some types of violence that would likely have been condemned by most previous thinkers about civil disobedience (Conway 2003).

5   On resulting tensions within the Canadian global justice movement, see Conway (2003).

6   Its opening salvo was probably the philosopher R.P. Wolff's pithy *In Defense of Anarchism* (1970). For concise overviews of the genre, see Horton (2010: 106–34) and Simmons (1996: 19–39).

7   His reading of Locke, as we will see, contrasts sharply with Arendt's. For Simmons, Locke is a philosophical anarchist and libertarian; for Arendt, he is a republican.

8   A tendency we observed in Zinn's writings, in part because of his anarchist inclinations.

9   Simmons tends to downplay facets of Thoreau's thinking that move in opposing directions – for example, Thoreau's delineation of his views from those of "no-government men" (Simmons 2010; Thoreau 1996: 2). For a non-anarchist interpretation of Thoreau, see Taylor (1996).

10 Thoreau, in fact, was probably only asked to pay the tax because he encountered the local Concord (Massachusetts) tax collector, Sam Staples, on his way to a cobbler to pick up some shoes. Staples seems to have offered to pay or loan the amount ($1.50) on Thoreau's behalf, who refused. The irritated Staples then took Thoreau into custody. The next morning Thoreau was released from jail, probably because an aunt paid the tax the previous evening. Thoreau might have been released shortly after his arrest, but an understandably annoyed Staples had already returned home and taken off his boots (Taylor 2015: 1–2).

11   Simmons, in contrast to many others (for example, Rawls), wants to interpret Thoreau as a legitimate and perhaps paradigmatic theorist of civil disobedience (2005, 2010; see also Lyons 2013: 130–47). For an illuminating conceptual history that underlines some potential problems with this move, see Hanson (2017).

12   Brown unsuccessfully used force to ignite a slave rebellion.

13   A problem also plaguing Robert Paul Wolff's (1970) version of philosophical anarchism (Reiman 1972).

14   See, however, the important exchange between Simmons and Horton on the "associative" model of obligation (Horton 2010; Simmons 2001: 65–92).

15   Habermas penned a book entitled *Legitimation Crisis* (1975 [1973]); Arendt thought contemporary liberal democracy faced serious crises. Unfortunately, Anglophone philosophical anarchists seem uninterested in a broad range of identifiably democratic theorists of civil disobedience.

16   Some anarchists offer accounts of civil disobedience barely distinguishable from those discussed in previous chapters (Woodcock 1966).

5.   Postnationalization and Privatization

1   On November 15, 2011, New York City police forcibly cleared Zuccotti Park. Protestors were arrested and later rearrested when trying to reoccupy the park.

2   On anarchist strands among Occupy activists, see Barber (2011).

3   For a defense of this strategy against state authorities that in many countries interpreted Occupy as having illegitimately and illegally privatized public space, see Kohn (2013).

4   Bernard E. Harcourt, for example, interprets Occupy as rejecting civil disobedience (in favor of what he calls political disobedience), but only because he narrowly defines it as accepting "the legitimacy of the political structure and of our political institutions" (2012: 33).

5   For a prescient discussion of some of the issues covered in this chapter, see Carter (2005: 107–75). I use the term "political authority" to refer to collectively binding decision making that claims legitimacy and sometimes, for sound reasons, is perceived as such by those impacted. Political authority here is both an empirical and a normative concept, i.e., it refers to organized structures of binding (and, typically, legally based) decision making and to normative tests (for example, an ideal of justice or democratic legitimacy) we expect such structures to meet.

6 Such claims always rest on some idealizations. The empirical research I summarize is chiefly concerned with general patterns among OECD states. This makes sense analytically because we can presuppose some empirical overlap between "developed" OECD states and those Rawls would have described as "nearly just" (that is, basically liberal and democratic). OECD members tend to be "developed" (though imperfect) liberal democracies having market economies and, in most cases, welfare states.

7 The state's capacity to mobilize sufficient power (and, if necessary, coercion) remains vital. I do not believe that the emerging postnational system corroborates fashionable anti-statist notions of "governance without government" (see Scheuerman 2014a; 2015).

8 And what of the obligations of citizens in rich and powerful countries versus those elsewhere (Ogunye 2015)?

9 My examples are taken almost exclusively from (western) Europe and North America not because I believe they successfully stand in for political experiences elsewhere, but only because this chapter focuses on shifts in so-called "nearly just" OECD countries.

10 I hesitate before making stronger generalizations. Even if our overall global order cannot be described as "nearly just," the specific political and institutional scenarios would-be law-breakers face vary significantly. Our multi-layered, decentered, postnational system is complicated; our theoretical account needs to acknowledge its complexities. The US, for example, occupies a very different position from most other countries within the World Bank. When US activists go to the streets to shape their country's policies vis-à-vis the World Bank or to protest it directly, their actions possess potentially more clout than those of activists elsewhere. In some but not all situations faced by disobedients, undemocratic postnational institutions may play a predominant or decisive role.

11 Following a similar line of reasoning, Caney (2015) outlines a "right to resistance" to global injustice, in part because he questions the relevance of Rawlsian civil disobedience in the context of a global status quo that fails the "nearly just" test. However, more elements of the original Rawlsian model of civil disobedience can be salvaged than Caney acknowledges.

12 Think, for example, of the nationalistic overtones of protests against EU austerity measures in Greece, Spain, and elsewhere.

13 Outside OECD countries as well, the "Arab Spring" uprisings, for example, were partly motivated by criticisms of state privatization (May 2015: 13).

14   This criticism also applies to non-Rawlsian versions (France-schet 2015).

15   See chapter 7 for the details.

16   Note that this view speaks powerfully against violence committed against persons but not perhaps against violence against objects or property.

17   Rawls still would have been right to recall the dangers of such approaches. Uncivil disobedience has been commonplace even in liberal democracies. Its record is extremely rocky (Kirkpatrick 2008).

18   Note his respectful rejection of Zinn's broader definition of civil disobedience (Rawls 1971: 364).

19   They also argued that accepting legal penalties was necessary to demonstrate respect for law. In principle, however, a willingness to face punishment may not be the only or always best way to do so.

20   See Scheuerman (1999) and Schneiderman (2001). For example, the EU response to the financial and euro crises, a target of recent activist groups, has entailed an assault on core features of the rule of law. According to the legal scholar Christian Joerges, the Union "is experiencing a kind of state of emergency in which the law is losing its integrity … [T]he European Central Bank is disregarding its statutes …; parliaments are convened to make fast-tracked decisions that cannot be meaningfully discussed; Greece, and other members of the Union, are being told that their sovereignty is now 'limited'; changes of government take place under exceptional circumstances" (2012: 12).

21   That new order will also likely require a substantial dose of global stateness, though not perhaps a centralized monopoly on legitimate violence (Scheuerman 2014a; 2015).

6.   Digitalization

1   For recent discussions, see Harcourt (2015), Owen (2015), Sauter (2014), and Züger (2015).

2   On Anonymous, see Coleman (2014); on WikiLeaks and the controversial figure of Julian Assange, see Leigh and Harding (2011).

3   When meeting familiar tests (for example, nonviolence, publicity, acceptance of legal consequences), disobedients sometimes face reduced legal penalties. This has only occurred after decades of political struggle; there is also ample evidence that the achievement remains fragile, particularly when the cause

in question is unpopular. Even disobedients who follow the usual script can face harsh penalties.

4 For the messy details, see Ludlow (2013). Brown did not aid his cause by threatening FBI agents in a YouTube video.

5 Ackroyd only served ten months, however. I know of no systematic study comparing how different national legal jurisdictions are confronting digital disobedience.

6 Preska's comments were widely discussed in the media, e.g., Kopstein (2013).

7 An extensive critical analysis of the CFAA is available at the Electronic Frontier Foundation website (https://www.eff.org/issues/cfaa). Nor is this worrisome statutory pattern distinctly US-American. The German Federal Republic's 2007 cybersecurity law (StGB 202) promulgates harsh penalties (for example, up to a ten-year prison sentence) for hacking, with computer experts understandably concerned about some excessively broad and vague legal categories.

8 Manning and Snowden illustrate how elements of competing models of civil disobedience are often fused in social reality. In a liberal democratic political context, political lawbreaking is likely to contain elements of competing (liberal, democratic) models.

9 For example, if Julian Assange and WikiLeaks abetted Russian intelligence in leaking materials that undercut Hillary Clinton's presidential candidacy, we cannot reasonably place their acts under the rubric of civil disobedience. In its religious, liberal, and democratic versions, civil disobedience was about countering injustices committed by the powerful and privileged, not advancing an authoritarian state's geopolitical interests against its global rivals. Here we face an example not of lawbreaking intended to demonstrate respect for law, but instead meant to disrupt and disable another country's legislative mechanisms for the sake of advancing an authoritarian state's power interests and destroying legitimate law-based government.

10 To this we might add cyberterrorism or cyberwar.

11 Neither the Manning Support Group, nor other activist groups to which donations were made, were able in fact to access the money (Coleman 2014: 277–83, 288–90, 337–63).

12 Whether some political systems presently being shaped by authoritarian populist movements still deserve to be categorized as liberal democratic seems unclear.

13 However, some commentators are skeptical that such legal protections will prove able to protect whistleblowers (Alford 2001).

7.   Tilting at Windmills?

1   For important exceptions, see Goodin (2005), Lefkowitz (2007).
2   Among many others: Brownlee (2016), Celikates (2013: 211–18), Douzinas (2013: 91–6), Lyons (2013: 112–29), Welchman (2001).
3   For example, Celikates offers what he concedes is a "less restrictive" definition of civil disobedience as "an intentionally unlawful and principled collective act of protest," in which citizens seek changes to laws, policies, or institutions. Though distinguished from conscientious objection and "full-scale revolutionary revolt," his definition "deliberately leaves open whether civil disobedience is public, nonviolent, [and] conscientious." Civil disobedience, Celikates adds, should also rest on a civil rather than martial or military logic, though he remains somewhat opaque about the specific contours of that logic (2016a: 39).
4   Some of the best empirical work, correspondingly, takes politically oriented lawbreaking's normative contours seriously (Sutterlüty 2014).
5   In contrast, Balibar, whom Celikates relies on, appears to endorse the view that civil disobedience is not "a matter, in the end, of weakening legality, but of reinforcing it, even if this way of defending law against itself ... can only be legally considered illegal" (2014: 176; also 2002). On the recent French debate on civil disobedience, see Moulin-Dos (2015).
6   See, for example, Smith's revealing reformulation of Rawls' definition ("disobedience to law within the limits of fidelity to the law") as "disobedience to law within the limits of deliberative intent" (2013: 32).
7   Complicated jurisprudential issues arise here. A defensible view of the rule of law should pursue a middle way between legal positivism and natural law: we should neither reduce the rule-of-law to the "rule of good law," nor rob it of any ethical or normative substance whatsoever. Nor do we want a conception that is either overly judicial or unduly legislative. The (always aspirational and thus incomplete) realization of rule of law standards (e.g., clarity, publicity, prospectiveness, generality, constancy) requires cooperation between and among legislatures, courts, and the executive if it is to prove sufficient.
8   See Scheuerman (2014b). For a critical rejoinder, see Brownlee (2016).

Conclusion

1 A chant apparently used by BLM activists at protests outside the Minnesota State Fair in August 2015.
2 For the list, see: https://joincampaignzero.org.
3 In St. Paul, Minnesota, in July 2016, violence erupted at protests following the police killing of an unarmed motorist, with many police officers reporting injuries. BLM activists blamed the escalation of violence on local anarchists, including some who allegedly pelted officers with stones and bricks. Their claims, however, ignored the group's own decentralized and heterogeneous structure, organizational contours that make it vulnerable to participation by groups whose goals and tactics diverge from BLM's nonviolent commitments.
4 In the case of refugees, the Universal Declaration of Basic Rights guarantees core legal protections. By describing refugees' acts as illegal, those placing their actions under the rubric of civil disobedience risk distorting the crucial point that *state* signatories to the Declaration are the real lawbreakers when they refuse to enforce those protections.
5 The term comes from the DREAM Act, US federal legislation – supported by then President Barack Obama and congressional Democrats, but never passed because of Republican opposition – aiming to grant legal status to undocumented immigrants who came to the US as children. As I write, the DREAMers remain in legal and political limbo, with Trump promising draconian measures to deport them.
6 Based on my discussion of political and philosophical anarchism (chapter 4), it should be clear why anarchism, including its right-wing libertarian variants, represents a more difficult case. Some anarchists participate in civil disobedience's common discourse; others reject it. Some implicitly express respect for others as political equals; in other cases, this is less clear.
7 In Murietta, California, in July 2014, an angry mob kept a bus operated by US Border Patrol, filled with undocumented migrant children and families, from reaching a processing center. In Clausnitz, Germany, in February 2016, a bus with refugees was forced to turn back by a mob, egged on by local racists and neo-fascists. A former hotel where refugees were to be housed was torched and destroyed.

References

Abrahamsen, Rita and Williams, Michael (2011). *Security Beyond the State: Private Security in International Politics*. Cambridge: Cambridge University Press.

Alford, C. Fred (2001). *Whistleblowers: Broken Lives and Organizational Power*. Ithaca, NY: Cornell University Press.

Allen, Francis A. (1967). "Civil Disobedience and the Legal Order," *University of Cincinnati Law Review* 36(1): 1–33.

Arato, Andrew and Cohen, Jean L. (1992). *Civil Society and Political Theory*. Cambridge, MA: MIT Press.

Arendt, Hannah (1958). *The Human Condition*. Chicago, IL: University of Chicago Press.

Arendt, Hannah (1963). *On Revolution*. New York: Penguin.

Arendt, Hannah (1972 [1970a]). "Civil Disobedience." In *Crises of the Republic*. New York: Harcourt, Brace, pp. 49–102.

Arendt, Hannah (1972 [1970b]). "On Violence." In *Crises of the Republic*. New York: Harcourt, Brace, pp. 103–99.

Arendt, Hannah (1972 [1971]). "Lying in Politics: Reflections on the Pentagon Papers." In *Crises of the Republic*. New York: Harcourt, Brace, pp. 1–48.

Arendt, Hannah (2016). *Denktagebuch, 1950–1973*, Vols. I–II. Munich: Piper Verlag.

Balibar, Etienne (2002). "Sur la désobéissance civique." In *Droit de cité*. Paris: Quadrige/PUF, pp. 17–22.

Balibar, Etienne (2012). "Lenin and Gandhi: A Missed Encounter?" *Radical Philosophy* 172: 9–17.

Balibar, Etienne (2014). *Equaliberty: Political Essays*. Durham, NC: Duke University Press.

Barber, Benjamin (2011). "Occupy Wall Street: 'We Are What Democracy Looks Like!'" *Logos* 10(4). Available at: http://logosjournal.com/2011/fall_barber/

Bay, Christian (1971 [1967]). "Civil Disobedience Prerequisites for Democracy in a Mass Society." In Jeffrie G. Murphy (ed.) *Civil Disobedience and Violence*. Belmont, CA: Wadsworth, pp. 73–92.

Bedau, Hugo A. (1961). "On Civil Disobedience," *Journal of Philosophy* 58: 653–65.

Bedau, Hugo A. (1991). "Introduction." In Hugo Bedau (ed.) *Civil Disobedience in Focus*. New York: Routledge, pp. 1–12.

Bedau, Hugo A. (1991 [1970]). "Civil Disobedience and Personal Responsibility for Injustice." In Hugo Bedau (ed.) *Civil Disobedience in Focus*. New York: Routledge, pp. 49–67.

Beitz, Charles (1979). *Political Theory and International Relations*. Princeton, NJ: Princeton University Press.

Bell, Duncan (2014). "What is Liberalism?" *Political Theory* 42: 682–715.

Benhabib, Seyla (2002). *The Reluctant Modernism of Hannah Arendt*. Lanham, MD: Rowman & Littlefield.

Bernstein, Jay (2009). "Promising and Civil Disobedience." In R. Berkowitz, J. Katz, and T. Keenan (eds.) *Thinking in Dark Times: Hannah Arendt on Ethics and Politics*. New York: Fordham University Press, pp. 115–27.

Bernstein, Richard J. (2013). *Violence: Thinking Without Banisters*. Cambridge: Polity.

Berrigan, Daniel (2009). *Essential Writings*. Maryknoll, NY: Orbis.

Biondi, Martha (2016). "The Radicalism of Black Lives Matter," *In These Times* (September). Available at: http://inthesetimes.com/features/black-lives-matter-history-police-brutality.html

Black Lives Matter (2015). "11 Major Misconceptions About the Black Lives Matter Movement." Available at: http://blacklivesmatter.com/11-major-misconceptions-about-the-black-lives-matter-movement/

Bleyer, Peter (2000). "The Other Battle in Seattle," *Studies in Political Economy* 62 (Summer): 25–33.

Bobbio, Norberto (1987). *The Future of Democracy: A Defense of the Rules of the Game*. Minneapolis, MN: University of Minnesota Press.

Bondurant, Joan V. (1958). *Conquest of Violence: The Gandhian Philosophy of Conflict*. Princeton, NJ: Princeton University Press.

Brouwer, Daniel C. (2001). "ACT-ing UP in Congressional Hearings." In Robert Asen and Daniel C. Brouwer (eds.) *Counterpublics and the State*. Albany, NY: SUNY Press, pp. 87–109.

Brown, Judith M. (1977). *Gandhi and Civil Disobedience: The Mahatma in Indian Politics 1928–1934*. Cambridge: Cambridge University Press.

Brown, Judith M. (1989). *Gandhi: Prisoner of Hope*. New Haven, CT: Yale University Press.

Brownlee, Kimberley (2012a). *Conscience and Conviction: The Case for Civil Disobedience*. Oxford: Oxford University Press.

Brownlee, Kimberley (2012b). "Conscientious Objection and Civil Disobedience." In Andrei Marmor (ed.) *The Routledge Companion to Philosophy of Law*. New York: Routledge, pp. 527–39.

Brownlee, Kimberley (2016). "The Civil Disobedience of Edward Snowden: A Reply to William Scheuerman," *Philosophy and Social Criticism* 42(10): 965–70.

Cabrera, Luis (2010). *The Practice of Global Citizenship*. Cambridge: Cambridge University Press.

Caney, Simon (2015). "Responding to Global Injustice: On the Right of Resistance," *Social Philosophy & Policy* 32(1): 51–73.

Carter, April (1971). *The Political Theory of Anarchism*. New York: Harper & Row.

Carter, April (1973). *Direct Action and Liberal Democracy*. New York: Harper & Row.

Carter, April (2005). *Direct Action and Democracy Today*. Cambridge: Polity.

Cate, Fred (2015). "Edward Snowden and the NSA: Law, Policy, and Politics." In David P. Fidler (ed.) *The Snowden Reader*. Bloomington, IN: Indiana University Press, pp. 26–44.

Caygill, Howard (2013). *On Resistance*. London: Bloomsbury.

Celikates, Robin (2010). "Ziviler Ungehorsam und radikale Demokratie. Konstituierende vs. konstituierte Macht?" In Thomas Bedorf and Kurt Röttgers (eds.) *Das Politische und die Politik*. Berlin: Suhrkamp, pp. 274–300.

Celikates, Robin (2013). "Civil Disobedience as a Practice of Civil Freedom." In James Tully (ed.) *Global Citizenship: James Tully in Dialogue*. London: Bloomsbury, pp. 211–28.

Celikates, Robin (2016a). "Rethinking Civil Disobedience as a Practice of Contestation: Beyond the Liberal Paradigm," *Constellations* 23(1): 37–45.

Celikates, Robin (2016b). "Democratizing Civil Disobedience," *Philosophy and Social Criticism* 42(10): 982–94.

Chakrabarty, Bidyut (2013). *Confluence of Thought: Mahatma Gandhi and Martin Luther King, Jr.* Oxford: Oxford University Press.

Chenoweth, Erica and Stephan, Maria J. (2013). *Why Civil Resistance Works: The Strategic Logic of Nonviolent Conflict*. New York: Columbia University Press.

Chumley, Cheryl K. (2013). "Donald Trump on Edward Snowden: Kill the 'Traitor'," *Washington Times*, July 2.

Cidam, Cigdem (2017). "Radical Democracy Without Risks? Habermas on Constitutional Patriotism and Civil Disobedience," *New German Critique* 44: 105–32.

Coady, C.A.J. (1986). "The Idea of Violence," *Journal of Applied Philosophy* 3(1): 3–19.

Cohen, Carl (1966). "Civil Disobedience and the Law," *Rutgers Law Review* 21(1): 1–17.

Cohen, Carl (1971). *Civil Disobedience: Conscience, Tactics, and the Law*. New York: Columbia University Press.

Cohen, Marshall (1969). "Civil Disobedience in a Constitutional Democracy," *Massachusetts Review* 10: 211–26.

Cohen, Marshall (1972). "Liberalism and Disobedience," *Philosophy and Public Affairs* 1: 283–314.

Coleman, Gabriella (2014). *Hacker, Hoaxer, Whistleblower, Spy: The Many Faces of Anonymous*. New York: Verso.

Conway, Janet (2003). "Civil Resistance and the 'Diversity of Tactics' in the Anti-Globalization Movement: Problems of Violence, Science, and Solidarity in Activist Politics," *Osgoode Hall Law Journal* 41(2–3): 506–30.

Cooke, Maeve (2016). "Civil Obedience and Disobedience," *Philosophy and Social Criticism* 42(10): 995–1003.

Cooke, Maeve (2017). "Conscience in Public Life." In Cécile Laborde and Aurélia Bardo (eds.) *Religion in Liberal Political Philosophy*. Oxford: Oxford University Press, pp. 295–308.

Cutler, Claire (2003). *Private Power and Global Authority: Transnational Merchant Law in the Global Political Economy*. Cambridge: Cambridge University Press.

Dalton, Dennis (1993). *Mahatma Gandhi: Nonviolent Power in Action*. New York: Columbia University Press.

Del Signore, John (2012). "Occupy Wall Street Activist Explains Why Protesters Break the Law," *Gothamist*, April 27.

Della Porta, Donatella, Andretta, Massimiliano, Mosca, Lorenzo, and Reiter, Herbert (2006). *Globalization from Below: Transnational Activists and Protest Networks*. Minneapolis, MN: University of Minnesota Press.

Delmas, Candice (2015). "The Ethics of Government Whistleblowing," *Social Theory and Practice* 14(1): 77–105.

Delmas, Candice (2016). "Civil Disobedience," *Philosophy Compass* 11: 681–91.

DiSalvo, Charles R. (1991). "Abortion and Consensus: The Futility of Speech, the Power of Disobedience," *Washington and Lee Law Review* 48: 219–34.

Douzinas, Costas (2013). *Philosophy and Resistance in the Crisis.* Cambridge: Polity.

Dreier, Ralf (1983). "Widerstand und ziviler Ungehorsam im Rechtsstaat." In Peter Glotz (ed.) *Ziviler Ungehorsam im Rechtsstaat.* Frankfurt: Suhrkamp, pp. 54–75.

Dworkin, Ronald (1977). *Taking Rights Seriously.* Cambridge, MA: Harvard University Press.

Dworkin, Ronald (1985). *A Matter of Principle.* Cambridge, MA: Harvard University Press.

Dyer, Justin B. and Stuart, Kevin E. (2013). "Rawlsian Public Reason and the Theological Framework of Martin Luther King's 'Letter from Birmingham City Jail'," *Politics and Religion* 6: 145–63.

Dyson, Michael E. (2000). *I May Not Get There with You: The True Martin Luther King, Jr.* New York: Free Press.

Edgar, Harold and Schmidt, Benno C. Jr. (1973) "The Espionage Statutes and Publication of Defense Information," *Columbia Law Review* 73(5): 929–1087.

Egoumenides, Magda (2014). *Philosophical Anarchism and Political Obligation.* London: Bloomsbury Academic.

Engler, Mark and Engler, Paul (2016). *This is an Uprising: How Nonviolent Revolt is Shaping the Twenty-First Century.* New York: Nation Books.

Epstein, Barbara (1991). *Political Protest and Cultural Revolution: Nonviolent Direct Action in the 1970s and 1980s.* Berkeley, CA: University of California Press.

Farmer, James (1965). *Freedom, When?* New York: Random House.

Feinberg, Joel (1979). "Civil Disobedience in the Modern World," *Humanities in Society* 2(1): 37–60.

Ferrara, Alessandro (2014). *The Democratic Horizon: Hyperpluralism and the Renewal of Political Liberalism.* Cambridge: Cambridge University Press.

Foley, Michael S. (2003). *Confronting the War Machine: Draft Resistance During the Vietnam War.* Chapel Hill, NC: University of North Carolina Press.

Fortas, Abe (1968). *Concerning Dissent and Civil Disobedience.* New York: Signet.

Fraenkel, Ernst (2017 [1941]). *The Dual State: A Contribution to the Theory of Dictatorship* (with introduction by Jens Meierhenrich). Oxford: Oxford University Press.

Franceschet, Antonio (2015). "Theorizing State Civil Disobedience in International Politics," *Journal of International Political Theory* 11(2): 239–56.

Frankenberg, Günter (1984). "Ziviler Ungehorsam und rechtsstaatliche Demokratie," *JuristenZeitung* 39(6): 266–75.

Fraser, Nancy (2009). *Scales of Justice: Reimagining Political Space in a Globalizing World*. New York: Columbia University Press.

Freeman, Harrop (1966). "Civil Disobedience and the Law," *Rutgers Law Review* 21(1): 17–27.

Freeman, Jody and Minow, Martha (eds.) (2009). *Government by Contract: Outsourcing and American Democracy*. Cambridge, MA: Harvard University Press.

Fuller, Lon (1964). *The Morality of Law*. New Haven, CT: Yale University Press.

Galtung, Johan (1969). "Violence, Peace, and Peace Research," *Journal of Peace Research* 6(3): 167–91.

Gandhi, Mohandas K. (1986a). *The Moral and Political Writings of Mahatma Gandhi*, Vol. I, Raghavan Iyer (ed.). Oxford: Oxford University Press.

Gandhi, Mohandas K. (1986b). *The Moral and Political Writings of Mahatma Gandhi*, Vol. II, Raghavan Iyer (ed.). Oxford: Oxford University Press.

Gandhi, Mohandas K. (1987). *The Moral and Political Writings of Mahatma Gandhi*, Vol. III, Raghavan Iyer (ed.). Oxford: Oxford University Press.

Gandhi, Mohandas K. (1993 [1957]). *An Autobiography: The Story of My Experiments with Truth*. Boston, MA: Beacon Press.

Gandhi, Mohandas K. (2008). *The Essential Writings*, Judith M. Brown (ed.). Oxford: Oxford University Press.

Gans, Chaim (1992). *Philosophical Anarchism and Political Disobedience*. Cambridge: Cambridge University Press.

Garber, Megan (2015). "The Revolutionary Aims of Black Lives Matter," *The Atlantic*, September 30. Available at: https://www.theatlantic.com/politics/archive/2015/09/black-lives-matter-revolution/408160/

Genschel, Philipp and Zangl, Bernhard (2008). "Metamorphosen des Staates – vom Herrschaftsmonopolisten zum Herrschaftsmanager," *Leviathan* 36: 430–54.

Ginsberg, Benjamin (2013). *The Value of Violence*. Amherst, NY: Prometheus Books.

Goodin, Robert (2005). "Toward an International Rule of Law: Distinguishing International Law-Breakers from Would-be Lawmakers," *Journal of Ethics* 9(1): 225–46.

Goodman, Paul (1970). *New Reformation: Notes of a Neolithic Conservative*. New York: Random House.

Goodway, David (2012). "Not Protest But Direct Action: Anarchism Past and Present," *History & Policy*. Available at: http://www.historyandpolicy.org/policy-papers/papers/not-protest-but-direct-action-anarchism-past-and-present

Gould-Wartofsky, Max (2015). *The Occupiers: The Making of the 99 Percent Movement*. New York: Oxford University Press.

Graeber, David (2002). "The New Anarchists," *New Left Review* 13: 61–73.

Graeber, David (2009). *Direct Action: An Ethnography*. Edinburgh: AK Press.

Green, Leslie (1988). *The Authority of the State*. Oxford: Clarendon Press.

Green, Leslie (2002). "Globalization, Disobedience, and the Rule of Law." Available at: http://www.iilj.org/wp-content/uploads/2016/11/Green-Globalization-Civil-Disobedience-and-the-Rule-of-Law-2006.pdf

Greenawalt, Kent (1989). *Conflicts of Law and Morality*. Oxford: Oxford University Press.

Greenberg, Andy (2012). *This Machine Kills Secrets: Julian Assange, the Cypherpunks, and Their Fight to Empower Whistleblowers*. New York: Penguin.

Greenwald, Glenn, Ewan, MacAskill, and Poitras, Laura (2013). "Edward Snowden: The Whistleblower Behind the NSA Surveillance Revelations," *The Guardian*, June 9.

Gregg, Richard B. (1970 [1959]). *The Power of Nonviolence*. New York: Schocken Books.

Guggenberger, Bernd and Offe, Claus (eds.) (1984). *An den Grenzen der Mehrheitsdemokratie*. Opladen: Westdeutscher Verlag.

Habermas, Jürgen (1975 [1973]). *Legitimation Crisis*, Thomas McCarthy (trans.). Cambridge, MA: MIT Press.

Habermas, Jürgen (1985a [1979]). "Introduction." In *Observations on "The Spiritual Situation of the Age,"* Andrew Buchwalter (trans.). Cambridge, MA: MIT Press, pp. 1–30.

Habermas, Jürgen (1985b [1983]). "Civil Disobedience: Litmus Test for the Democratic Constitutional State," John Torpey (trans.). *Berkeley Journal of Sociology* 30: 95–116.

Habermas, Jürgen (1985c [1984]). "Right and Violence: A German Trauma," Martha Calhoun (trans.). *Cultural Critique* 1: 125–39.

Habermas, Jürgen (1986 [1976]). "Hannah Arendt's Communications Concept of Power." In Steven Lukes (ed.) *Power*. New York: New York University Press, pp. 75–93.

Habermas, Jürgen (1987 [1986]) "Über Moral, Recht, ziviler Ungehorsam und Moderne." In *Eine Art Schadensabwicklung*. Frankfurt: Suhrkamp, pp. 64–9.

Habermas, Jürgen (1989 [1962]). *The Structural Transformation of the Public Sphere: An Inquiry into a Category of Bourgeois Society*, Thomas Burger (trans.). Cambridge, MA: MIT Press.

Habermas, Jürgen (1996 [1992]). *Between Facts and Norms: Contributions to a Discourse Theory of Law and Democracy*, William Rehg (trans.). Cambridge, MA: MIT Press.

Habermas, Jürgen (2004). "Religious Tolerance: The Pacemaker for Cultural Rights," *Philosophy* 79: 5–18.

Haksar, Vinit (1986). *Civil Disobedience, Threats and Offers: Gandhi and Rawls*. Delhi: Oxford University Press.

Haksar, Vinit (2003). "The Right to Civil Disobedience," *Osgoode Hall Law Journal* 41(2–3): 408–26.

Hanson, Russell L. (2017). "A Brief Conceptual History of Civil Disobedience, from Thoreau to Gandhi and King," presented at Midwest Political Science Association Annual Meeting, Chicago, April 6–9.

Harcourt, Bernard E. (2012). "Political Disobedience," *Critical Inquiry* 39(1): 33–55.

Harcourt, Bernard E. (2015). *Exposed: Desire and Disobedience in the Digital Age*. Cambridge, MA: Harvard University Press.

Harris, Edward A. (1991). "Fighting Philosophical Anarchism with Fairness: The Moral Claims of Law in the Liberal State," *Columbia Law Review* 91: 919–64.

Hatzopoulos, Pavlos and Patelis, Korinna (2013). "The Comrade is Violent: Liberal Discourse of Violence in Anti-Austerity Greece," *Theory & Event*, 16(1).

Held, David (2006). *Models of Democracy*, 3rd edn. Cambridge: Polity.

Hill, Jason (2013). *Civil Disobedience and the Politics of Identity: When We Should Not Get Along*. New York: Palgrave.

Horton, John (2010). *Political Obligation*, 2nd edn. London: Palgrave.

Hughes, Michael L. (2014). "Civil Disobedience in Transnational Perspective: American and West German Anti-Nuclear-Power Protesters, 1975–1982," *Historical Social Research* 39: 236–53.

Hurrelmann, Achim, Leibfried, Stephan, Martens, Kerstin, and Mayer, Peter (eds.) (2007). *Transforming the Golden-Age Nation State*. Basingstoke: Palgrave Macmillan.

Isaac, Jeffrey (1992). *Arendt, Camus, and Modern Rebellion*. New Haven, CT: Yale University Press.

Isserman, Maurice (1987). *If I Had a Hammer ...: The Death of the Old Left and the Birth of the New Left*. New York: Basic Books.

Jackson, Thomas F. (2007). *From Civil Rights to Human Rights: Martin Luther King, Jr., and the Struggle for Economic Justice*. Philadelphia, PA: University of Pennsylvania Press.

James, Gene G. (1973). "The Orthodox Theory of Civil Disobedience," *Social Theory and Practice*, 2(4): 475–98.

Joerges, Christian (2012). "Europe's Economic Constitution in Crisis." Bremen: ZenTra Working Papers in Transnational Studies 06/2012.

Kalyvas, Andreas (2008). *Democracy and the Politics of the Extraordinary: Max Weber, Carl Schmitt, and Hannah Arendt.* New York: Cambridge University Press.

Kapur, Sudarshan (1992). *Raising Up a Prophet: The African-American Encounter with Gandhi.* Boston, MA: Beacon Press.

Kateb, George (1983). *Hannah Arendt: Politics, Conscience, Evil.* Totowa, NJ: Rowman & Allanheld.

Kateb, George (2006). *Patriotism and other Mistakes.* New Haven, CT: Yale University Press.

Kennedy, Randall (2015). "Lifting as We Climb: a Progressive Defense of Respectability Politics," *Harper's Magazine*, October: 24, 26–34.

King, Martin Luther (1986a [1958]). *Stride Toward Freedom: The Montgomery Story.* New York: Harper & Row.

King, Martin Luther (1986b). *A Testament of Hope: The Essential Writings and Speeches of Martin Luther King, Jr.*, James M. Washington (ed.). New York: Harper & Row.

King, Martin Luther (1991 [1963]). "Letter from Birmingham City Jail." In Hugo Bedau (ed.) *Civil Disobedience in Focus.* New York: Routledge, pp. 68–84.

King, Martin Luther (2016). *The Radical King*, Cornel West (ed.). Boston, MA: Beacon Press.

Kirkpatrick, Jennet (2008). *Uncivil Disobedience: Studies in Violence and Democratic Politics.* Princeton, NJ: Princeton University Press.

Kohn, Margaret (2013). "Privatization and Protest: Occupy Wall Street, Occupy Toronto, and the Occupation of Public Space in a Democracy," *Perspectives on Politics*, 11(1): 99–109.

Kopstein, Joshua (2013). "Hacker with a Cause," *The New Yorker*, November 21. Available at: http://www.newyorker.com/tech/elements/hacker-with-a-cause

Kornhauser, Anne M. (2015). *Debating the American State: Liberal Anxieties and the New Leviathan, 1930–1970.* Philadelphia, PA: University of Pennsylvania Press.

Kosek, Joseph Kip (2008). *Acts of Conscience: Christian Nonviolence and Modern American Democracy.* New York: Columbia University Press.

Kramnick, Isaac and Moore, R. Laurence (2005). *The Godless Constitution: A Moral Defense of the Secular State.* New York: Norton.

Kraut, Richard (1984). *Socrates and the State.* Princeton, NJ: Princeton University Press.

Laker, Thomas (1986). *Ziviler Ungehorsam. Geschichte–Begriff–Rechtfertigung*. Baden-Baden: Nomos.

Laudani, Raffaele (2013). *Disobedience in Western Political Thought: A Genealogy*. Cambridge: Cambridge University Press.

Lefkowitz, David (2007). "On a Moral Right to Civil Disobedience," *Ethics* 117: 202–33.

Leigh, David and Harding, Luke (2011). *Wikileaks: Inside Julian Assange's War on Secrecy*. New York: PublicAffairs.

Lovell, Jarret S. (2009). *Crimes of Dissent: Civil Disobedience, Criminal Justice, and the Politics of Conscience*. New York: New York University Press.

Lowery, Wesley (2016). *"They Can't Kill Us All": Ferguson, Baltimore, and a New Era in America's Racial Justice Movement*. New York: Little, Brown and Company.

Ludlow, Peter (2013). "The Strange Case of Barrett Brown," *The Nation*, June 18. Available at: https://www.thenation.com/article/strange-case-barrett-brown/

Lyons, David (2013). *Confronting Injustice: Moral History and Political Theory*. Oxford: Oxford University Press.

MacCallum, Gerald C. (1970). "Some Truths and Untruths About Civil Disobedience." In J. Roland Pennock and John Chapman (eds.) *Political and Legal Obligation*. New York: New York University Press, pp. 370–400.

Madar, Chase (2013). *The Passion of Bradley Manning*. London: Verso.

Mantena, Karuna (2012). "Another Realism: The Politics of Gandhian Nonviolence." *American Political Science Review* 106(2): 455–70.

Markovits, Daniel (2005). "Democratic Disobedience," *Yale Law Journal* 114: 1897–952.

Maus, Ingeborg (1992). *Zur Aufklärung der Demokratietheorie*. Frankfurt: Suhrkamp.

Maxwell, Carol J.C. (2002). *Pro-Life Activists in America: Meaning, Motivation, and Direct Action*. Cambridge: Cambridge University Press.

May, Todd (2015). *Nonviolent Resistance: A Philosophical Introduction*. Cambridge: Polity.

McWilliams, Wilson Carey (1969). "Civil Disobedience and Contemporary Constitutionalism: The American Case," *Comparative Politics* 1(2): 211–27.

Medsger, Betty (2014). *The Burglary: The Discovery of J. Edgar Hoover's Secret FBI*. New York: Vintage.

Metzger, Gillian E. (2009). "Private Delegations, Due Process, and the Duty to Supervise." In Jody Freeman and Martha Minow (eds.) *Government by Contract: Outsourcing and American Democracy*. Cambridge, MA: Harvard University Press, pp. 291–309.

Miller, David (1984). *Anarchism*. London: J.M. Dent.

Miller, Nathan (2015). "International Civil Disobedience: Unauthorized Interventions and the Conscience of the International Community," *Maryland Law Review* 74: 315–76.

Milligan, Tony (2013). *Civil Disobedience: Protest, Justification, and the Law*. London: Bloomsbury.

Moulin-Dos, Claire (2015). *Civic Disobedience: Taking Politics Seriously*. Baden-Baden: Nomos.

Neumann, Franz L. (1957). *The Democratic and Authoritarian State*. Glencoe, IL: Free Press.

Newman, Saul (2011). "Postanarchism: A Politics of Anti-Politics," *Journal of Political Ideologies* 16(3): 313–27.

Newman, Saul (2012). "Anarchism and Law: Towards a Post-Anarchist Ethics of Disobedience," *Griffith Law Review* 21(2): 307–29.

Newman, Saul (2016). *Postanarchism*. Cambridge: Polity.

Nimtz, August (2016). "Violence and/or Nonviolence in the Success of the Civil Rights Movement: The Malcolm X–Martin Luther King, Jr. Nexus," *New Political Science* 38(1): 1–22.

Ogunye, Temi (2015). "Transnational Civil Disobedience and Global Justice," *Ethics and Global Politics* 8(1): 1–23.

Owen, Taylor (2015). *Disruptive Power: The Crisis of the State in the Digital Age*. New York: Oxford University Press.

Parekh, Bhikhu (1989). *Gandhi's Political Philosophy: A Critical Examination*. New York: Springer.

Pateman, Carole (1970). *Participation and Democratic Theory*. Cambridge: Cambridge University Press.

Pateman, Carole (1985 [1979]). *The Problem of Political Obligation: A Critique of Liberal Theory*. Berkeley, CA: University of California Press.

Perrine, Aaron (2001). "The First Amendment Versus the World Trade Organization: Emergency Powers and the Battle of Seattle," *Washington Law Review*, 76 (2001): 635–68.

Perry, Lewis (2013). *Civil Disobedience: An American Tradition*. New Haven, CT: Yale University Press.

Peterson, Andrea (2015). "Edward Snowden Says He Would Go to Jail to Come Back to the US," *Washington Post*, October 6.

Petherbridge, Danielle (2016). "Between Thinking and Action: Arendt on Conscience and Civil Disobedience," *Philosophy and Social Criticism* 42(10): 971–81.

Pettit, Philip (1997). *Republicanism: A Theory of Freedom and Government*. New York: Oxford University Press.

Pineda, Erin (2015). "Civil Disobedience and Punishment: (Mis) reading Justification and Strategy from SNCC to Snowden," *History of the Present* 5(1): 1–30.

Pogge, Thomas (1988). *Realizing Rawls*. Ithaca, NY: Cornell University Press.

Preuss, Ulrich (1995). *Constitutional Revolution: The Link Between Constitutionalism and Progress*. Atlantic Highlands, NJ: Humanities Press.

Quint, Peter (2008). *Civil Disobedience and the German Courts: The Pershing Missile Protests in Comparative Perspective*. Abingdon: Routledge-Cavendish.

Rawls, John (1969 [1966]). "The Justification of Civil Disobedience." In Hugo A. Bedau (ed.) *Civil Disobedience: Theory and Practice*. Indianapolis, IN: Bobbs-Merrill, pp. 240–55.

Rawls, John (1971). *A Theory of Justice*. Cambridge, MA: Harvard University Press.

Rawls, John (1993). *Political Liberalism*. Cambridge, MA: Harvard University Press.

Raz, Joseph (2009 [1979]). *The Authority of Law*. Oxford: Oxford University Press.

Reiman, Jeffrey H. (1972). *In Defense of Political Philosophy*. New York: Harper & Row.

Reynolds, Barbara (2015). "I Was a Civil Rights Activist in the 1960s. But it's Hard for Me to Get Behind Black Lives Matter," *Washington Post*, August 24.

Richards, David A.J. (2004). "Ethical Religion and the Struggle of Human Rights: The Case of Martin Luther King, Jr.," *Fordham Law Review* 72(5): 2105–52.

Risen, James and Thomas, Judy L. (1998). *Wrath of Angels: The American Abortion War*. New York: Basic Books.

Ritter, Alan (1980). *Anarchism: A Theoretical Analysis*. Cambridge: Cambridge University Press.

Roberts, Adam and Garton Ash, Timothy (eds.) (2011). *Civil Resistance and Power Politics: The Experience of Non-violent Action from Gandhi to the Present*. Oxford: Oxford University Press.

Rosa, Hartmut and Scheuerman, William E. (eds.) (2009). *High-Speed Society: Social Acceleration, Power, and Modernity*. University Park, PA: Pennsylvania State University Press.

Rosen, Michael (2012). *Dignity: Its History and Meaning*. Cambridge, MA: Harvard University Press.

Rosenblum, Nancy (1981). "Thoreau's Militant Conscience," *Political Theory* 9(1): 81–110.

Rudolph, Susanne Hoeber and Rudolph, Lloyd (1967). *Gandhi: The Traditional Roots of Charisma*. Chicago, IL: University of Chicago Press.

Russell, Bertrand (1961). "Civil Disobedience," *New Statesman* 61: 245–6.

Sabl, Andrew (2001). "Looking Forward to Justice: Rawlsian Civil Disobedience and Its Non-Rawlsian Lessons," *Journal of Political Philosophy* 9(3): 307–30.

Sauter, Molly (2014). *The Coming Swarm: DDoS Actions, Hacktivism, and Civil Disobedience on the Internet.* London: Bloomsbury.

Scalmer, Sean (2011). *Gandhi in the West: The Mahatma and the Rise of Radical Protest.* Cambridge: Cambridge University Press.

Schauer, Frederick (2015). *The Force of Law.* Cambridge, MA: Harvard University Press.

Scheuerman, William E. (1995). "Majority Rule and the Environmental Crisis: Critical Reflections on the German Debate," *German Politics & Society* 13(2): 35–59.

Scheuerman, William E. (1999). "Economic Globalization and the Rule of Law," *Constellations* 6(1): 3–25.

Scheuerman, William E. (2004). *Liberal Democracy and the Social Acceleration of Time.* Baltimore, MD: Johns Hopkins University Press.

Scheuerman, William E. (2014a). "Cosmopolitanism and the World State," *Review of International Studies* 40(3): 419–41.

Scheuerman, William E. (2014b). "Whistleblowing as Civil Disobedience: The Case of Edward Snowden," *Philosophy and Social Criticism* 40(7): 609–28.

Scheuerman, William E. (2015). "From Global Governance to Global Stateness." In Robert Schuett and Peter M.R. Stirk (eds.) *The Concept of the State in International Relations: Philosophy, Sovereignty, Cosmopolitanism.* Edinburgh: Edinburgh University Press, pp. 187–220.

Scheuerman, William E. (2016). "Crises and Extralegality from Above and from Below." In Poul F. Kjaer and Niklas Olsen (eds.) *Critical Theories of Crisis in Europe.* Lanham, MD: Rowman & Littlefield, pp. 197–212.

Scheuerman, William E. (2017). "What is Political Resistance?" Available at: http://www.publicseminar.org/2017/02/what-is-political-resistance/#.WSBqd9y1uUk

Schneiderman, David (2001). "Investment Rules and the Rule of Law," *Constellation* 8(4): 521–37.

Schock, Kurt (2005). *Unarmed Insurrections: People Power Movements in Nondemocracies.* Minneapolis, MN: University of Minnesota Press.

Schock, Kurt (2015). *Civil Resistance Today.* Cambridge: Polity.

Schuppert, Gunnar (2010). *Staat als Prozess.* Frankfurt: Campus.

Sebastian, Simone (2015). "Don't Criticize Black Lives Matter for Provoking Violence. The Civil Rights Movement Did, Too," *Washington Post*, October 1.

Senor, Thomas D. (1987). "What If There Are No Political Obligations? A Reply to A.J. Simmons," *Philosophy and Public Affairs*, 16(3): 260–8.

Sharp, Gene (1973). *The Politics of Nonviolent Action*. Boston, MA: Sargent Publishers.

Shelby, Tommie (2007). "Justice, Deviance, and the Dark Ghetto," *Philosophy and Public Affairs*, 35(2): 126–60.

Shelby, Tommie (2016). *Dark Ghettos: Injustice, Dissent, and Reform*. Cambridge, MA: Belknap Press of Harvard University Press.

Shklar, Judith N. (1986 [1964]). *Legalism: Law, Morals, and Political Trials*. Cambridge, MA: Harvard University Press.

Shorrock, Tim (2008). *Spies for Hire: The Secret World of Intelligence Outsourcing*. New York: Simon & Schuster.

Shridharani, Krishnalal (1972 [1939]). *War Without Violence: A Study of Gandhi's Method and Its Accomplishments*. New York: Garland.

Sibley, Mulford Q. (1972 [1965]). "On Political Obligation and Civil Disobedience." In Michael P. Smith and Kenneth L. Deutsch (eds.) *Political Obligation and Civil Disobedience: Readings*. New York: Thomas Crowell, pp. 21–34.

Simmons, A. John (1979). *Moral Principles and Political Obligation*. Princeton, NJ: Princeton University Press.

Simmons, A. John (1987). "The Anarchist Position," *Philosophy and Public Affairs* 16(3): 269–79.

Simmons, A. John (1993). *On the Edge of Anarchy: Locke, Consent, and the Limits of Society*. Princeton, NJ: Princeton University Press.

Simmons, A. John (1996). "Philosophical Anarchism." In John T. Sanders and Jan Narveson (eds.) *For and Against the State: New Philosophical Readings*. Lanham, MD: Rowman & Littlefield, pp. 19–39.

Simmons, A. John (2001). *Justification and Legitimacy: Essays on Rights and Obligations*. Cambridge: Cambridge University Press.

Simmons, A. John (2005). "Civil Disobedience and the Duty to Obey the Law." In R.G. Frey and Christopher Heath Wellman (eds.) *A Companion to Applied Ethics*. Chichester: Wiley.

Simmons, A. John (2010). "Disobedience and Its Objects," *Boston University Law Review* 90: 1805–31.

Singer, Peter (1973). *Democracy and Disobedience*. Oxford: Clarendon Press.

Sitze, Adam (2013). "Foreword." In Raddaele Laudani, *Disobedience in Western Political Thought: A Genealogy*. Cambridge: Cambridge University Press, pp. vii–xxvi.

Smart, Barry (1991 [1978]). "Defining Civil Disobedience." In Hugo A. Bedau (ed.) *Civil Disobedience in Focus*. New York: Routledge, pp. 189–211.

Smith, Jackie (2007). *Social Movements for Global Democracy*. Baltimore, MD: Johns Hopkins University Press.

Smith, M.B.E. (1973). "Is There a Prima Facie Obligation to Obey the Law?" *Yale Law Journal* 82: 950–76.

Smith, Verity (2009). "Hannah Arendt on Civil Disobedience and Constitutional Patriotism." In Roger Berkowitz, Jeffrey Katz, and Thomas Keenan (eds.) *Thinking in Dark Times: Hannah Arendt on Ethics and Politics*. New York: Fordham University Press, pp. 105–12.

Smith, William (2008). "Civil Disobedience and Social Power: Reflections on Habermas," *Contemporary Political Theory* 7: 72–89.

Smith, William (2012). "A Constitutional Niche for Civil Disobedience? Reflections on Arendt." In Marco Goldoni and Christopher McCorkindale (eds.) *Hannah Arendt and the Law*. Oxford: Hart, pp. 133–50.

Smith, William (2013). *Civil Disobedience and Deliberative Democracy*. Abingdon: Routledge.

Smith, William (2015). "Global Civil Disobedience: Cabrera on Unauthorized Economic Migration," *Contemporary Political Theory* 14: 90–9.

Snowden, Edward (2013). "Statement by Edward Snowden to Human Rights Groups at Moscow's Sheremetyevo Airport," July 12. Available at: https://wikileaks.org/Statement-by-Edward-Snowden-to.html

Sorabji, Richard (2014). *Moral Conscience Through the Ages: Fifth Century BCE to the Present*. Chicago, IL: University of Chicago Press.

Sparks, Holloway (1997). "Dissident Citizenship: Democratic Theory, Political Courage, and Activist Women," *Hypatia* 12(1): 74–110.

Specter, Matthew G. (2010). *Habermas: An Intellectual Biography*. New York: Cambridge University Press.

Starnes, Todd (2016). "Hey, Black Lives Matter, Stop Terrorizing Our Cities," July 11. Available at: http://www.foxnews.com/opinion/2016/07/11/hey-black-lives-matter-stop-terrorizing-our-cities.html

Stevick, Daniel B. (1969). *Civil Disobedience and the Christian*. New York: Seabury Press.

Stone, Geoffrey (2004). *Perilous Times: Free Speech in Wartime – From the Sedition Act of 1798 to the War on Terrorism*. New York: Norton.

Storing, Herbert (1991 [1969]). "The Case Against Civil Disobedience." In Hugo A. Bedau (ed.) *Civil Disobedience in Focus*. New York: Routledge, pp. 85–102.

Sutterlüty, Ferdinand (2014). "The Hidden Morale of the 2005 French and 2011 English Riots," *Thesis Eleven* 121(1): 38–56.

Tamanaha, Brian (2004). *On the Rule of Law: History, Politics, Theory*. New York: Cambridge University Press.

Tarrow, Sidney (2005). *The New Transnational Activism*. Cambridge: Cambridge University Press.

Taylor, Bob Pepperman (1996). *America's Bachelor Uncle: Thoreau and the American Polity*. Lawrence, KS: University of Kansas Press.

Taylor, Bob Pepperman (2015). *The Routledge Guidebook to Thoreau's Civil Disobedience*. London: Routledge.

Terchek, Ronald J. (1998). *Gandhi: Struggling for Autonomy*. Lanham, MD: Rowman & Littlefield.

Thomassen, Lasse (2007). "Within the Limits of Deliberative Reason Alone: Habermas, Civil Disobedience and Constitutional Democracy," *European Journal of Political Theory* 6(2): 200–18.

Thoreau, Henry (1996). *Thoreau: Political Writings*, Nancy Rosenblum (ed.). New York: Cambridge University Press.

Tolstoy, Leo (1967). *Tolstoy's Writings on Civil Disobedience and Non-Violence*. New York: Signet.

Velasco, Juan Carlos (2016). "Revitalizing Democracy Through Civil Disobedience," *Filosofia Unisinos* 17(2): 111–20.

Verkuil, Paul R. (2007). *Outsourcing Sovereignty: Why Privatization of Government Functions Threatens Democracy and What We Can Do About It*. New York: Cambridge University Press.

Vinthagen, Stellan (2015). *A Theory of Nonviolent Action: How Civil Resistance Works*. London: Zed Books.

Volpp, Leti (2014). "Civility and the Undocumented Alien." In Austin Sarat (ed.) *Civility, Legality, and Justice in America*. New York: Cambridge University Press, pp. 69–106.

Waldron, Jeremy (1999). *The Dignity of Legislation*. New York: Cambridge University Press.

Waldron, Jeremy (2011). "The Rule of Law and the Importance of Procedure." In James E. Fleming (ed.) *Getting to the Rule of Law*. New York: New York University Press, pp. 3–31.

Walzer, Michael (1970 [1969]). *Obligations: Essays on Disobedience, War, and Citizenship*. New York: Simon & Schuster.

Weber, Max (2004 [1919]). "Politics as a Vocation." In David Owen and Tracy Strong (eds.), *The Vocation Lectures*. Indianapolis, IN: Hackett.

Weber, Thomas (2004). *Gandhi as Disciple and Mentor*. Cambridge: Cambridge University Press.

Welchman, Jennifer (2001). "Is Ecosabotage Civil Disobedience?" *Philosophy and Geography* 4(1): 97–107.

White, Jonathan (2015). "Emergency Europe," *Political Studies* 63(2): 300–18.

White, Stephen and Farr, Eva Robert (2012). "'No-Saying' in Habermas," *Political Theory* 40(19): 32–57.

Whittington, Keith (2000). "In Defense of Legislatures," *Political Theory* 28: 690–702.

Wolff, Robert Paul (1970). *In Defense of Anarchism*. New York: Harper & Row.

Woodcock, George (1966). *Civil Disobedience*. Toronto: Canadian Broadcasting Corporation.

Woozley, A.D. (1976). "Civil Disobedience and Punishment," *Ethics* 86(4): 323–31.

Yingling, M. Patrick (2016). "Civil Disobedience to Overcome Corruption: The Case of Occupy Wall Street," *Indiana Journal of Law and Social Equality* 4(2): 121–34.

Zashin, Elliot M. (1972). *Civil Disobedience and Democracy*. New York: Free Press.

Zerilli, Linda (2014). "Against Civility: A Feminist Perspective." In Austin Sarat (ed.) *Civility, Legality, and Justice in America*. New York: Cambridge University Press, pp. 107–31.

Zinn, Howard (1971). "The Conspiracy of Law." In Robert P. Wolff (ed.) *The Rule of Law*. New York: Simon & Schuster, pp. 1–12.

Zinn, Howard (1990). *Declarations of Independence: Cross-Examining American Ideology*. New York: HarperCollins.

Zinn, Howard (2002 [1968]). *Disobedience and Democracy: Nine Fallacies on Law and Order*. Cambridge, MA: South End Press.

Zohlhöfer, Reimut and Ohringer, Herbert (2006). "Selling Off the 'Family Silver': The Politics of Privatization." *World Political Science Review* 2: 30–52.

Züger, Theresa (2015). "Three Ways to Understanding Civil Disobedience in a Digitized World," June 19. Available at: https://www.hiig.de/blog/three-ways-to-understanding-civil-disobedience-in-a-digitized-world/

Zwiebach, Burton (1975). *Civility and Disobedience*. Cambridge: Cambridge University Press.

Index